MathFlare

Name: _______________________

Class: __________

Teacher: _______________________

Introduction

As parents and educators, we recognize the pivotal role mathematics plays in shaping a child's academic journey and future success. Yet, the path to mathematical proficiency can often seem daunting, fraught with challenges and complexities. That's where the transformative power of MathFlare Workbooks shine through, illuminating the way forward with clarity, precision, and purpose.

Introducing MathFlare Workbooks – a beacon of guidance, a testament to excellence, and a catalyst for achievement. Crafted with meticulous care and expertise, MathFlare Workbooks stand as paragons of educational excellence, designed to nurture young minds, ignite a passion for learning, and develop a deep-rooted understanding of mathematical concepts.

Picture this: your child eagerly delves into the pages of Mathflare Workbook, greeted by a step-by-step guide illuminated with vivid examples that demystify complex mathematical concepts. With each turn of the page, they embark on a journey of discovery, encountering thoughtfully curated practice questions that reinforce learning and hone problem-solving skills. And when they unveil the answers to those very questions, a sense of accomplishment blossoms within them – a tangible reward for their hard work and dedication.

But MathFlare Workbooks are more than just tools for learning; they are pathways to comprehension, fostering a deep-seated understanding of mathematical concepts through a sequential, logical flow. From fundamental principles to advanced problem-solving strategies, every chapter builds upon the last, ensuring a robust foundation upon which future knowledge can be constructed.

As parents, we yearn for nothing more than to see our children thrive, to witness the spark of inspiration ignited within them as they conquer academic challenges with confidence and poise. MathFlare Workbooks serve as partners in this noble endeavor, offering not just practice questions, but the keys to unlocking a world of opportunity.

And for teachers, MathFlare Workbooks stand as invaluable allies in the quest to cultivate mathematical proficiency in the classroom. With answers readily available, instructors can focus on guiding and nurturing their students, confident in the knowledge that MathFlare Workbooks provide a solid framework upon which to build.

In the pages of MathFlare Workbooks, we find not just the promise of academic excellence, but the seeds of a brighter tomorrow. So let us embrace the power of mathematics, let us champion the journey of learning, and let us pave the way for a generation of young minds poised to shape the world. With MathFlare Workbooks as our guide, the possibilities are infinite, and the future, bright.

Table of Contents

MathFlare
Grade 1-2
MATH WORKBOOK
Step by Step Guide and Essential Practice with Answers
Counting and Numbers
Addition and Subtraction
Place Value and Expanded Notations
Understanding Time
MathFlare Publishing

MathFlare
Grade 2
MATH WORKBOOK
Step by Step Guide and Essential Practice with Answers
Addition Subtraction
Multiplication
Place Value and Expanded Notations
Geometry
MathFlare Publishing

MathFlare
Grade 2-3
MATH WORKBOOK
Step by Step Guide and Essential Practice with Answers
Addition Subtraction
Multiplication and Division
Place Value and Expanded Notations
Geometry
MathFlare Publishing

MathFlare
Grade 3
MATH WORKBOOK
Step by Step Guide and Essential Practice with Answers
Multiplication and Division
Decimals
Place Value and Expanded Notations
Fractions and Geometry
MathFlare Publishing

MathFlare
Grade 3-4
MATH WORKBOOK
Step by Step Guide and Essential Practice with Answers
Addition Subtraction
Multiplication Division
Place Value and Expanded Notations
Fractions and Geometry
MathFlare Publishing

MathFlare
Grade 4
MATH WORKBOOK
Step by Step Guide and Essential Practice with Answers
Addition Subtraction
Multiplication Division
Place Value and Expanded Notations
Fractions and Geometry
MathFlare Publishing

MathFlare
Grade 4-5
MATH WORKBOOK
Step by Step Guide and Essential Practice with Answers
Multiplication Division
Place Value and Expanded Notations
Fractions and Geometry
Unit Conversion
MathFlare Publishing

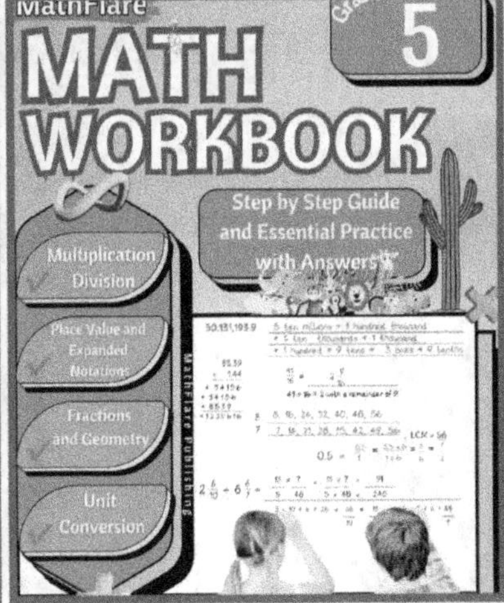

MathFlare
Grade 5
MATH WORKBOOK
Step by Step Guide and Essential Practice with Answers
Multiplication Division
Place Value and Expanded Notations
Fractions and Geometry
Unit Conversion
MathFlare Publishing

MathFlare
Grade 5-6
MATH WORKBOOK
Step by Step Guide and Essential Practice with Answers
Multiplication Division
Place Value and Expanded Notations
Fractions and Geometry
Units and Statistics
MathFlare Publishing

MathFlare
MATH WORKBOOK
6
Step by Step Guide and Essential Practice with Answers
Integers and Statistics
Arithmetic and Pre-Algebra
Fractions and Geometry
Ratio and Percentage
MathFlare Publishing

MathFlare
MATH WORKBOOK
6-7
Step by Step Guide and Essential Practice with Answers
Arithmetic and Pre-Algebra
Ratio, Percent Proportion
Geometry
Statistics
MathFlare Publishing

MathFlare
MATH WORKBOOK
7
Step by Step Guide and Essential Practice with Answers
Pre-Algebra
Ratio, Percent Proportion
Geometry
Statistics
MathFlare Publishing

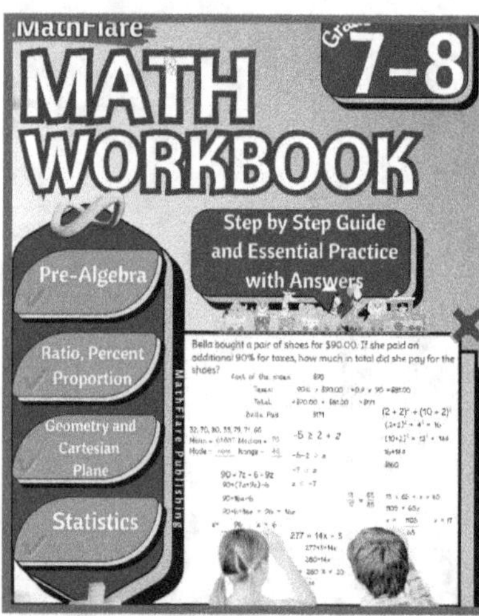

MathFlare
MATH WORKBOOK
7-8
Step by Step Guide and Essential Practice with Answers
Pre-Algebra
Ratio, Percent Proportion
Geometry and Cartesian Plane
Statistics
MathFlare Publishing

MathFlare
MATH WORKBOOK
8
Step by Step Guide and Essential Practice with Answers
Pre-Algebra
Percentage
Linear Equations
Geometry
MathFlare Publishing

MathFlare
MATH WORKBOOK
8-9
Step by Step Guide and Essential Practice with Answers
Pre-Algebra
Ratio, Proportion and Percentage
Linear Equations
Geometry and Cartesian Plane
MathFlare Publishing

MathFlare
MATH WORKBOOK
9
Step by Step Guide and Essential Practice with Answers
Equations and Expressions
Linear Equations and Systems
Quadratic Equations
Geometry
MathFlare Publishing

MathFlare
MATH WORKBOOK
9-10
Step by Step Guide and Essential Practice with Answers
Equations and Expressions
Linear Equations and Systems
Quadratic Equations
Polynomials Geometry
MathFlare Publishing

MathFlare
MATH WORKBOOK
10
Step by Step Guide and Essential Practice with Answers
Equations and Expressions
Linear Equations and Systems
Quadratic Equations
Polynomials Scientific Notations
MathFlare Publishing

Chapter. 01

Equations and Expressions

Simplifying expressions

It involves combining like terms and performing operations to make the expression easier to understand and work with.

Let's simplify the expression:

$$2x - 2x + 8 + 4$$

- **Combine like terms:** First, we look for terms with the same variable and exponent. In this expression, $2x$ and $-2x$ are like terms, so they can be combined:

$$2x - 2x = 0$$

- **Substitute the simplified terms:** After combining the like terms, the expression becomes:

$$0 + 8 + 4$$

- **Combine the remaining terms:** Now, we add the constants together:

$$8 + 4 = 12$$

Let's solve another problem:

$$-7m - 3 - 3 - 6m$$

combine like terms

$$-7m - 6m - 3 - 3$$

$$13m - 6$$

Solving Equations

Evaluating expressions involves substituting given values for variables in an expression and then performing the indicated operations to find the result.

For example: Let's evaluate $4x - 10$, when $x = 3$:

Step 1: Substitute the given value for the variable:

Replace every occurrence of x in the expression $4x - 10$ with the given value, which is 3:

$$= 4(3) - 10$$

Step 2: Perform the operations:

Perform the indicated operations according to the order of operations (PEMDAS - Parentheses, Exponents, Multiplication and Division, Addition and Subtraction):

$$= 4 \times 3 - 10$$

Step 3: Simplify:

Calculate the result:

$$12 - 10 = 2$$

Solving Equations (One Side)

Solving one-step equations involves performing a single operation to isolate the variable and find its value.

Let's solve an equation step by step: $16 + x = 31$

1. **Identify the Goal:**

     The goal is to isolate the variable x on one side of the equation.

2. **Simplify the Equation**: Combine like terms on both sides of the equation, if necessary.

   The equation is already simplified.

3. **Undo Addition or Subtraction**: If there's addition or subtraction involving the variable, undo it by performing the opposite operation on both sides of the equation.

   Since x is being added to 16, we'll undo this operation by subtracting 16 from both sides of the equation:

   $$16 + x - 16 = 31 - 16$$

4. **Isolate the Variable**: Ensure that the variable is alone on one side of the equation.

   $$x = 15$$

5. **Check Your Solution**: Substitute the value of x back into the original equation to verify that it satisfies the equation.

   $$16 + 15 = 31$$

   $$31 = 31$$

   The equation is balanced.

Equations (Two Sides)

A two-sided equation is an equation where both sides have expressions with variables and constants. The goal when solving a two-sided equation is to find the value of the variable that makes both sides equal.

For example: Let's solve an equation:

$$9 + 8x + 8 = 64 + x + 2$$

- **Combine Like Terms:** Simplify each side of the equation by combining like terms (terms with the same variable or constants).

$$9 + 8x + 8 = 64 + x + 2$$

$$17 + 8x = 66 + x$$

- **Isolate the Variable:** Use inverse operations to isolate the variable on one side of the equation.

subtract x from both sides:

$$17 + 8x - x = 66 + x - x$$

$$17 + 7x = 66$$

subtracting 17 from both sides:

$$17 - 17 + 7x = 66 - 17$$

$$7x = 49$$

divide both sides by 7:

$$\frac{7x}{7} = \frac{49}{7} = x = 7$$

- **Check Solution:** Once you find the solution, substitute it back into the original equation to ensure it makes the equation true.

Substitute $x = 7$ back into the original equation:

$$9 + 8(7) + 8 = 64 + 7 + 2$$

$$9 + 56 + 8 = 64 + 7 + 2$$

$$73 = 73$$

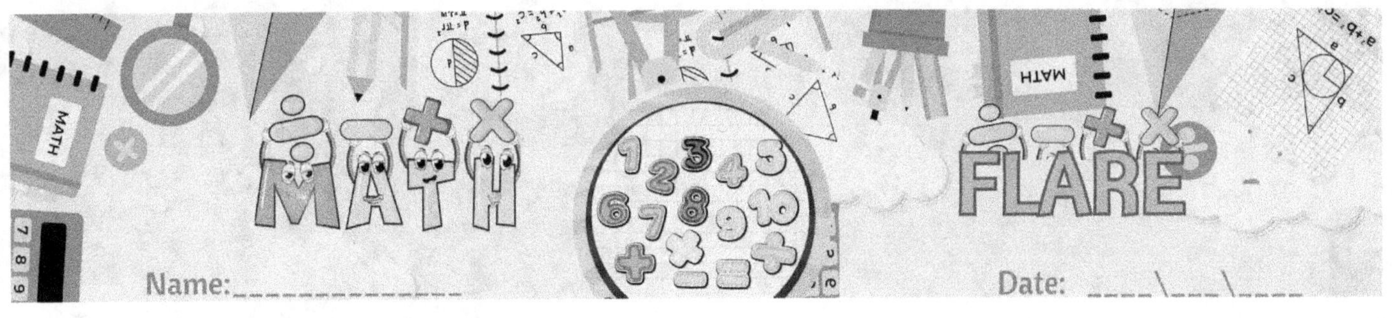

Simplify Expressions

1. $3z - 20z + 8z - 1 + 3$

2. $7 + 16k - 17 + 2k - 3 + 7k$

3. $-19m - 4 + 8 - 9m$

4. $6 + 8 + 13m - 20m + 16 - 7m$

5. $15z + 6 - 7z + 8 + 5z + 14$

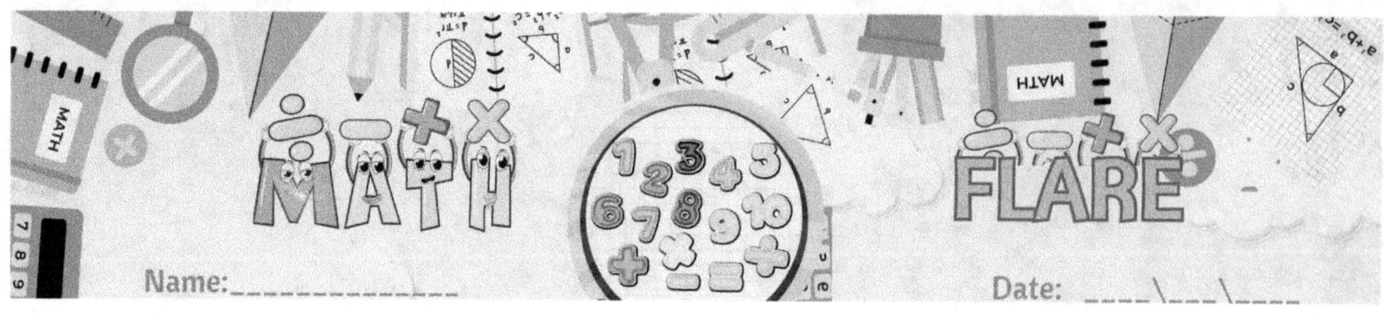

6. $11x - x + 6 + 12$

7. $-2x - 20 - 16 - 20x$

8. $1 + 9 + 12y - 2y + 4 - 19y$

9. $9y - 16y + 8 + 14$

10. $6k + 15 + k$

11. $4k - 6 + 3k - 2 + 9k + 18$

12. $-12z + 12 + 5z + 18 + 16z - 12$

13. $7y + 6 - 12 - 13y + 5y$

14. $11z - 18 - 13z + 17$

15. $y - 19y$

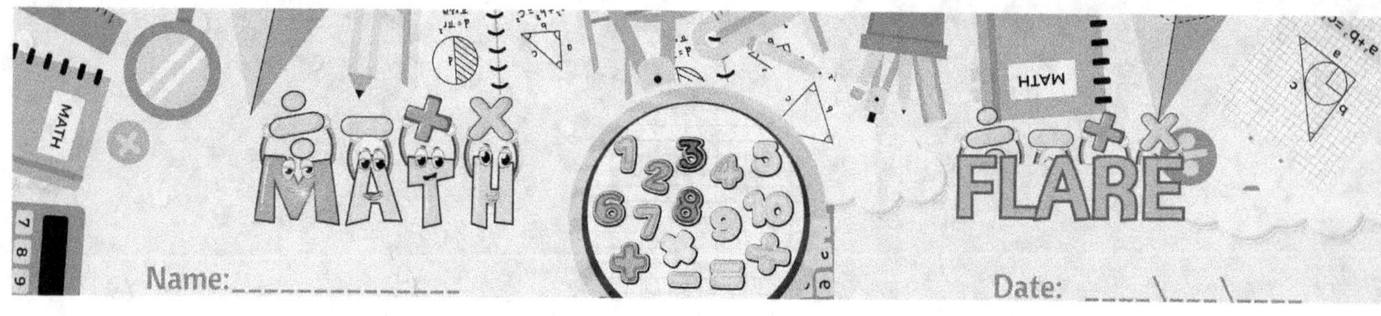

16. $-9z + 6 + 18z + 17 + 4z - 12$

17. $-8x + 18x$

18. $18m + 12 + 4m$

19. $18z - 18z$

20. $18m + 4 - 17m + 13 + 11m + 3$

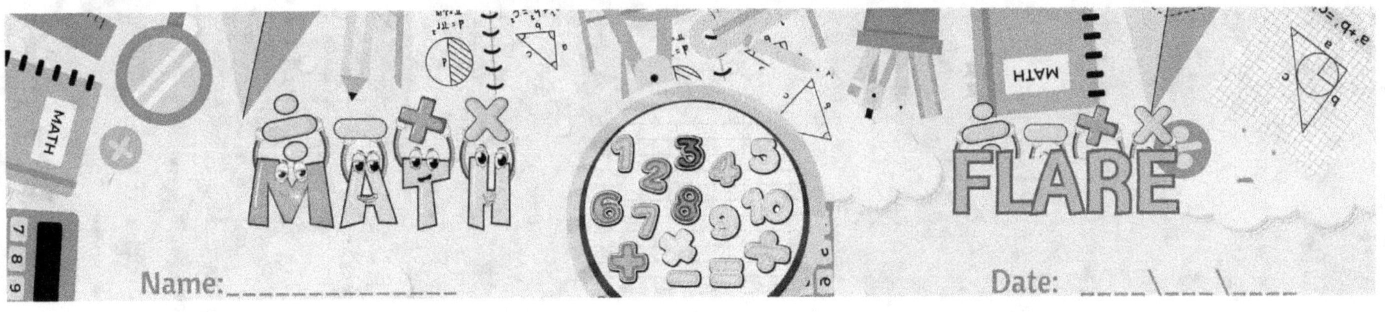

21. $y + 13 + 13y$

22. $-4x + 4 + 14x$

23. $-7z - z$

24. $11k + 3 + 3k$

25. $14z - 15 + 4z - 5 + 7z + 7$

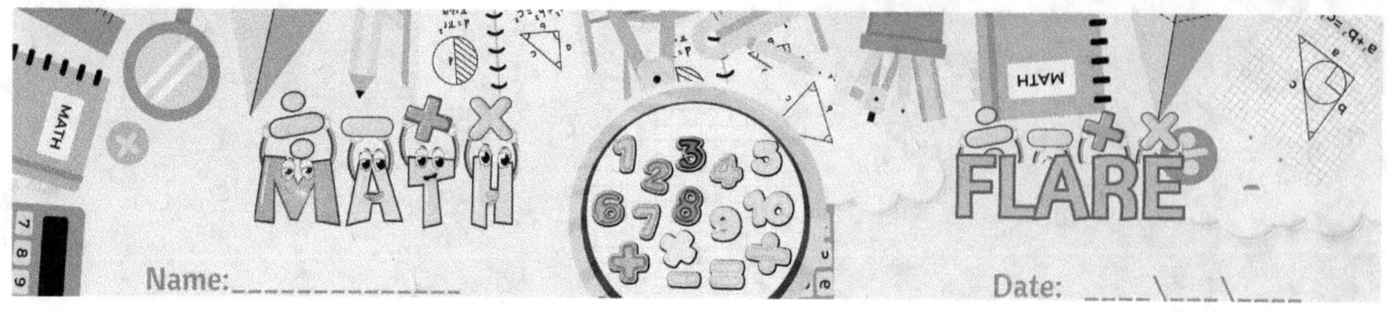

26. 9k – 2 + 2k – 14 + k + 1

27. –16 + 12 – 4m + 17m – 19 + 3m

28. –16 + 4k – 9k – 8 – 17k

29. 5 + 11z – 2z

30. 15y + 1 + y

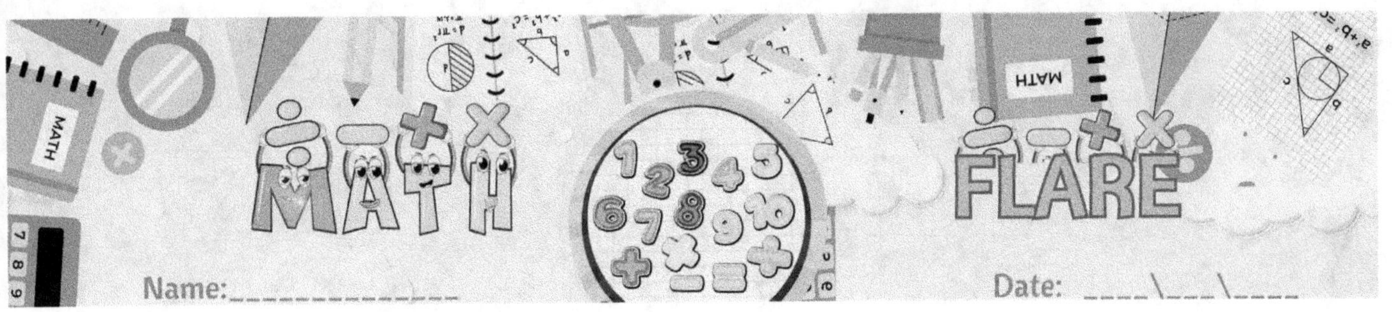

31. $4k + 11 + 20k + 13 + 7k + 4$

32. $15 + z - 12 + 12z$

33. $y + 20 + 4y$

34. $19z - 12z + 9 + 13$

35. $-4k + k$

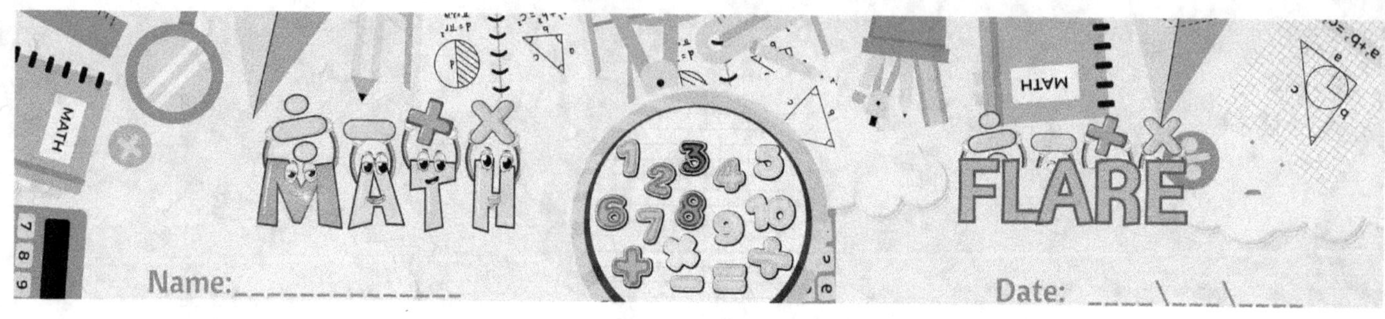

36. $x + 4 + 4x$

37. $16z + 10 - 3 - 18z + 18z$

38. $-y - 7y$

39. $19 - 1(17k - 1)$

40. $4x + 11 + 15x$

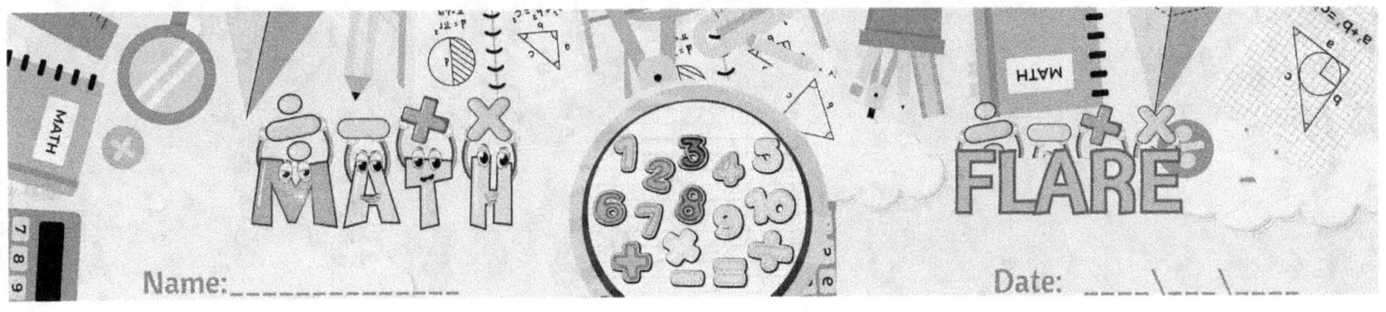

41. $-x - 11x$

42. $-12y + 19 + 8y + 14 + 7y - 16$

43. $9 - 13(3m - 1)$

44. $6x - 7 - 4x + 16$

45. $17z + 17 + 7z$

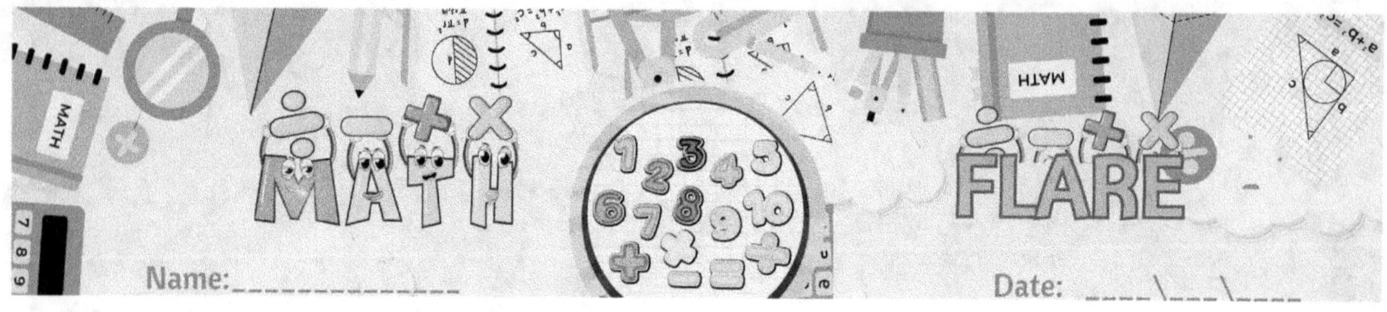

46. $13k - 12 - 19k + 7 - 13$

47. $15 - 8y + 3 - 10y + 12 - 8y$

48. $-13 - 5y + 10 - 17y$

49. $z + 2 + 10z$

50. $7y - y$

51. $8k + 12k$

52. $-20 + 15z - 14z - 15 + 14z$

53. $12m + 20 - 14 - 8m + 10m$

54. $8 + 14(-2m + 14)$

55. $20m + 9 + 18m$

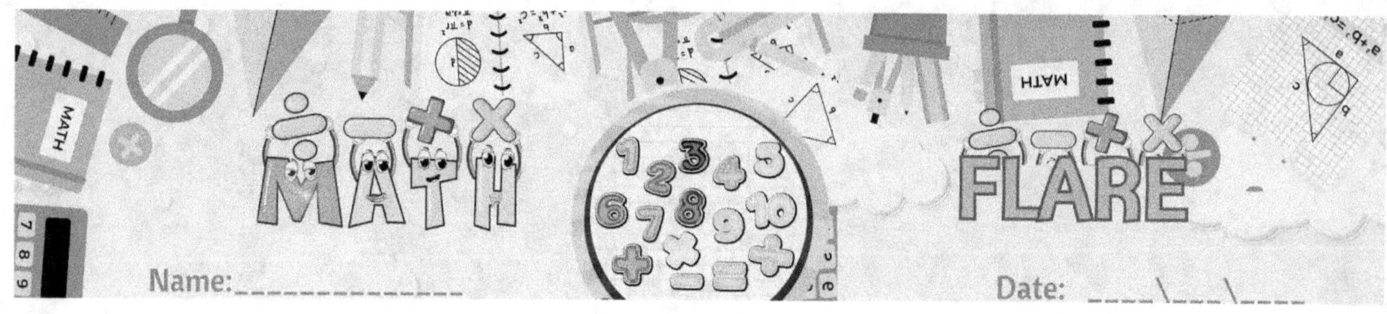

56. $-14 + 2m + 7 - 20m$

57. $6m + 17 - 6 - 2m + 5m$

58. $-18m + 13 - 20m$

59. $-8m + m$

60. $9 - 17(20z - 13)$

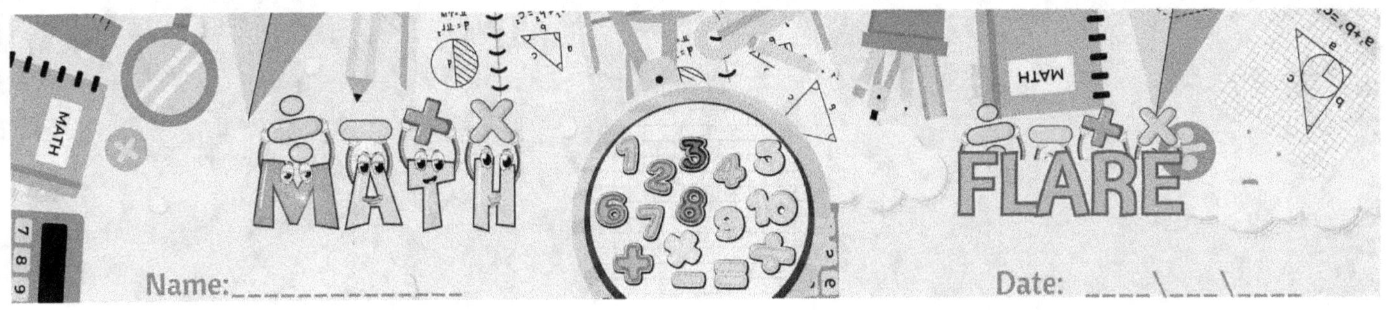

61. $12k - 20 - 10k + 3 - 20$

62. $10m + 5 - 5m + 13 + 15m + 7$

63. $13y - 7y + 15 + 9$

64. $-17k - 15 + 13k$

65. $3z - 14z + 2 + 3$

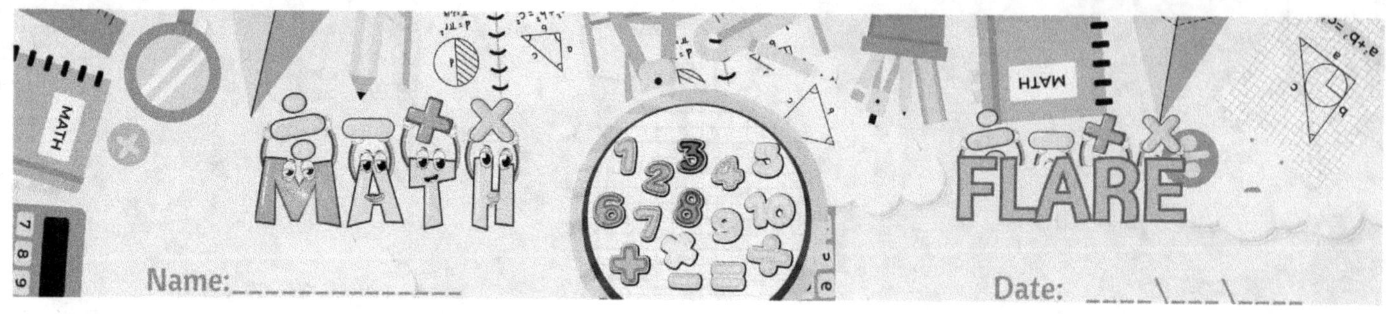

66. $-13 - 7m + 7 - 10m$

67. $15k - 11 - 16k + 7$

68. $-11y - 16y$

69. $8 + 12y + 20 + 6y$

70. $20 + 7k - 14 + 20k - 14 + 8k$

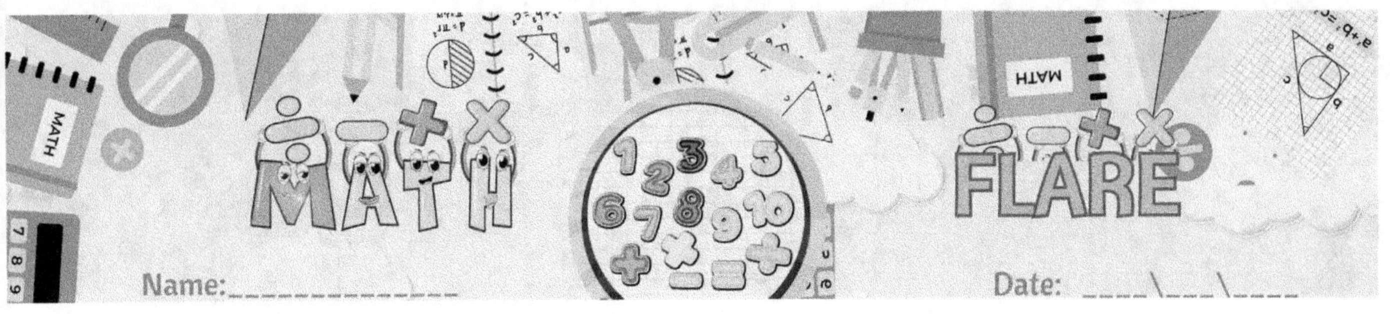

71. $3k - k$

72. $-y + 19y$

73. $8m + 17 + 2m$

74. $18 + 17(-8m + 19)$

75. $3z - 6 - 3z + 19 - 1$

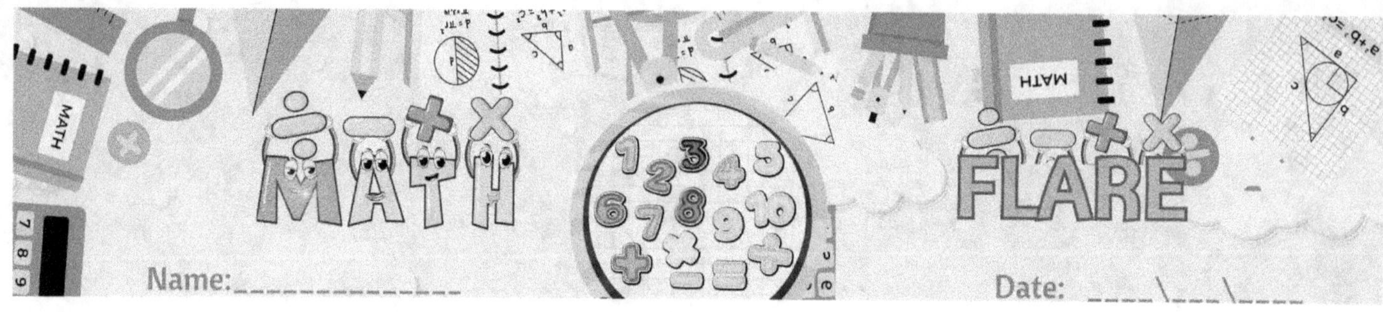

76. $4 + k - 2 + 20k$

77. $-3k + 4 + 6k$

78. $14m - 15m + 19 + 8$

79. $18 - 19(7k - 3)$

80. $-12z - z$

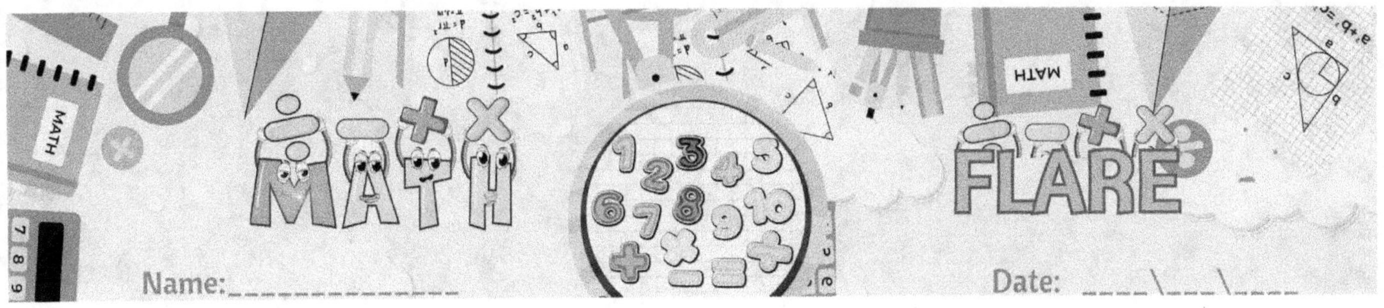

81. $19 + 15(2m - 12)$

82. $-5x + x + 3 - 20x$

83. $1 + 5m + 20 + 10m$

84. $3m - 17m$

85. $16x - x$

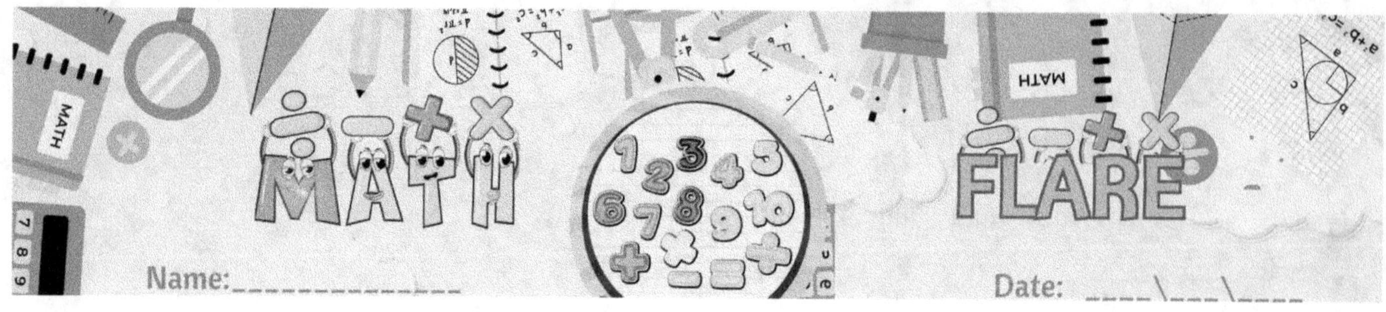

86. $-5k - k$

87. $4x + 3 + 18x + 20 + 15x + 1$

88. $-17x + 3 - 11x$

89. $11y + 10 + y$

90. $-4 + 4y - 18y - 12 - 3y$

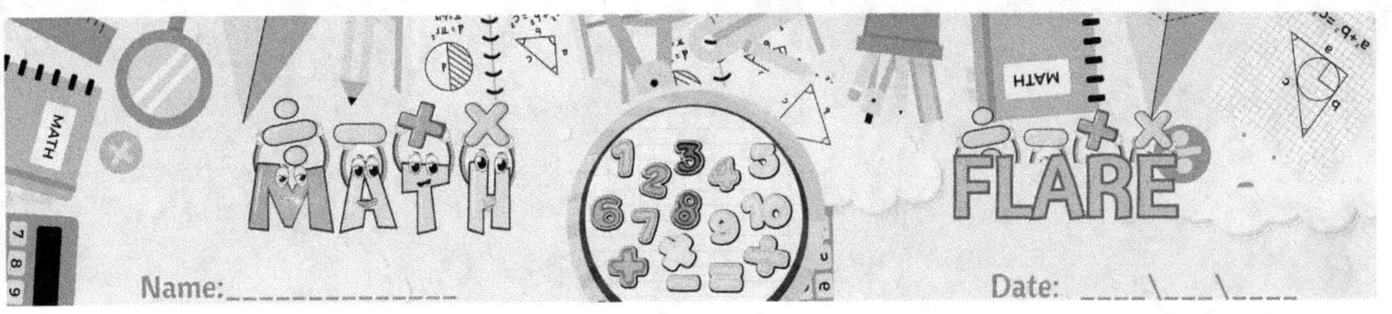

91. $-4m + 15m + 10 - 4m$

92. $8 + 8y - 5 + 3y$

93. $-7x + x$

94. $4 - 17(12m - 15)$

95. $14m - 10m + 1 + 7$

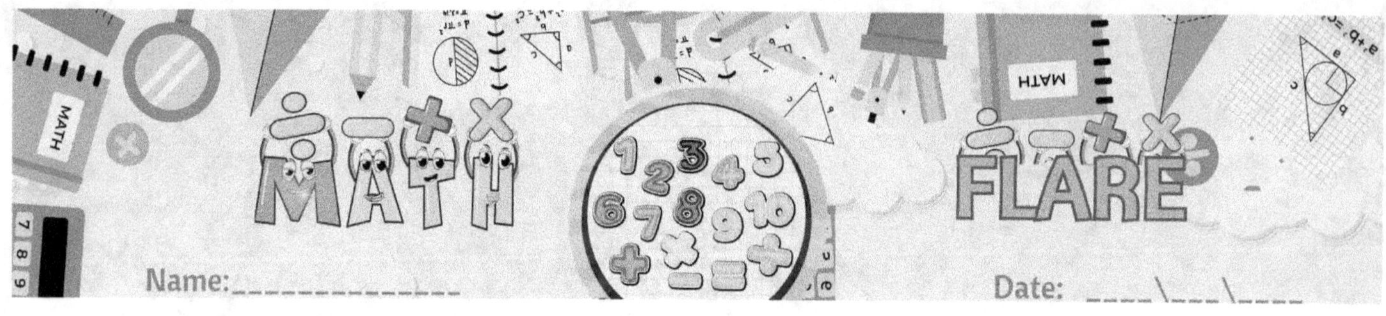

96. $-19k + 15 + 5k$

97. $19z - 19z$

98. $18 + 8m - 13m + 2 - 19m$

99. $-y + 12y$

100. $-14 + 14 - 13y + 5y - 12 + 20y$

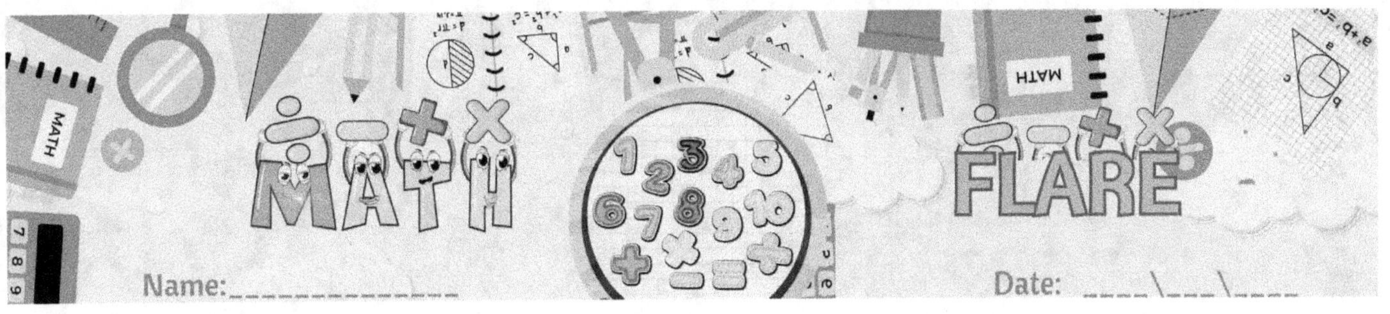

Solving Equations

Evaluate each expression when: x = 2

1. $2 \div x =$

2. $x \div 1 =$

3. $x^1 + x - 2 =$

4. $10 + x =$

5. $\dfrac{x}{2} =$

6. $5^1 + x^1 =$

7. $4 - x =$

8. $1 + x =$

9. $x^1 + x - 10 =$

10. $8(3 - x) =$

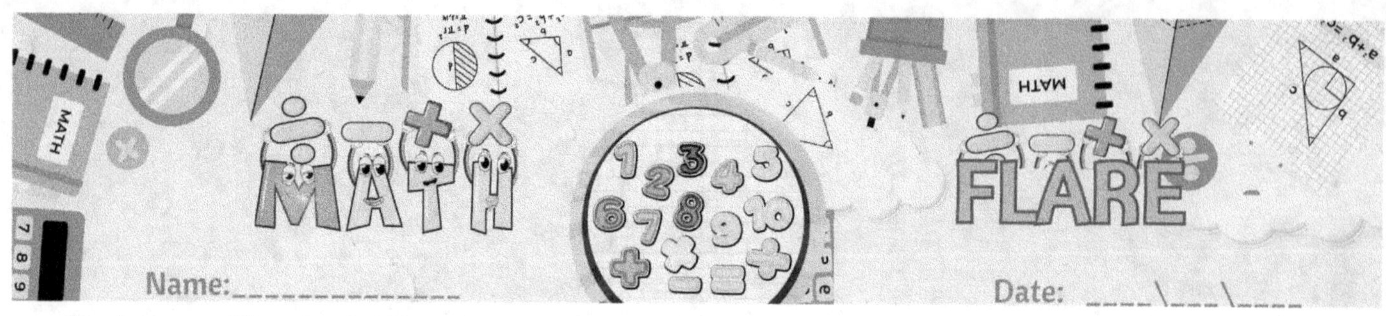

Solving Equations

Evaluate each expression when: x = 3

1. $6 \div x =$

2. $x - 5 =$

3. $3x + 5 =$

4. $10x + 7 - 8x =$

5. $10(4x - 8) + 10(10 + x) =$

6. $x + 4 =$

7. $\dfrac{9 + 27}{x + 3} =$

8. $x - 4 =$

9. $7x + 7 =$

10. $8 \div (x + 5) =$

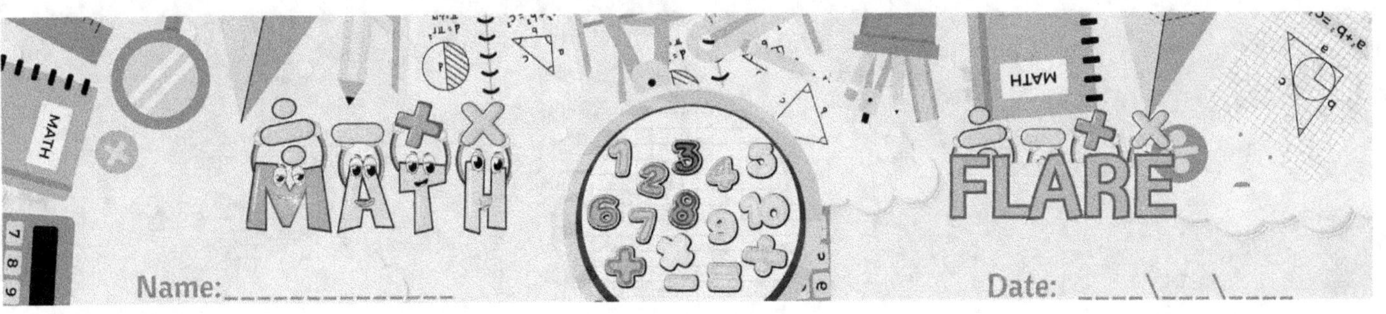

Solving Equations

Evaluate each expression when: x = 2

1. $3 \div (x + 1) =$

2. $x^1 + x - 4 =$

3. $4 + (6x + 10) =$

4. $x + 9 =$

5. $\dfrac{4 + 36}{x + 8} =$

6. $x + 6 + 2x =$

7. $2^1 + x^1 =$

8. $(4 + 5x) + (8x - 6) - (8 + 4x) =$

9. $(x + 3) \div 5 =$

10. $1 - x =$

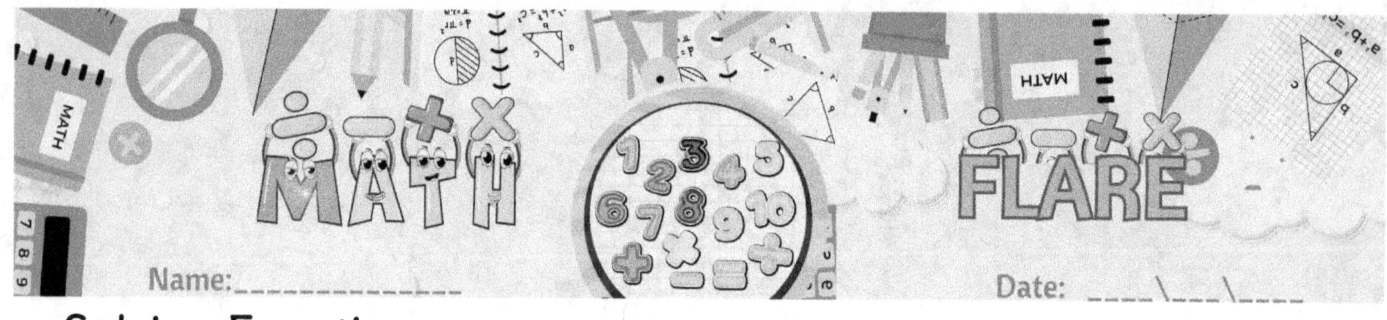

Solving Equations

Evaluate each expression when: $x = 5$

1. $x^1 + x - 2 =$

2. $8 + 7x =$

3. $8 + (5x + 8) =$

4. $10 \div x =$

5. $x - 4 =$

6. $\dfrac{x}{1} + 10 =$

7. $4 + (6x + 5) - 6 + (10x) =$

8. $3x + 4 =$

9. $4x + 7 =$

10. $1 \div (x + 10) =$

Solving Equations

Evaluate each expression when: x = 4

1. $x + x =$

2. $9(6x) =$

3. $x + 8 - 10x =$

4. $9(10x - 7) + 7(2 + x) =$

5. $5 + \dfrac{9 + x}{4x} - 10 =$

6. $10(8x) =$

7. $(6 + x) + (5x - 5) - (8 + 3x) =$

8. $10(10 + x) =$

9. $2(9 + x) =$

10. $2 + \dfrac{2 + x}{4x} - 9 =$

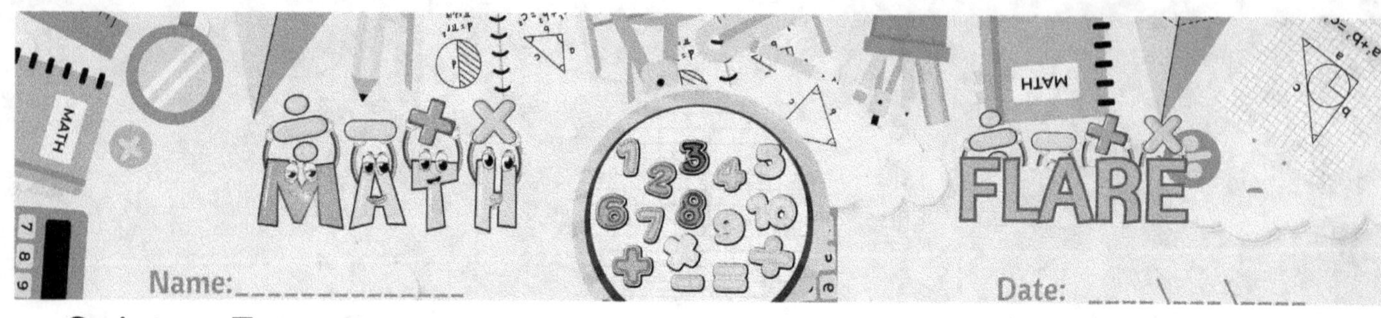

Solving Equations

Evaluate each expression when: $x = 3$

1. $5x + x =$

2. $x \div 3 =$

3. $\dfrac{4 + x}{x + 4} =$

4. $6 \div x =$

5. $x - 10 + 4x =$

6. $6x + x =$

7. $x + 7 =$

8. $9x + x - 7 =$

9. $\dfrac{2 + 30}{x + 1} =$

10. $\dfrac{3}{x} =$

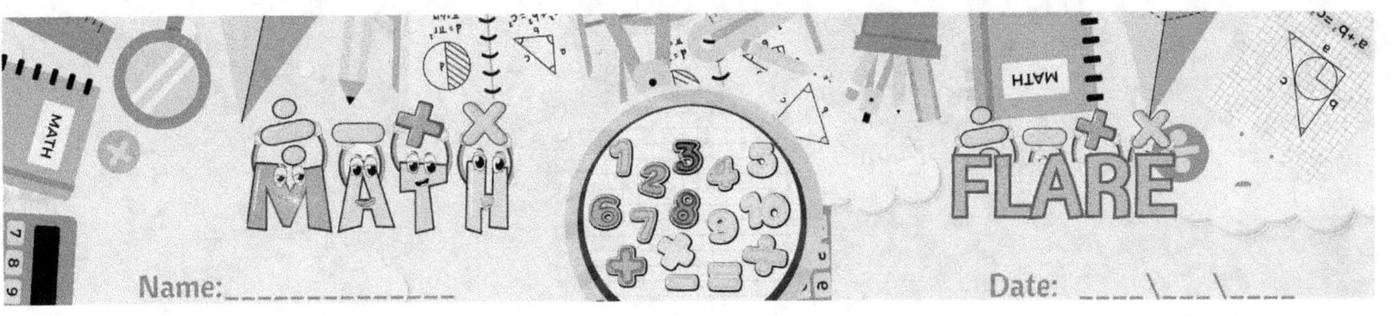

Solving Equations

Evaluate each expression when: x = 7

1. $4 \div (x + 9) =$

2. $6x + 4 =$

3. $\dfrac{14}{x} =$

4. $4x + 6 =$

5. $9(5 + x) =$

6. $x + 5x - 7 =$

7. $9x + 5 =$

8. $\dfrac{4 + x}{x + 4} =$

9. $x + 3x - 5 =$

10. $4x^1 + 9x^1 =$

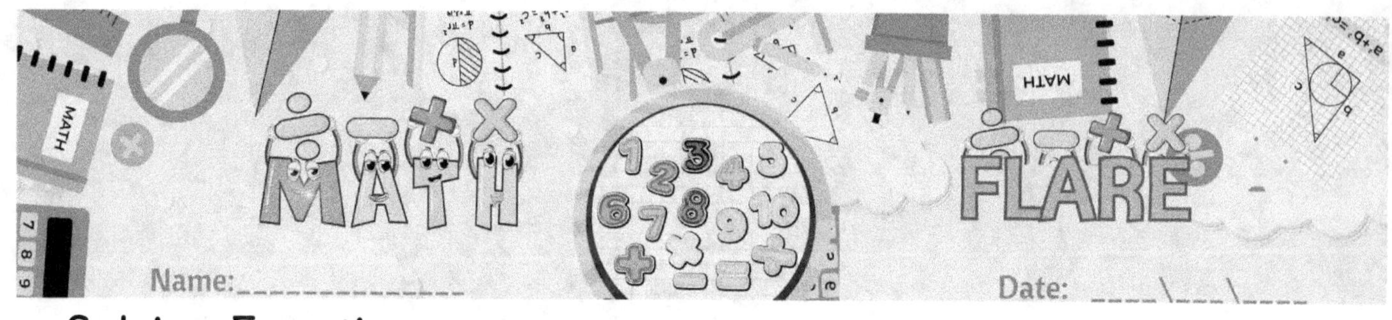

Solving Equations

Evaluate each expression when: $x = 6$

1. $7(4 + x) =$

2. $x - 3 =$

3. $\dfrac{9 + x}{x + 9} =$

4. $x + 2 =$

5. $6 \div x =$

6. $6x + x =$

7. $2x + 6x + 6x =$

8. $(1 + x) + (5x - 4) - (1 + 8x) =$

9. $x + 3 =$

10. $6(6 - x) =$

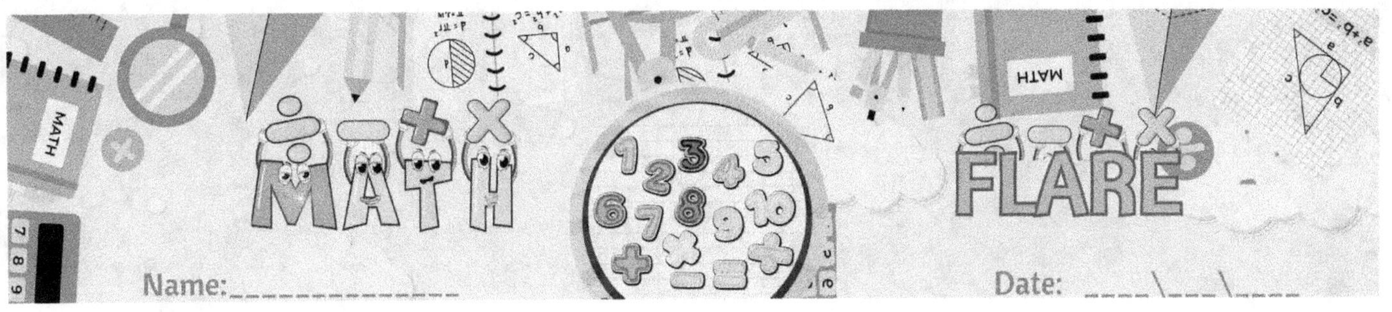

Solving Equations

Evaluate each expression when: $x = 1$

1. $(5x + 2) + (5x + 6) =$

2. $(5x)^1 =$

3. $x - 7 =$

4. $8 + \dfrac{7 + x}{x} - 9 =$

5. $7x + 9 =$

6. $4 - x =$

7. $6(3x) =$

8. $9(10x) =$

9. $x^1 + x - 5 =$

10. $x(8 + x) =$

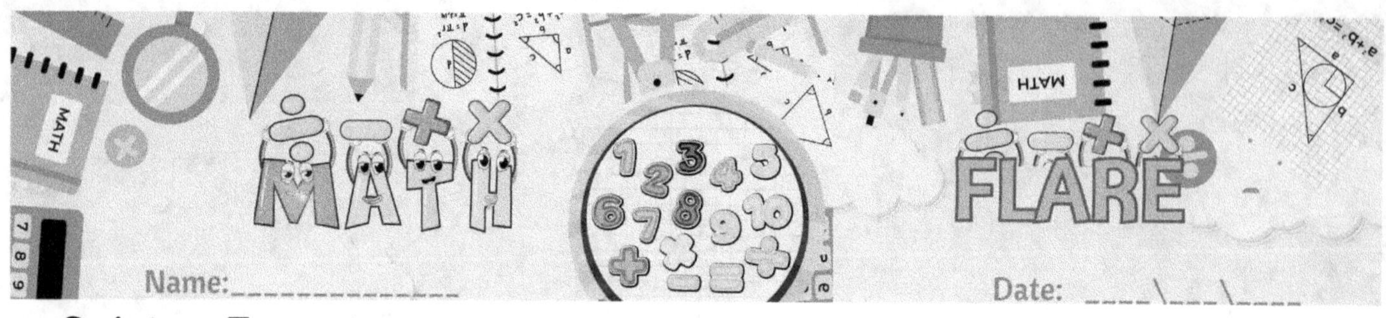

Solving Equations

Evaluate each expression when: x = 4

1. $7(2x) =$

2. $9 + \dfrac{x}{4} =$

3. $4 \div x =$

4. $7x + 7x + 9x =$

5. $4x - x =$

6. $2x + 4 =$

7. $4x + 3 - 8x =$

8. $5x + 7 - 10x =$

9. $(8x + 7) + (3x + 5) =$

10. $x - 7 =$

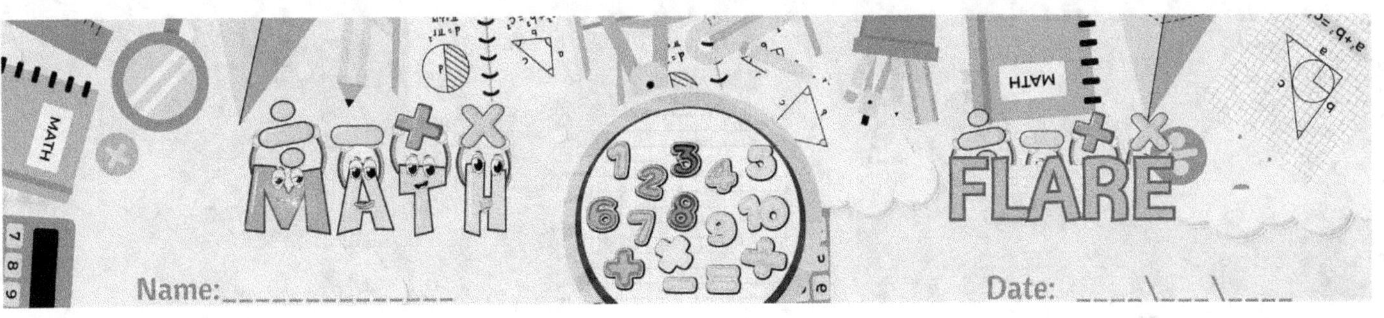

Solving Equations

Evaluate each expression when: $x = 4$

1. $x + 10 =$

2. $x - 7 =$

3. $2^1 + x^1 =$

4. $4x + x =$

5. $4 + 9x =$

6. $6x + 9x + 5x =$

7. $7 + \dfrac{4}{x} + 5^1 =$

8. $10(4 + x) =$

9. $9(2 - x) =$

10. $x + 5 + 9x =$

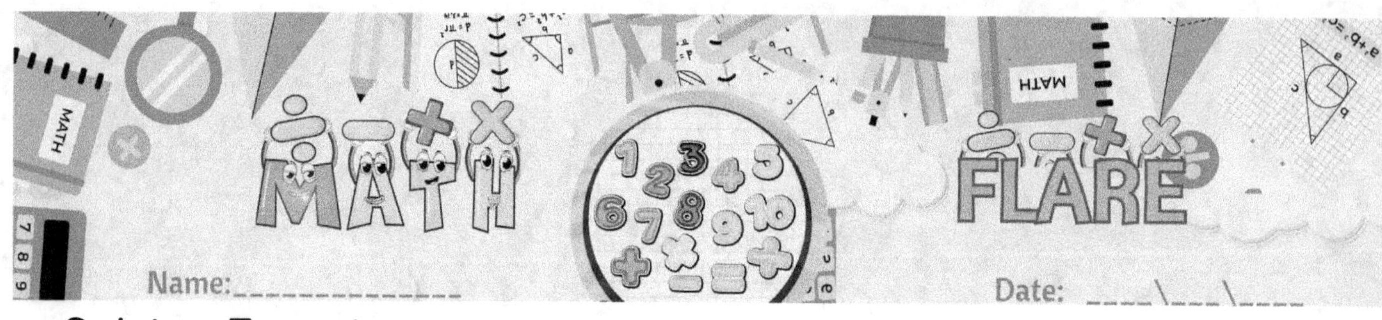

Solving Equations

Evaluate each expression when: x = 4

1. $4x^1 + 3x^1 =$

2. $x + 3 =$

3. $9(3x) =$

4. $8(9x) =$

5. $(5 + 7x) + (5x - 8) - (7 + 6x) =$

6. $3x + 1 =$

7. $x^1 + x - 3 =$

8. $5(8 - x) =$

9. $3x + x + 2x =$

10. $3 + \dfrac{8 + x}{x} - 5 =$

Solving Equations

Evaluate each expression when: $x = 2$

1. $7(2 - x) =$

2. $\dfrac{x}{1} =$

3. $x + 2 =$

4. $(2x)^1 =$

5. $(x + 4) + (10x + 3) =$

6. $\dfrac{7 + 38}{x + 1} =$

7. $4 + 2x =$

8. $x + 4 + (6x - 6) =$

9. $1 + x =$

10. $5 + \dfrac{30}{x} + 1^1 =$

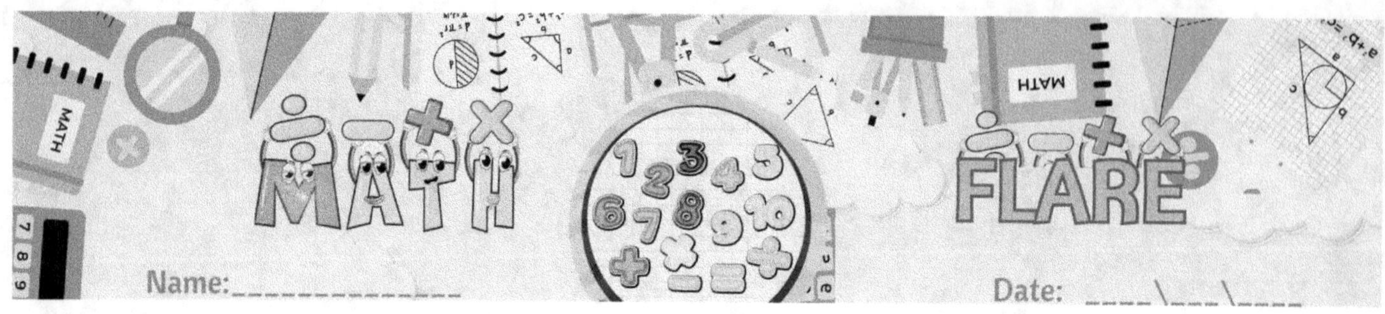

Name:______________

Date: ____________

Equations (One Side)

Solve for the variable.

1. $122 = 5z + 4z - 13$

2. $(15m)(8m) = 38{,}880$

3. $12y - y = 154$

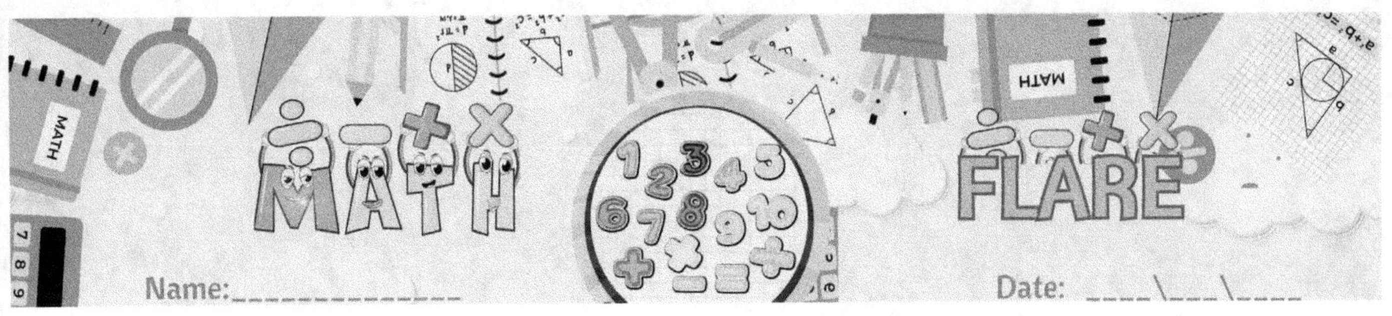

4. $0.263 = 10 \div (m + 18)$

5. $277 = 15y - 8$

6. $12 - z = 5$

7. $1 = \dfrac{y}{15}$

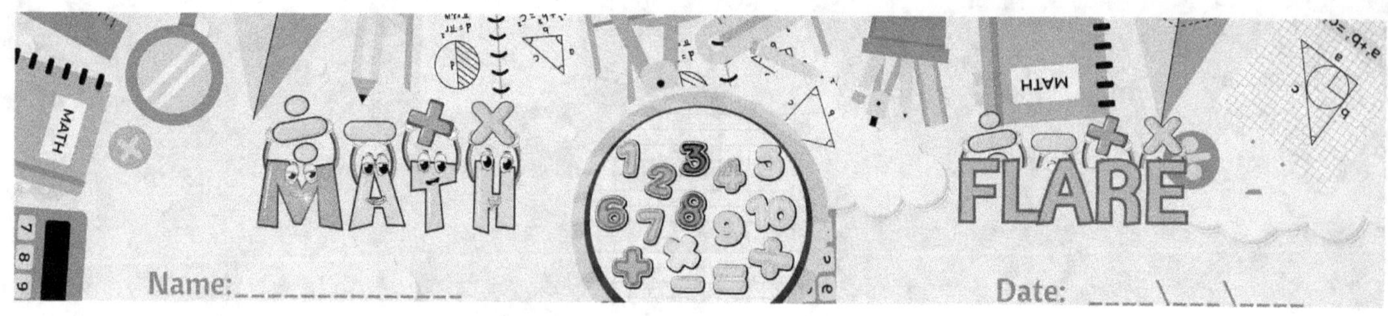

8. $(11m + 3) + (10m - 6) = 207$

9. $8(4m - 13) + 16(1 + m) = 344$

10. $3 = (z + 16) \div 8$

11. $206 = 11x + 8$

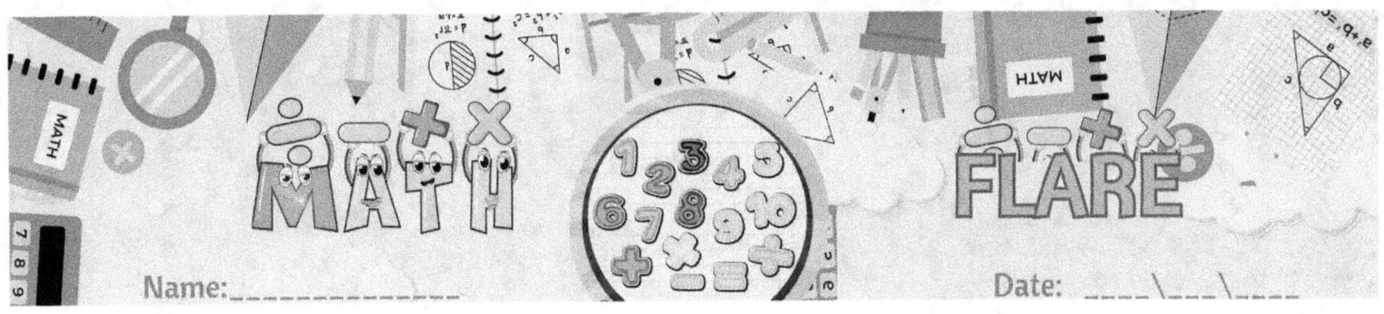

12. $3k - 7 + 12k = 98$

13. $10 \div k + 14 = 14.556$

14. $-162 = 18(2 - k)$

15. $y(14 + y) = 627$

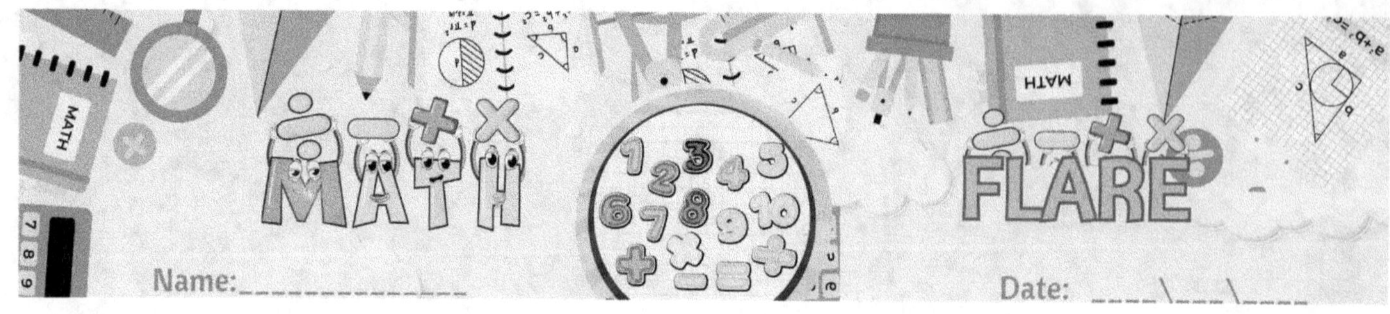

16. $20 + z = 36$

17. $12 \div y = 0.857$

18. $7 + (7z + 20) = 132$

19. $370 = 20x + 10$

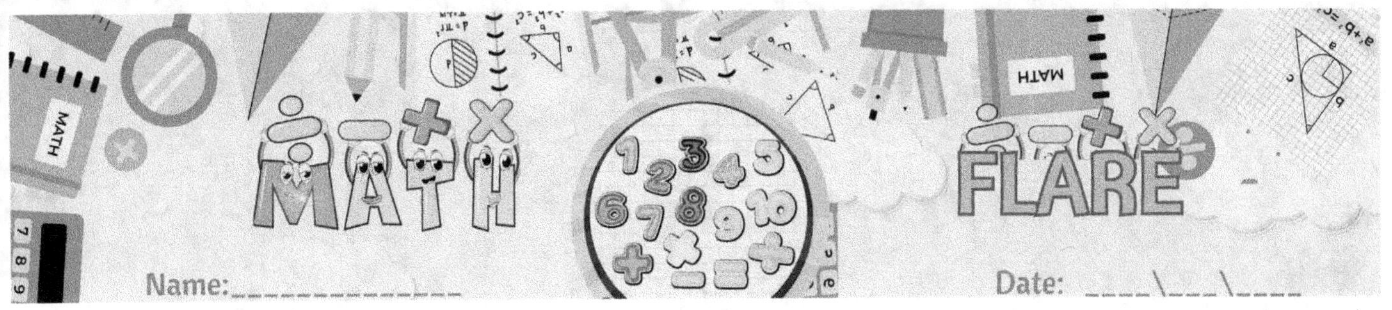

20. $18 + (19z + 17) = 73$

21. $12k - 2 + 9k = 19$

22. $42 = (18 + 12y) + (4y - 11) - (20 + 5y)$

23. $(11y + 16) + (16y + 14) = 165$

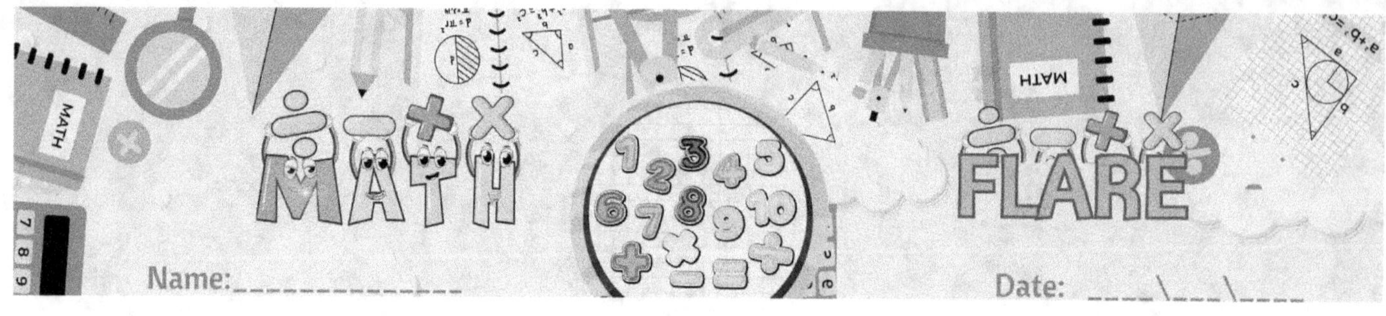

24. $y + 9 = 20$

25. $9 + k = 26$

26. $6.25 = 16 + \dfrac{14 + m}{2m} - 12$

27. $-56 = 14(3 - k)$

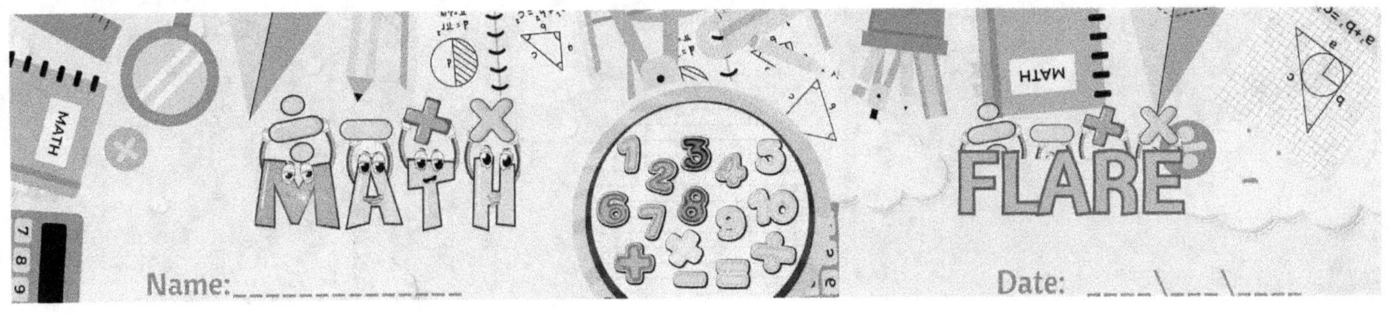

28. $87 = m^2 + m - 3$

29. $90 = (13 + 4z) + (3z - 2) - (17 + z)$

30. $2(2 + z) = 8$

31. $\dfrac{k}{8} = 2$

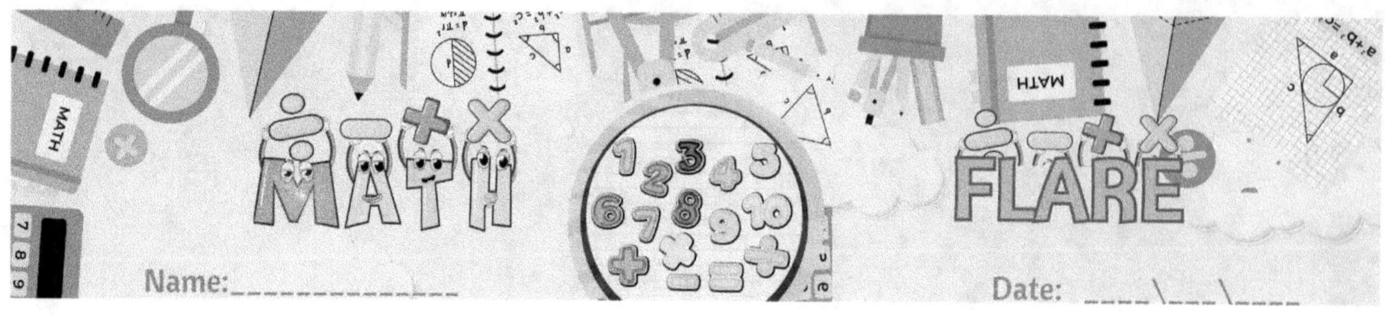

32. $14 = 13 + k$

33. $1.4 = y \div 10$

34. $4m + 4 = 24$

35. $19 - x = 9$

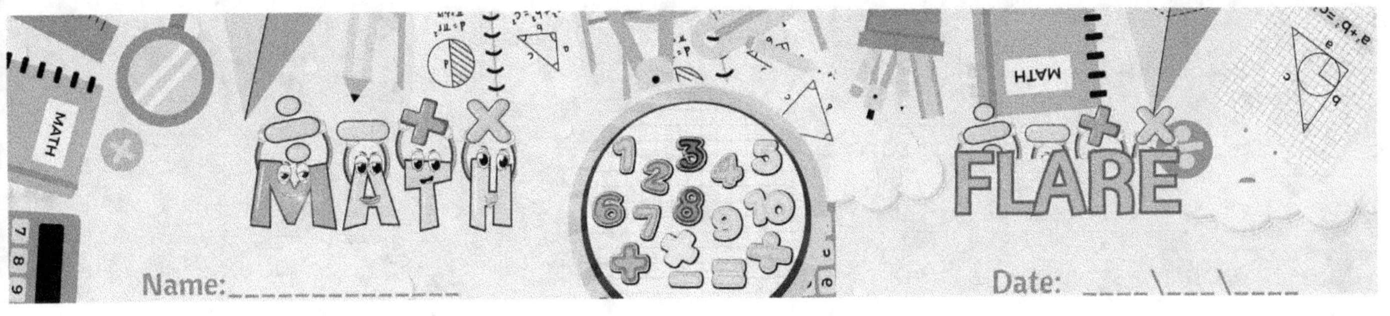

36. $\dfrac{x}{6} = 1$

37. $255 = 14m + m$

38. $(8y)^2 = 23{,}104$

39. $18m + 9 = 81$

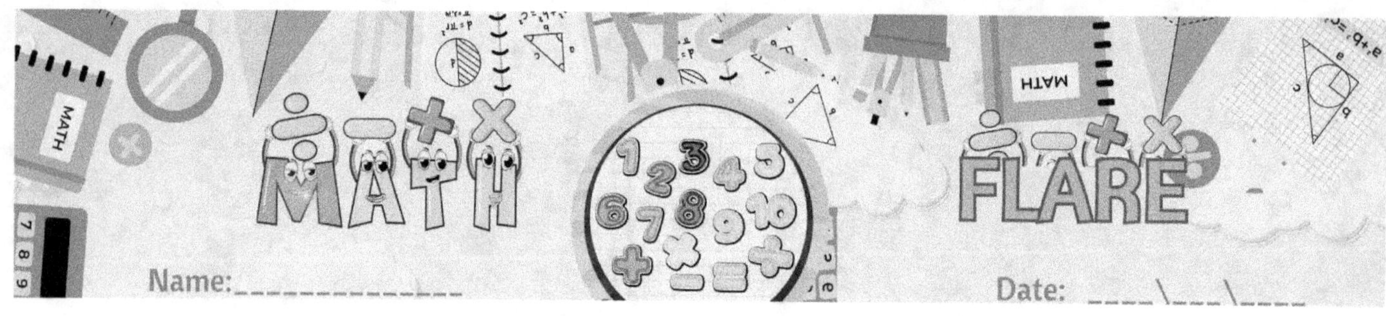

40. $-536 = -18(y + 9) + (-8(y - 2))$

41. $(15z + 14) + (19z - 14) = 102$

42. $(9y + 8) + (y + 11) = 89$

43. $15y + 2y - 15 = 325$

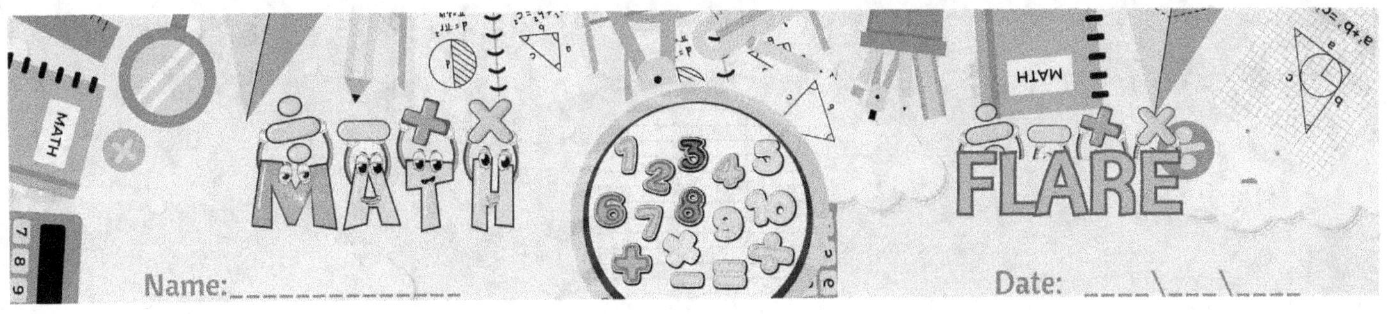

44. $k - 19 = -15$

45. $3z^2 + 4z^2 = 252$

46. $-10 = k - 13$

47. $123 = y^2 + y - 9$

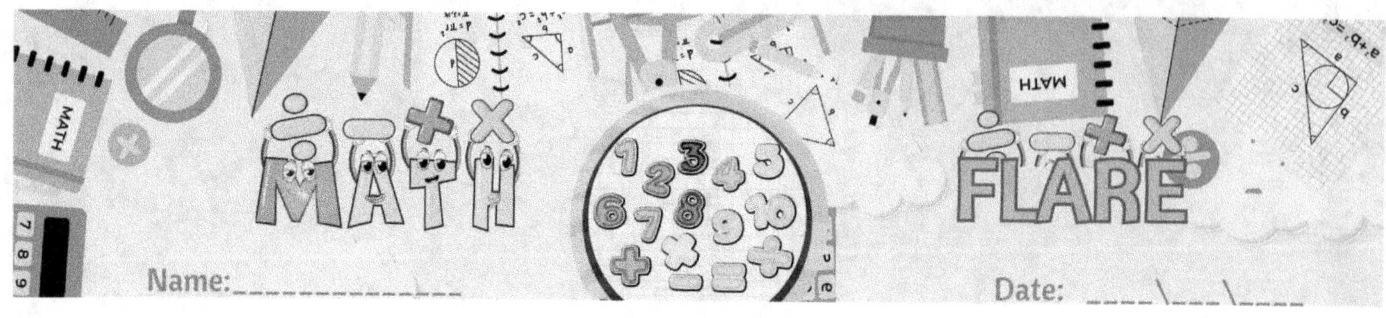

48. $14 = \dfrac{z}{1} + 4$

49. $18 + \dfrac{8}{k} + 10^2 = 126$

50. $37 = 11m + 4$

51. $4 + \dfrac{k}{1} = 12$

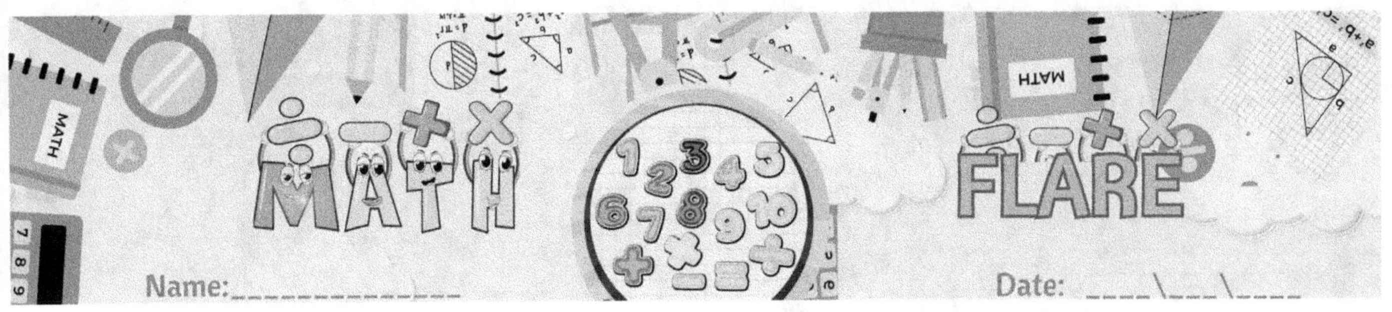

52. $2{,}916 = (18x)^2$

53. $106 = 1 + \dfrac{15}{y} + 10^2$

54. $5 + x = 10$

55. $(k + 14) \div 10 = 2.3$

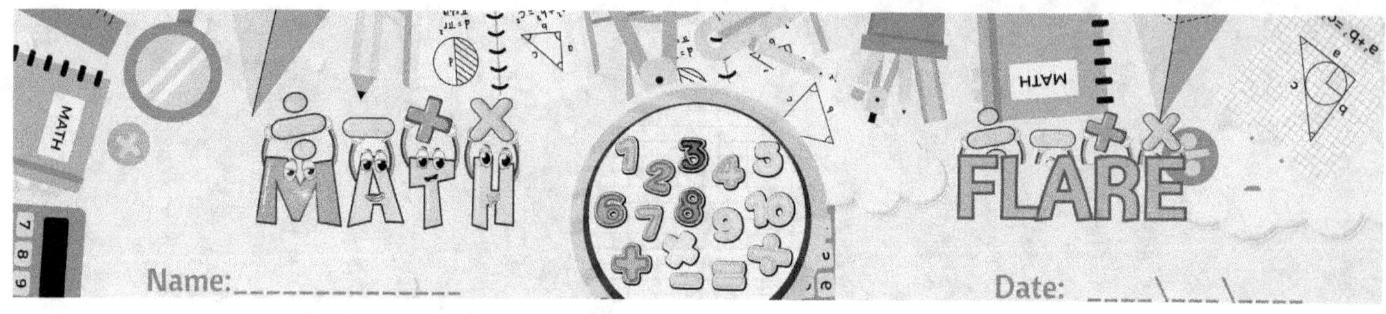

56. $47 = 9 + \dfrac{12}{x} + 6^2$

57. $10(15 - k) = 120$

58. $13x + x = 28$

59. $1.889 = \dfrac{14 + 20}{y + 14}$

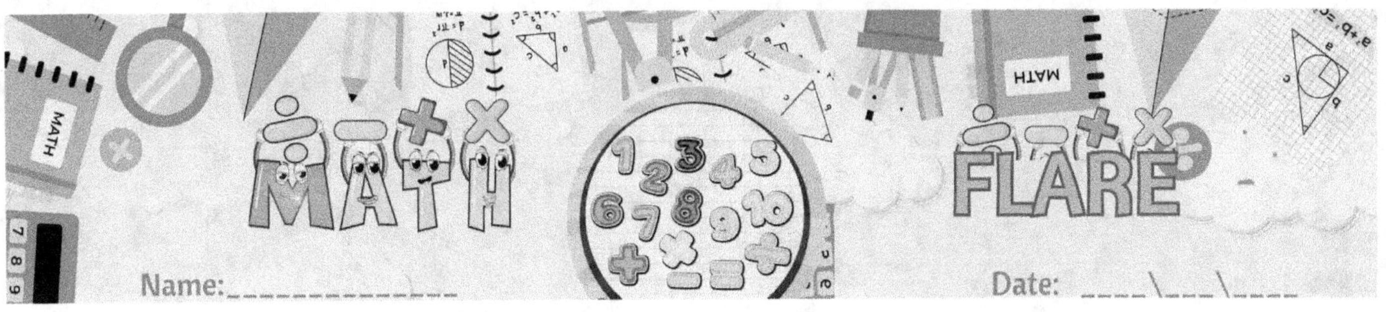

60. $290 = 17z + 17z - 16$

61. $\dfrac{14 + 1}{y + 10} = 1.364$

62. $21 = 6 + (6x + 3)$

63. $5 = k - 1$

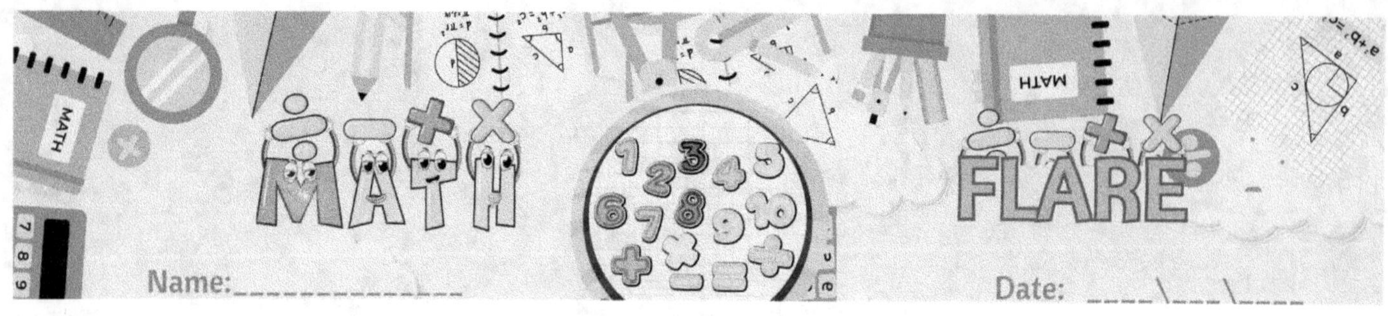

64. $-18 = 18(3 - y)$

65. $\dfrac{y}{3} + 9 = 12$

66. $k^2 + k - 14 = -8$

67. $3{,}332 = (17y)(y)$

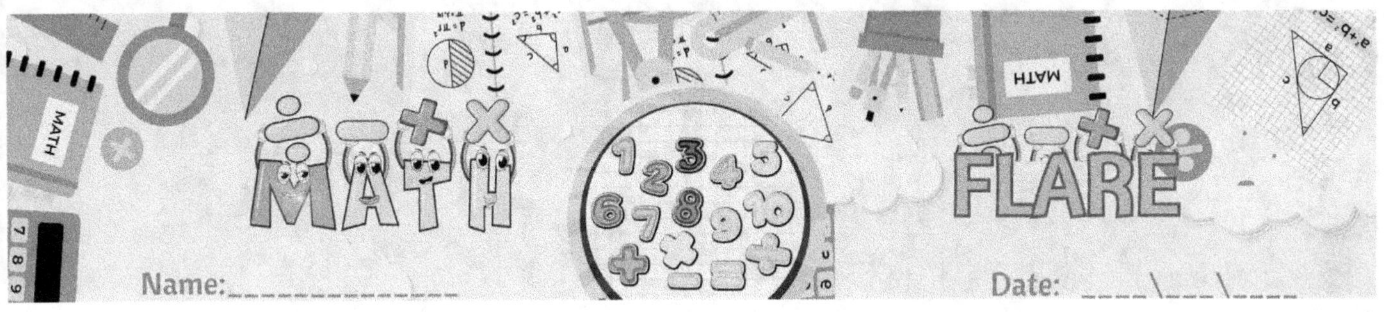

68. $347 = 18x + 5$

69. $41 = 14 + 9x$

70. $0.536 = 15 \div (y + 10)$

71. $-3.656 = 4 + \dfrac{14 + y}{8y} - 8$

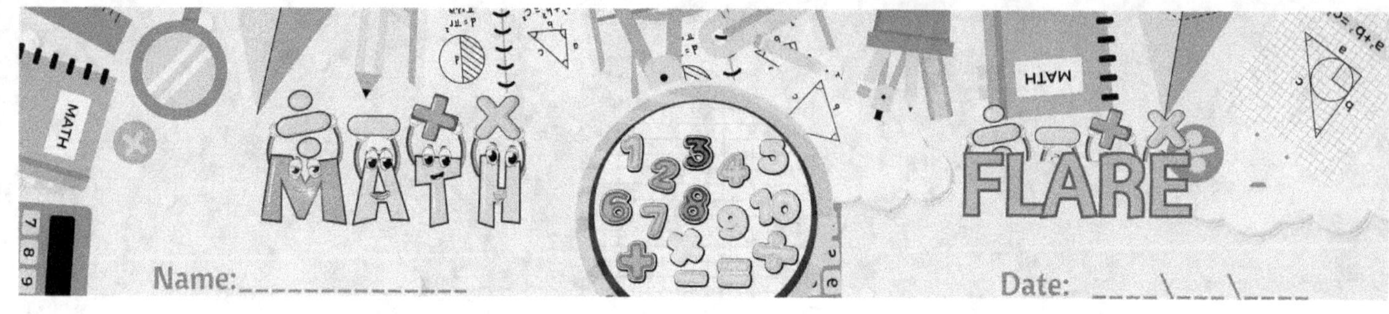

72. $0 = z - 7$

73. $x + 12 + 13x = 82$

74. $19x + 13 = 89$

75. $19 = 12 + k$

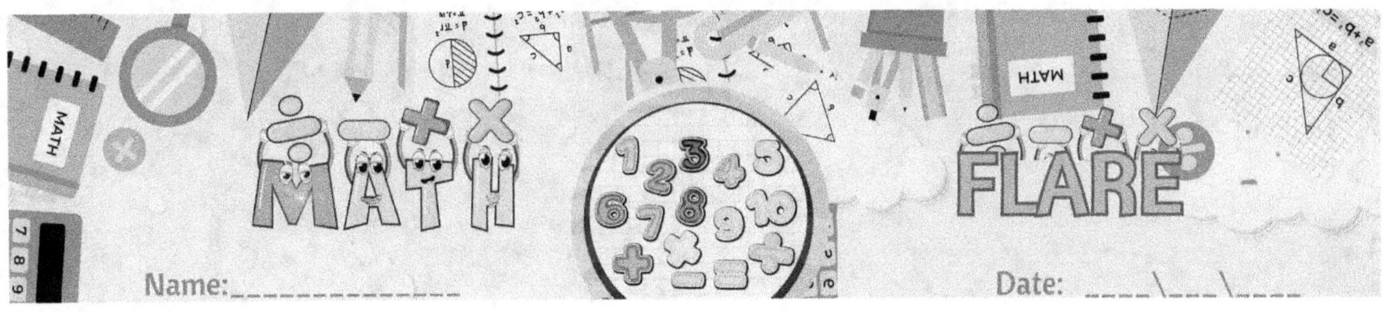

76. $4 + \dfrac{z}{9} = 5$

77. $160 = 20(17 - k)$

78. $54 = m^2 + m - 2$

79. $272 = 4^2 + z^2$

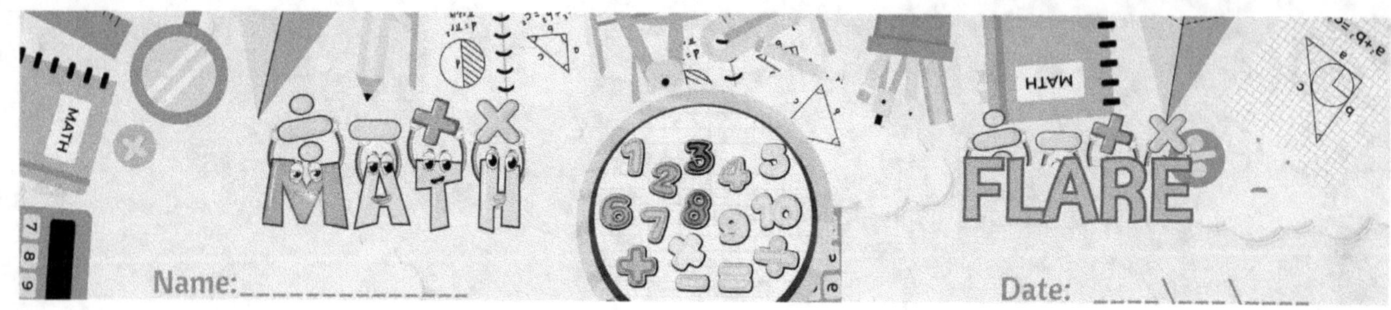

80. $9 = z + 8$

81. $300 = 8m + 15m + 2m$

82. $6x - 18 + 18x = 366$

83. $k \div 6 = 2.667$

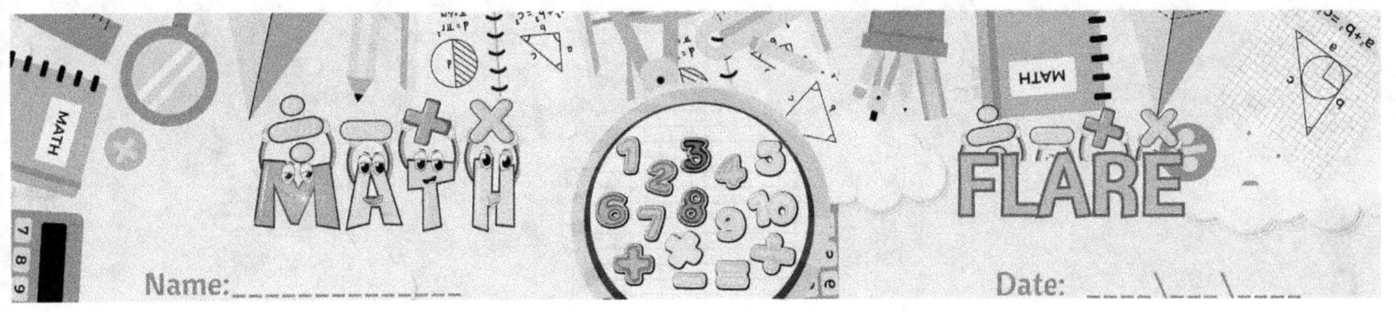

84. $1 + \dfrac{k}{1} = 17$

85. $23 = 5z + 9 - 3z$

86. $-84 = 12(13 - y)$

87. $k + 20 + 17k = 254$

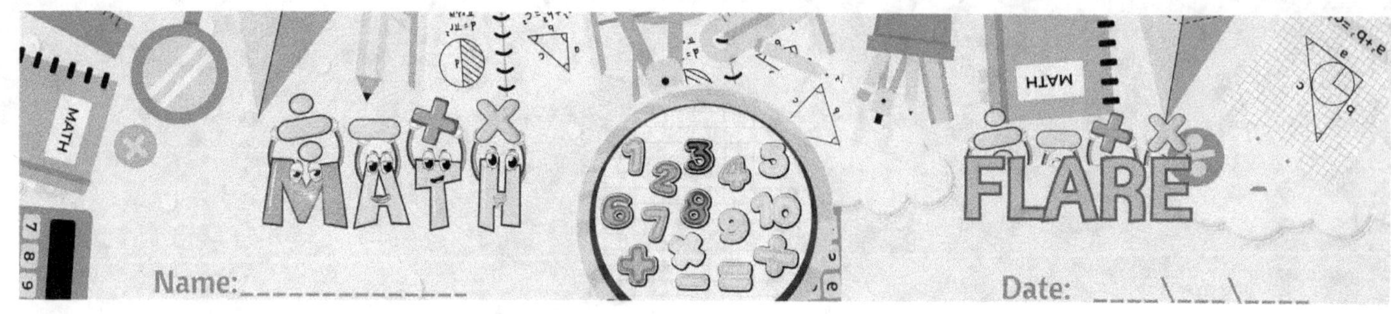

88. $16 = 18 \div z + 15$

89. $-4.75 = 8 + \dfrac{18 + m}{2m} - 14$

90. $372 = 9k + 15k - 12$

91. $(19m)^2 = 116{,}964$

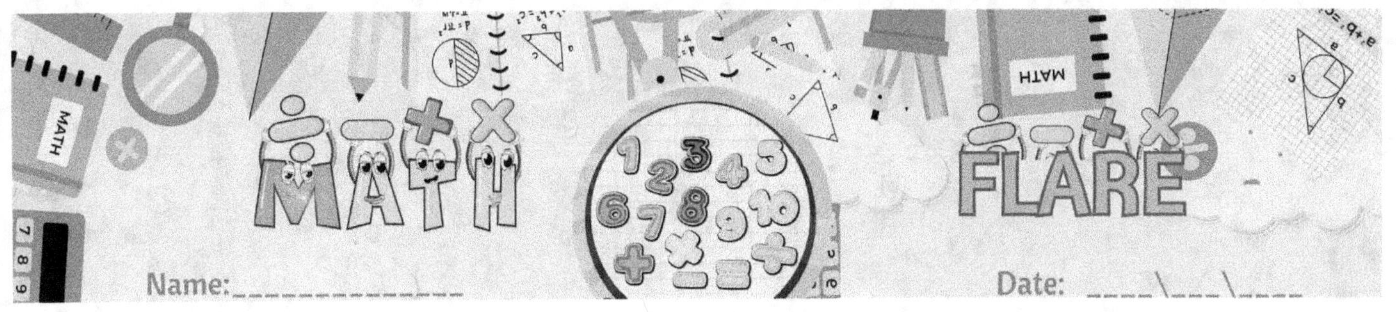

92. $-260 = -16(y + 5) + (-9(y - 5))$

93. $23 = \dfrac{k}{2} + 20$

94. $9 + \dfrac{12}{k} + 6^2 = 49$

95. $338 = 17x + 15$

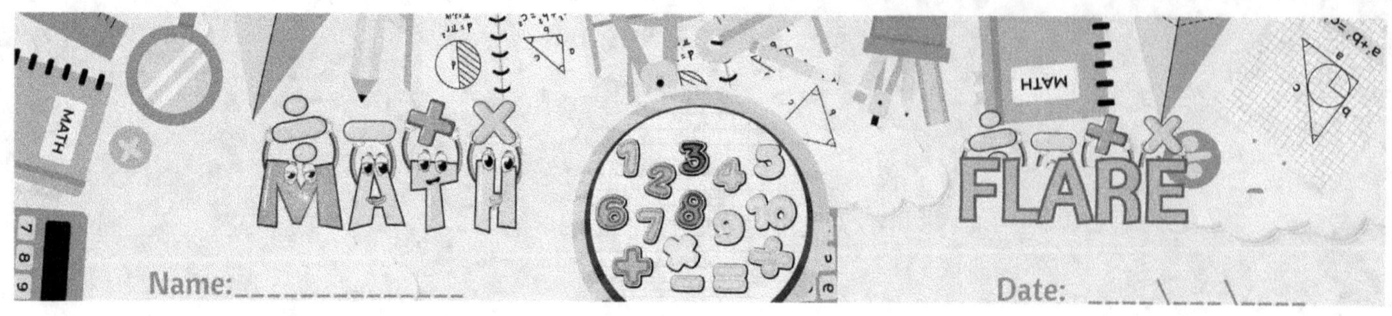

96. $15 = 9 + z$

97. $363 = z^2 + z - 17$

98. $2 = 20 - x$

99. $17 = 4 + m$

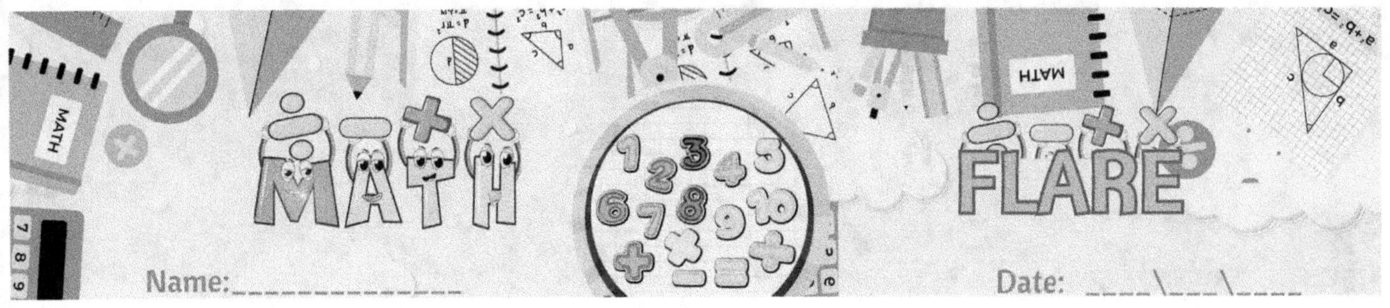

100. $y + 12 = 18$

101. $14(8k - 5) + 11(19 + k) = 754$

102. $(14x + 1) + (15x + 2) = 264$

103. $(k + 14) \div 12 = 2.167$

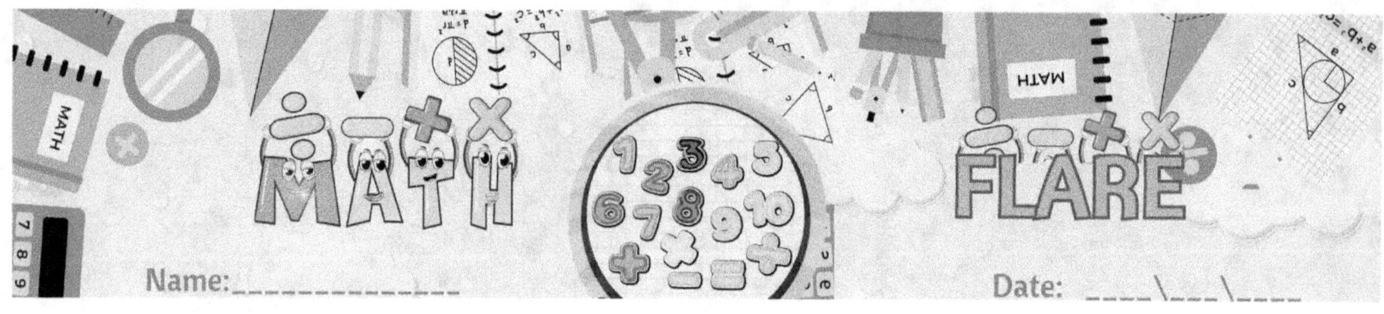

Equations (Two Sides)
Solve for the variable.

1. $8y + 8 = 58 - 2y$

2. $2 + 8y = 122 - 7y$

3. $21 - x = 2x + 9$

4. $3 + 7x = 2x + 8$

5. $10 + 2m = 5 + 3m$

6. $58 - m = 9 + 7m + 1$

7. $6 + 7z = 6z + 11$

8. $7 + 7m = 18 - 4m$

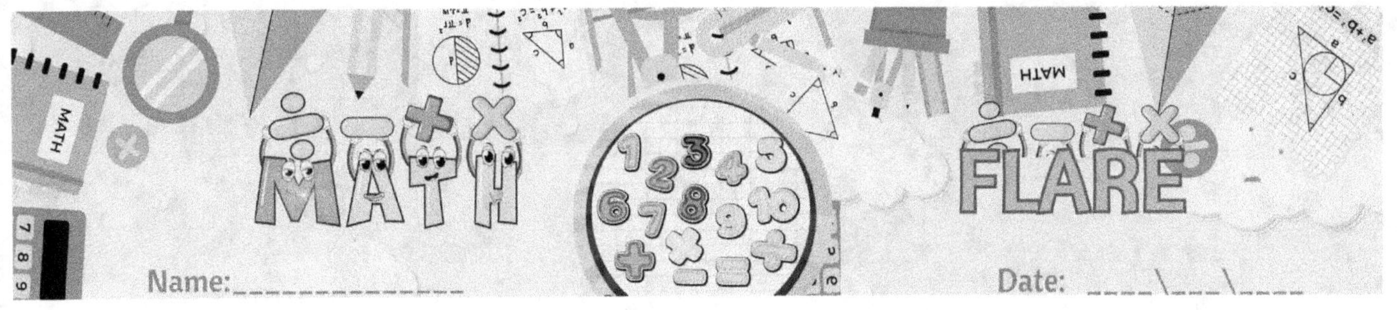

9. $34 + 3z = 9z + 4$

10. $7 + 2k + 1 = 19 + k + -5$

11. $19 + y = 8 + 2y + 4$

12. $4 + 7x + 8 = 46 - x + 14$

13. $19 - 6m = 7m + 6$

14. $17 + k + 1 = 4 + 5k + 2$

15. $17 + x = 3x + 1$

16. $4 + 6k = 7k + 2$

17. $4y + 15 = 3 + 8y$

18. $31 - x = 4 + 2x$

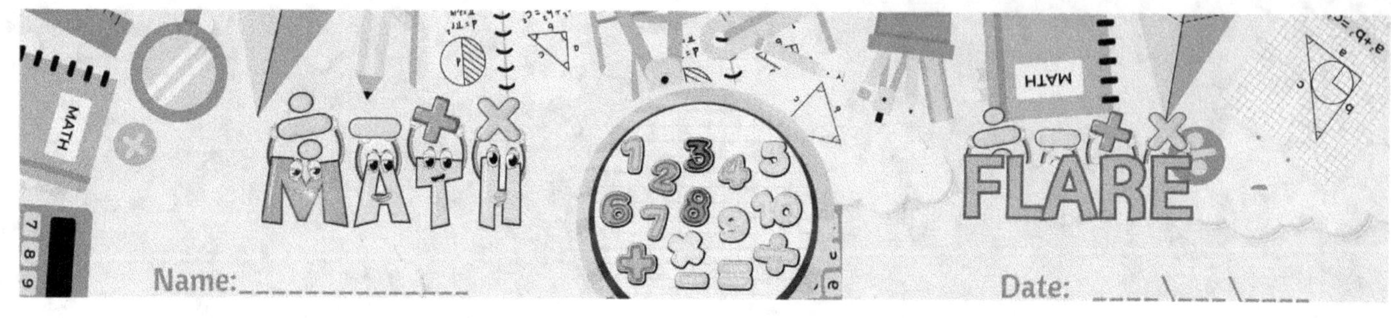

19. $38 + 2z = 7z + 3$

20. $29 + m = 4m + 8$

21. $2 + 2m = 8 + m$

22. $4 + 5z + 3 = 31 - z$

23. $11 + y = 2y + 3$

24. $66 + k = 3 + 8k$

25. $6 + 5m + 3 = 26 - m + 7$

26. $5 + 2m + 7 = 33 - m$

27. $47 - k = 5 + 6k$

28. $6 + 2m + 7 = 24 - m + 16$

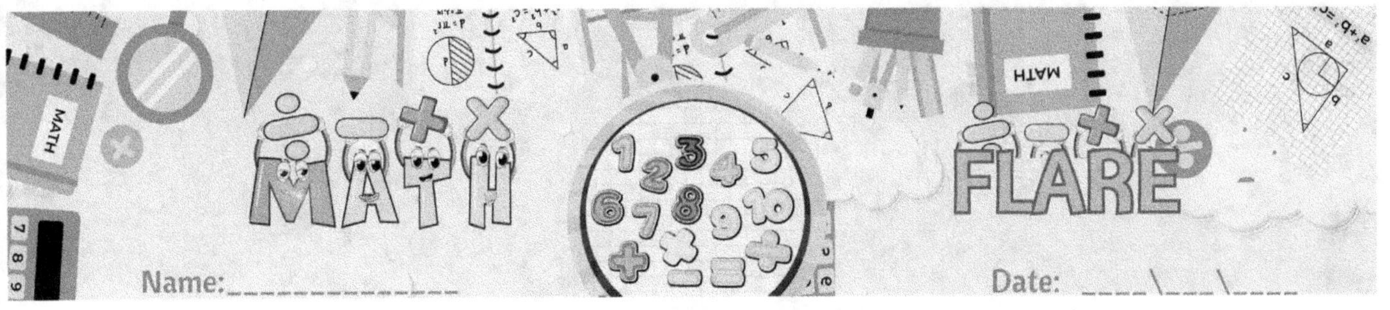

29. $2x + 1 = 5 + x$

30. $17 - k = 1 + 3k + 8$

31. $5 + 2x + 2 = 8 + x$

32. $45 + x = 9 + 8x + 1$

33. $8 + 3x = 10 + x$

34. $22 + x + -2 = 1 + 3x + 5$

35. $2 + 3z = 27 - 2z$

36. $40 + k = 8 + 5k$

37. $29 - 2z = 5 + 6z$

38. $14 - y = 4 + 4y$

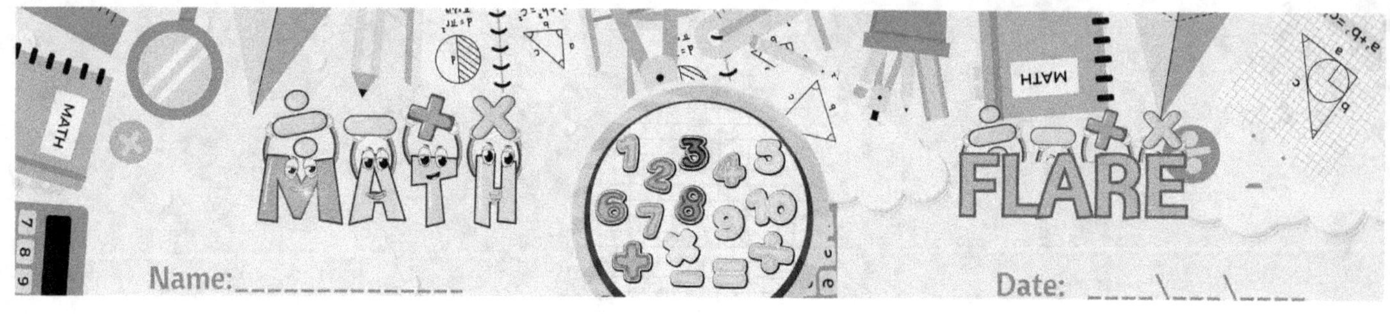

39. $27 - 2k = 7 + 8k$

40. $40 - y = 7 + 5y + 9$

41. $16 + m = 5m + 4$

42. $36 - k = 9 + 2k$

43. $59 + k + -2 = 7 + 6k + 5$

44. $13 + 7k = 8k + 6$

45. $2x + 5 = 9 + x$

46. $7y + 2 = 5y + 20$

47. $6 + 3k = 38 - k$

48. $28 - m + 9 = 6 + 7m + 7$

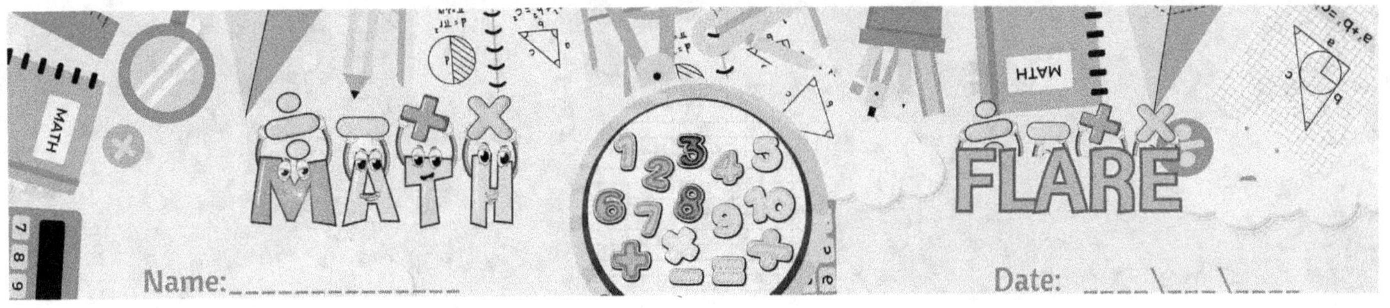

49. $8 + 6m = 18 + m$

50. $19 - k + 9 = 1 + 6k + 6$

51. $9 + 2z + 3 = 25 - z + 11$

52. $12 - z = 7z + 4$

53. $3 + 8m + 1 = 18 + m$

54. $145 - 7z = 9z + 1$

55. $51 - y = 7 + 5y + 8$

56. $42 + y = 8y + 7$

57. $15 + z = 6z + 5$

58. $9 + 4m = 12 + m$

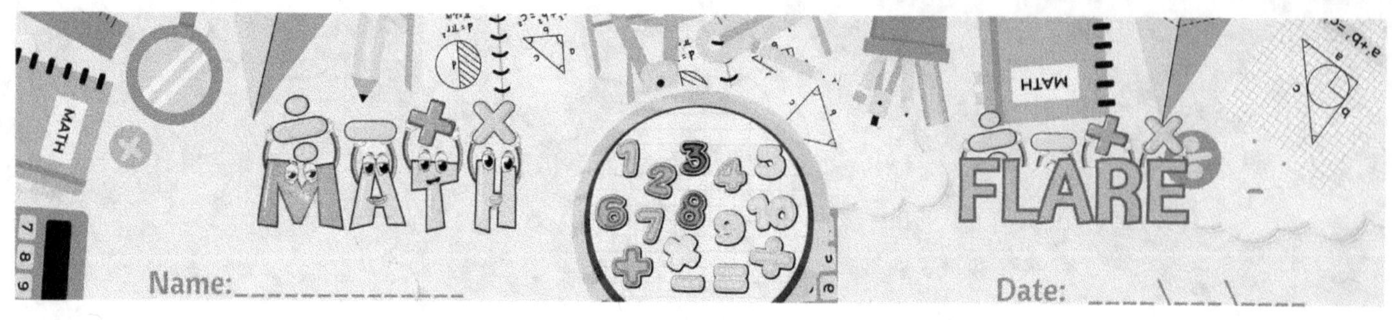

59. $2m + 1 = 6 + m$

60. $5z + 9 = 51 - z$

61. $9 + 5m = 15 + 3m$

62. $3 + 9x = 7x + 13$

63. $22 - z = 2 + 2z + 8$

64. $73 - y = 8 + 8y + 2$

65. $9x + 1 = 5x + 5$

66. $6 + 5m + 9 = 36 - m + 15$

67. $7 + 6z + 4 = 28 - z + 11$

68. $7z + 5 = 13 + 6z$

69. $8 + 2k + 7 = 24 + k$

70. $3 + 6x + 9 = 45 + x + -3$

71. $4k + 6 = 16 - k$

72. $3 + 5z + 8 = 47 - z$

73. $2m + 7 = 16 + m$

74. $4 + 7k = 68 - k$

75. $6z + 9 = 6 + 7z$

76. $22 + m = 8 + 3m + 6$

77. $6 + 4y + 7 = 48 - y$

78. $21 - y = 5y + 9$

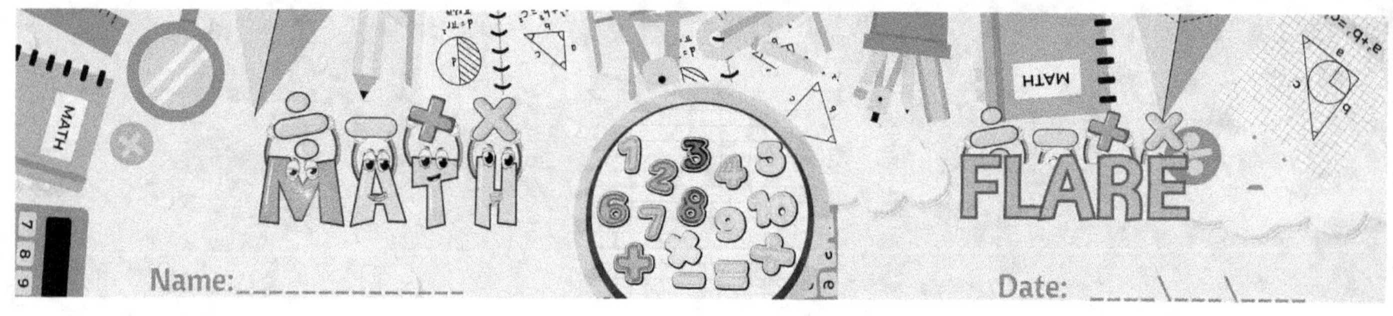

79. $8 + 7y + 3 = 35 - y$

80. $15 + y = 5 + 5y + 6$

81. $7 + 7k = 5k + 23$

82. $1 + 9z = 35 - 8z$

83. $41 - k = 6k + 6$

84. $71 - x = 7x + 7$

85. $16 + m = 2 + 5m + 2$

86. $1 + 3y = 36 - 2y$

87. $48 + k = 7 + 6k + 6$

88. $9 + 8y + 5 = 33 + y + 2$

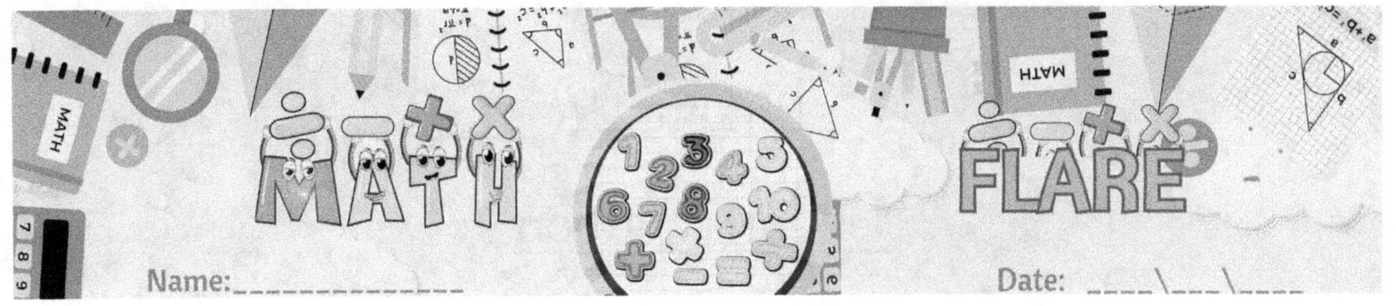

89. $16 + y = 6 + 2y + 2$

90. $30 - k = 2k + 3$

91. $7 + 3k = 43 - k$

92. $16 - x + 8 = 8 + 4x + 6$

93. $4 + 7x = 20 - x$

94. $4k + 9 = 14 - k$

95. $39 - x = 8 + 2x + 7$

96. $70 - y + 10 = 1 + 7y + 7$

97. $6 + 7k + 8 = 64 - k + 14$

98. $14 - x = 5 + 2x$

Chapter. 02

Linear Equation

Understanding Linear Functions

A linear equation is an algebraic equation that represents a straight line when graphed on a coordinate plane. It consists of variables raised to the power of 1 (i.e., no exponents higher than 1) and constant coefficients.

The general form of a linear equation in one variable x is:

$$ax + b = 0$$

Where a and b are constants, and x is the variable.

Let's solve the linear equation:

$$-2x + 9 = 5$$

- **Isolate the variable term:** We want to isolate the term containing x on one side of the equation. To do this, we'll move the constant term to the other side. Subtract 9 from both sides:

$$-2x + 9 - 9 = 5 - 9$$

$$-2x = -4$$

- **Divide by the coefficient of the variable:** To solve for x, divide both sides by the coefficient of x, which is -2:

$$\frac{-2x}{-2} = \frac{-4}{-2}$$

$$x = 2$$

<u>Slop from Two Points</u>

The slope between two points on a Cartesian coordinate system is a measure of the steepness of the line connecting those points. It's calculated by finding the change in the y-coordinates divided by the change in the x-coordinates.

- The coordinates of the first point as $(x_1, y_1) = (2, -30)$.

- The coordinates of the second point as $(x_2, y_2) = (-5, 40)$.

The formula to calculate the slope (m) between two points:

$$\frac{y_2 - y_1}{x_2 - x_1}$$

$$= \frac{40 - (-30)}{-5 - 2} = \frac{70}{-7}$$

$$\text{Slope} = -10$$

<u>Plotting Lines</u>

To plot the lines using the given points, we'll first locate each point on the coordinate plane, and then connect the points to form the lines. Let's plot each line one by one:

A = (-6, -3)	B = (0, 3)
C = (-4, -1)	D = (1, 4)
E = (4, 7)	F = (2, 5)

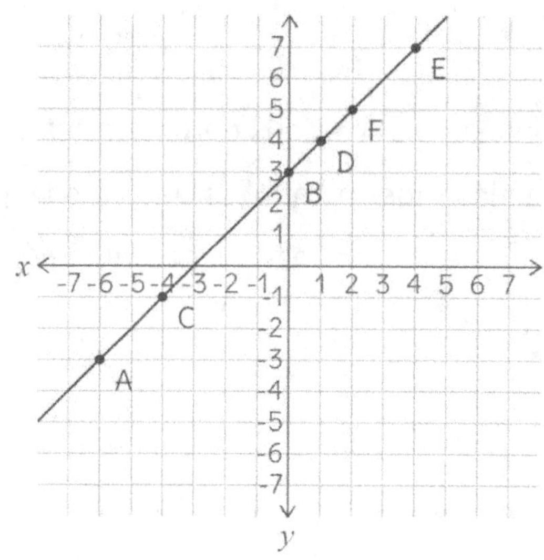

Graphing Linear Equation

Graphing a linear equation involves plotting the points that satisfy the equation on a coordinate plane and connecting them to form a straight line. Linear equations are equations of the form $y = mx + b$, where m represents the slope of the line, and b represents the y-intercept, the point where the line intersects the y-axis.

To graph a linear equation:

1. Identify the slope (m) and y-intercept (b) from the equation.

2. Plot the y-intercept $(0, b)$) as a point on the y-axis.

3. Use the slope to find additional points on the line. The slope represents the change in y for every unit change in x.

4. Connect the points to form a straight line.

For example, to graph the equation:

$$y = \frac{9}{4}x - 8$$

1. **Identify the slope and y-intercept:** The slope is $\frac{9}{4}$, and the y-intercept is -8.

2. **Plot the y-intercept:** Plot the point $(0, -8)$.

3. **Use the slope to plot additional points:** the slop is $\frac{9}{4}$ to find another point. we will move up 9 units and 4 units to the right from the y-intercept to find another point.

4. **Draw the line:** Once we have at least two points, we can draw a straight line.

We can continue this process to plot more points and extend the line further if needed.

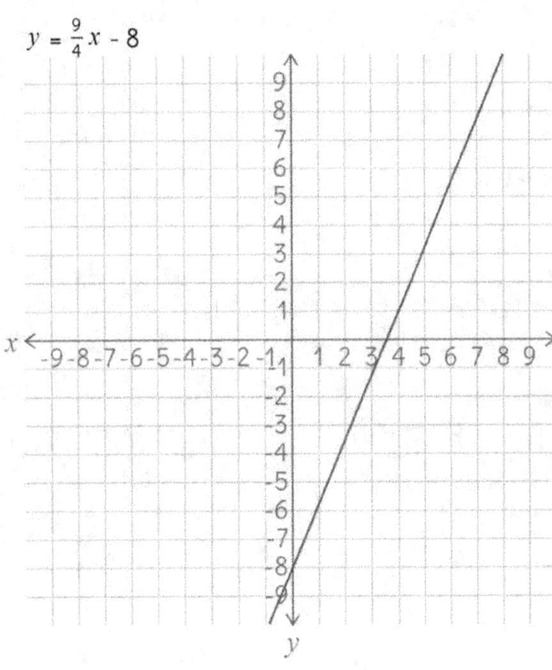

Understanding Linear Functions

1. $f(x) = -2x + -6$, find $f(-3)$

2. $f(x) = 3x + 9$, find $f(8)$

3. $f(x) = -1x + -6$, find $f(-3)$

4. $f(x) = 1x + -6$, find $f(-9)$

5. $f(x) = -5x + -2$, find $f(3)$

6. $f(x) = 0x + 4$, find $f(-3)$

7. $f(x) = -3x + 2$, find $f(-4)$

8. $f(x) = -5x + 3$, find $f(-5)$

9. $f(x) = -2x + 4$, find $f(-10)$

10. $f(x) = -4x + -6$, find $f(-3)$

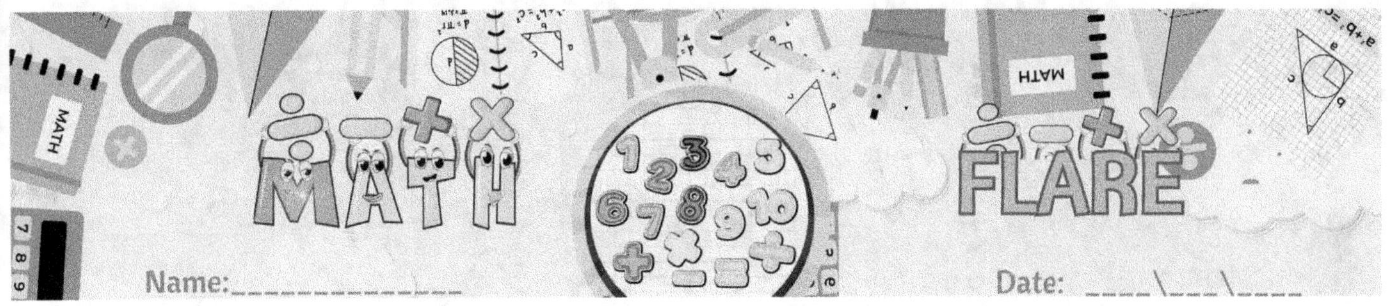

11. f(x) = -2x + 0, find f(9)

16. f(x) = 1x + 3, find f(10)

12. f(x) = 2x + 2, find f(-5)

17. f(x) = 3x + 2, find f(10)

13. f(x) = 4x + -2, find f(0)

18. f(x) = -2x + 8, find f(5)

14. f(x) = -1x + -5, find f(-7)

19. f(x) = -3x + -10, find f(-4)

15. f(x) = 1x + 3, find f(-10)

20. f(x) = -2x + 1, find f(-8)

21. f(x) = -1x + 2, find f(-9)

26. f(x) = 5x + -6, find f(5)

22. f(x) = 1x + 1, find f(-3)

27. f(x) = 2x + -5, find f(10)

23. f(x) = 0x + -9, find f(-9)

28. f(x) = 4x + 1, find f(-6)

24. f(x) = -4x + 0, find f(-2)

29. f(x) = -2x + 5, find f(8)

25. f(x) = -5x + 6, find f(0)

30. f(x) = -4x + -5, find f(0)

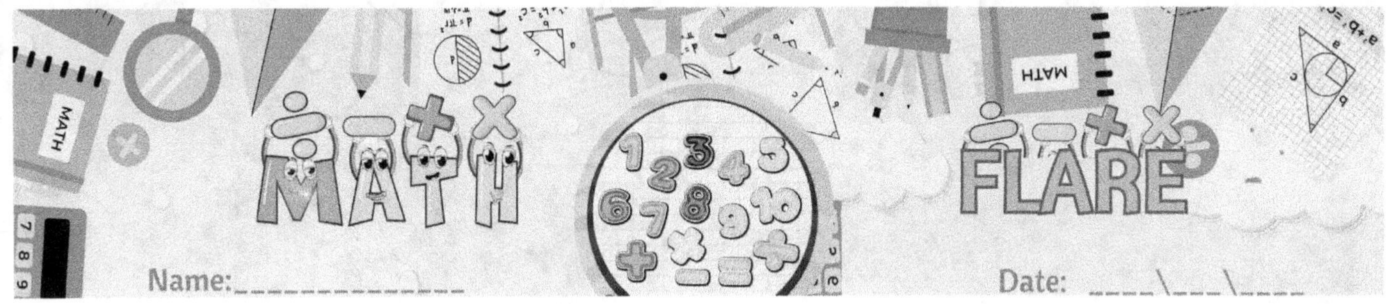

31. $f(x) = 4x + -10$, find $f(-3)$

36. $f(x) = 0x + 3$, find $f(0)$

32. $f(x) = -5x + -7$, find $f(-1)$

37. $f(x) = -3x + 3$, find $f(7)$

33. $f(x) = 5x + 8$, find $f(-2)$

38. $f(x) = -2x + 1$, find $f(-4)$

34. $f(x) = 0x + -2$, find $f(-10)$

39. $f(x) = 1x + -9$, find $f(-10)$

35. $f(x) = -3x + -7$, find $f(4)$

40. $f(x) = 0x + 7$, find $f(5)$

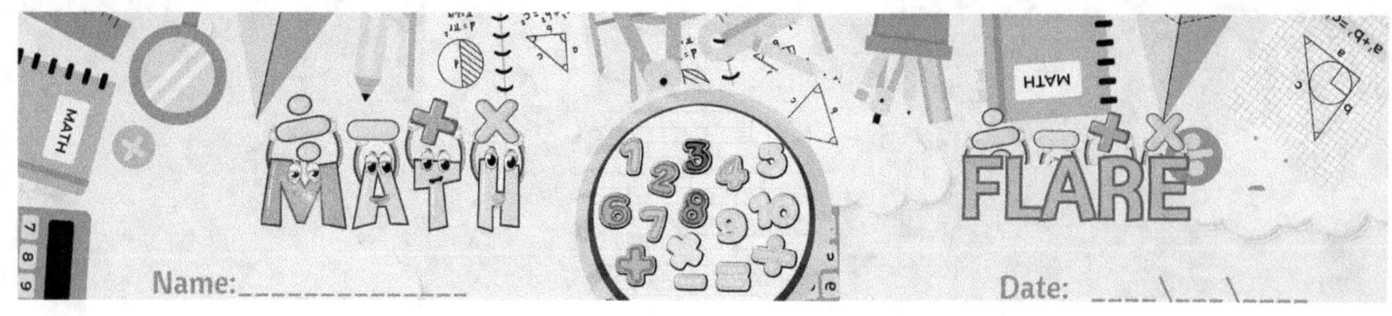

41. f(x) = -4x + -2, find f(-8)

42. f(x) = -2x + 4, find f(-5)

43. f(x) = -2x + -5, find f(-3)

44. f(x) = -4x + -7, find f(-2)

45. f(x) = 4x + 7, find f(2)

46. f(x) = -2x + -4, find f(0)

47. f(x) = 2x + 2, find f(-7)

48. f(x) = 4x + -5, find f(9)

49. f(x) = 4x + -5, find f(-1)

50. f(x) = 1x + 5, find f(3)

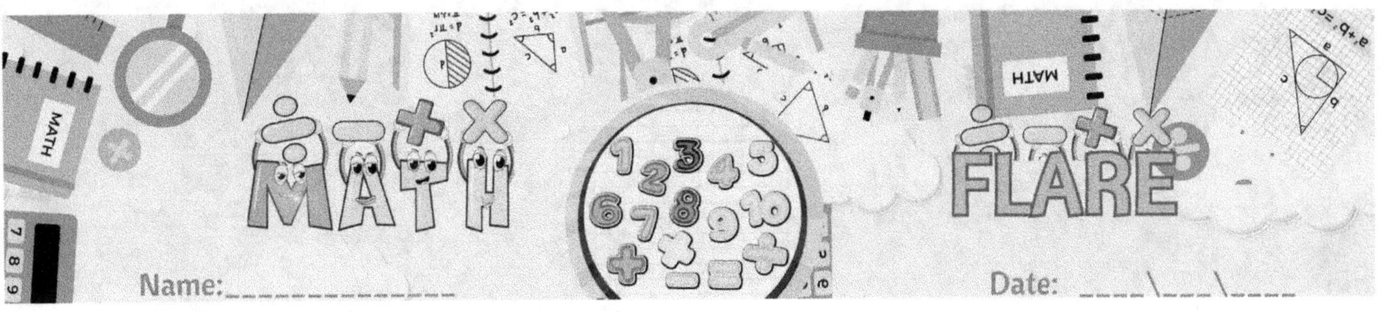

Solving Linear Functions

1. $-1x + 6 = -1$

2. $4x + 9 = 1$

3. $6x + 3 = -9$

4. $10x + 9 = 29$

5. $4x + -9 = -1$

6. $-4x + -8 = -20$

7. $-7x + -3 = 46$

8. $-6x + -7 = 11$

9. $-5x + 6 = -39$

10. $6x + -8 = -32$

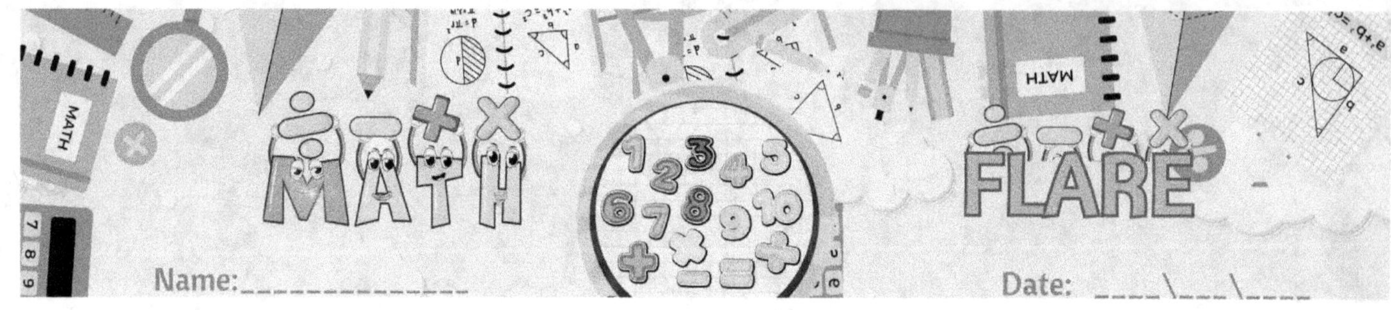

11. 7x + 3 = 45

12. 6x + -7 = 47

13. -8x + 9 = 33

14. -5x + -5 = -50

15. -1x + 9 = 19

16. -7x + -1 = -43

17. 5x + -9 = -39

18. 9x + 5 = -58

19. -7x + -2 = -9

20. 3x + 0 = 15

21. $4x + 10 = 30$

22. $3x + -3 = -27$

23. $6x + 9 = -39$

24. $-2x + 2 = 18$

25. $2x + -1 = -17$

26. $-3x + -9 = 21$

27. $-6x + 10 = -44$

28. $9x + -2 = 52$

29. $8x + 0 = 64$

30. $-7x + -4 = 38$

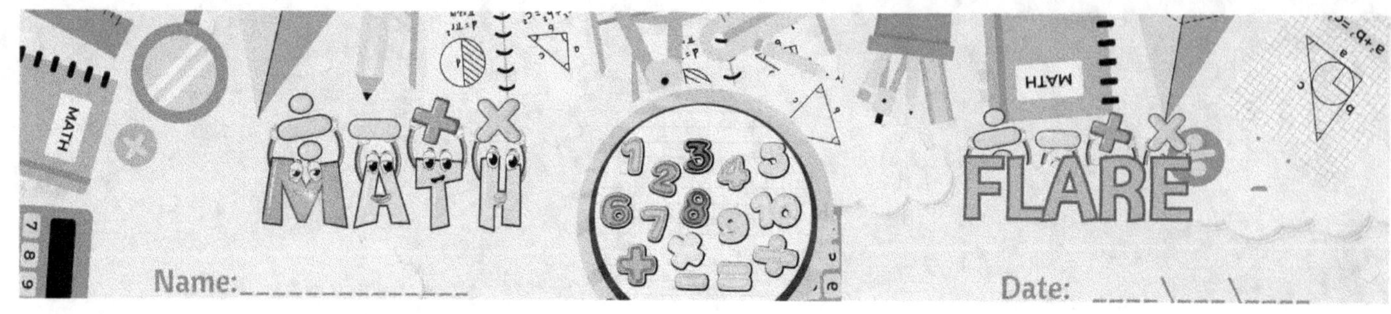

31. -1x + 3 = 1

36. 4x + -8 = -48

32. -5x + -2 = 3

37. 9x + 0 = -45

33. -10x + -9 = -59

38. 8x + 7 = 79

34. 2x + 7 = -1

39. -4x + 0 = -12

35. -10x + -10 = 40

40. -3x + -1 = -13

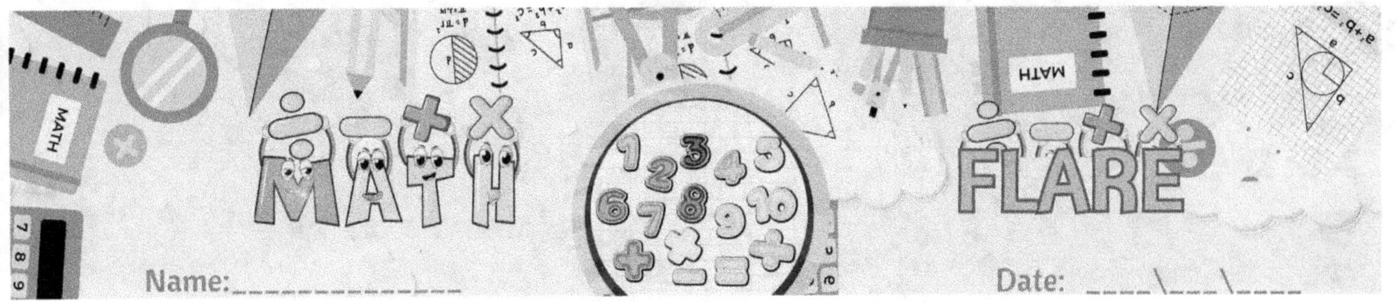

41. $-6x + 8 = 68$

42. $-9x + -9 = 9$

43. $10x + -8 = 72$

44. $6x + -4 = -52$

45. $4x + -4 = -8$

46. $6x + 9 = -39$

47. $-7x + -6 = -27$

48. $-2x + -6 = -20$

49. $9x + -10 = 35$

50. $-2x + 10 = 6$

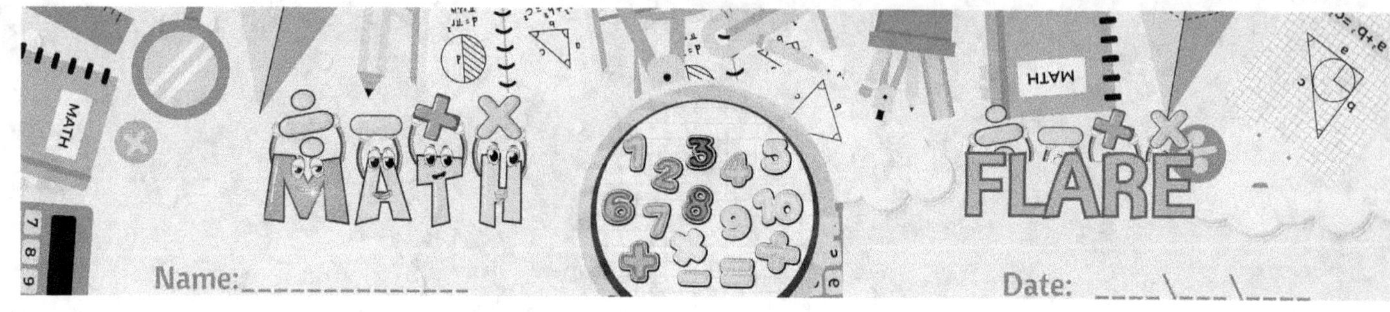

51. -6x + 2 = 8

52. 5x + -4 = -4

53. -6x + 1 = 49

54. 1x + 0 = 4

55. -10x + 8 = -62

56. -3x + 4 = 22

57. -1x + 9 = 19

58. -1x + 2 = 10

59. -8x + 0 = 72

60. 9x + 10 = 1

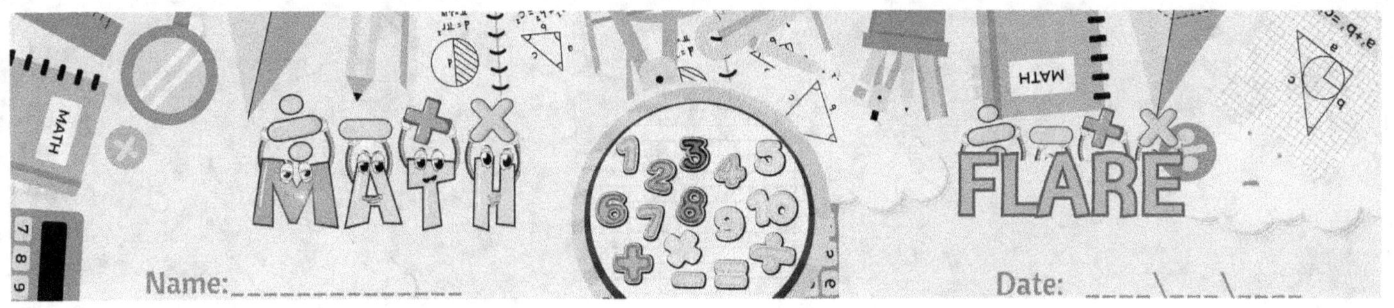

61. $-9x + -7 = -52$

62. $-6x + -3 = 51$

63. $-2x + -9 = -23$

64. $2x + 7 = 13$

65. $1x + 5 = 10$

66. $-9x + -1 = -37$

67. $2x + 9 = -11$

68. $-10x + 4 = 74$

69. $8x + 3 = 27$

70. $6x + 9 = 39$

71. -6x + -8 = 10

76. 5x + 3 = -22

72. 9x + 2 = -43

77. 5x + -10 = 20

73. 1x + -1 = 6

78. 9x + -10 = 62

74. 6x + -3 = -57

79. -9x + -9 = -27

75. 8x + -4 = 52

80. -2x + -10 = 8

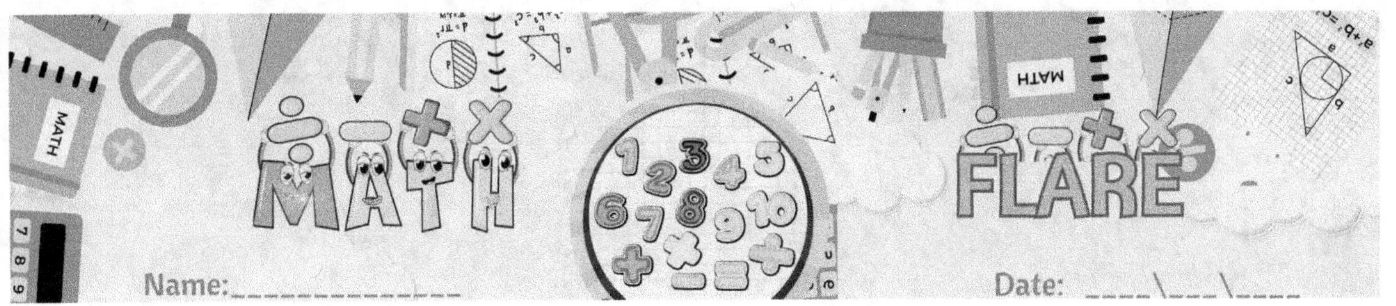

81. $8x + 10 = 26$

86. $-5x + 6 = 6$

82. $-10x + -6 = 44$

87. $4x + -8 = -40$

83. $6x + -1 = -43$

88. $6x + 7 = 49$

84. $-9x + 10 = -62$

89. $-1x + -1 = -7$

85. $4x + -2 = -18$

90. $5x + 4 = -6$

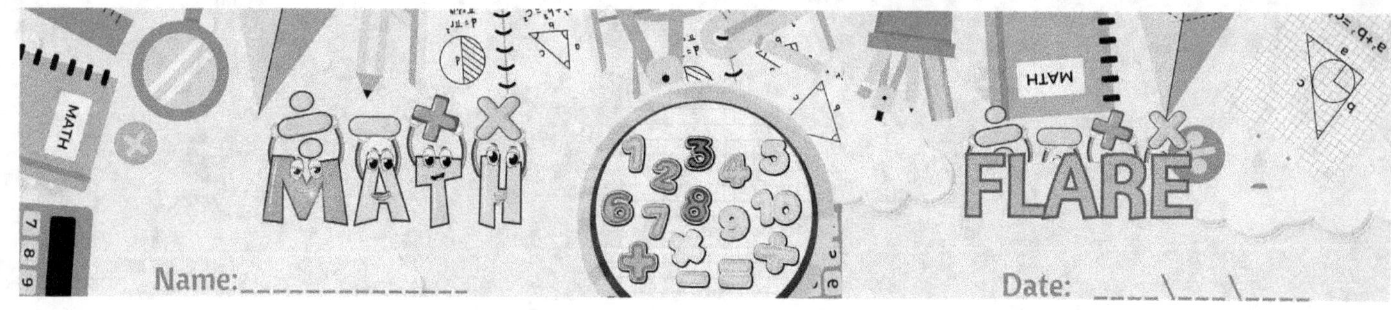

91. $9x + -5 = 76$

92. $-8x + -6 = 2$

93. $-1x + 0 = 1$

94. $2x + -1 = 3$

95. $9x + 9 = 27$

96. $-2x + 0 = -6$

97. $-6x + 2 = 38$

98. $5x + -1 = 39$

99. $-9x + 4 = 94$

100. $3x + -4 = 2$

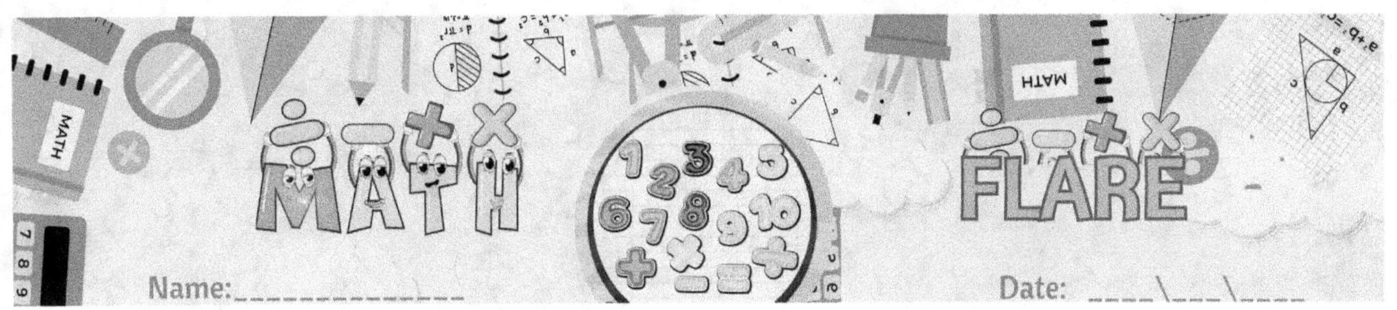

Find Slope from Two Points

1. (0, 0) and (10, -70)

2. (-1, -9) and (2, 21)

3. (8, -74) and (-2, 26)

4. (-2, 17) and (5, -32)

5. (10, -55) and (5, -30)

6. (8, 50) and (7, 43)

7. (7, -31) and (-6, 21)

8. (-7, -57) and (7, 69)

9. (0, 2) and (1, 1)

10. (2, -1) and (-9, 21)

11. (7, -37) and (3, -17)

12. (9, 88) and (10, 97)

13. (-4, -24) and (-10, -54)

14. (-4, 29) and (10, -41)

15. (4, 24) and (-1, -6)

16. (-10, 5) and (10, 5)

17. (-10, 62) and (4, -36)

18. (-5, 16) and (2, -5)

19. (8, -32) and (-9, 19)

20. (0, 2) and (-3, -7)

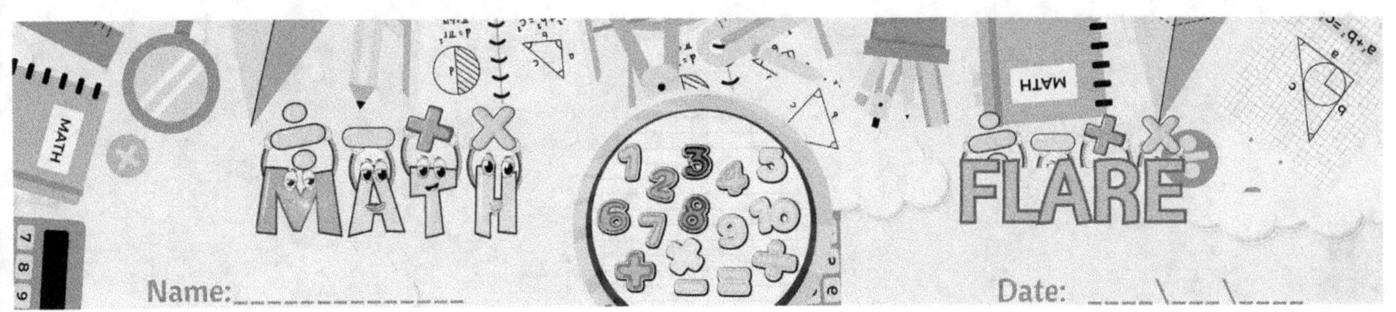

21. (-3, 31) and (-10, 80)

22. (3, -30) and (-1, -2)

23. (9, -26) and (-10, 50)

24. (-6, -9) and (-8, -15)

25. (1, -5) and (-3, -5)

26. (-5, 31) and (9, -81)

27. (10, -8) and (-9, -8)

28. (9, -27) and (2, 1)

29. (5, 17) and (-6, -16)

30. (-9, 97) and (6, -53)

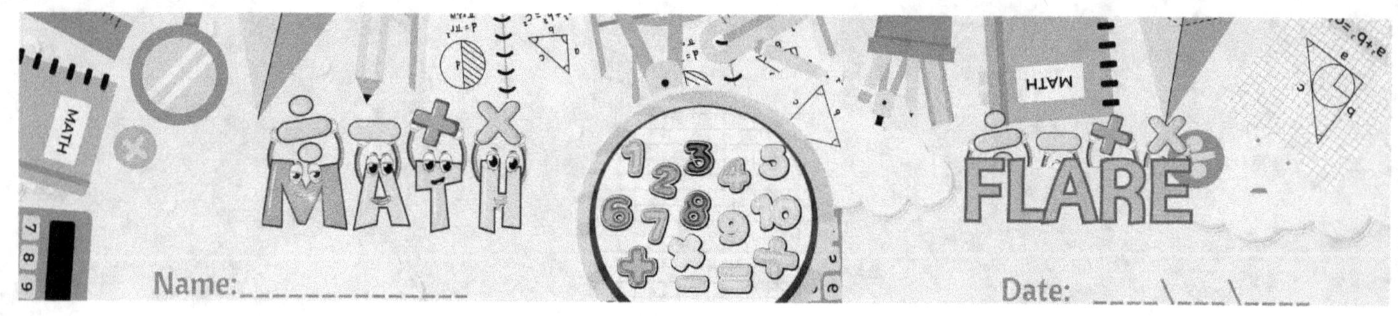

31. (10, -82) and (1, -1)

32. (8, 65) and (-5, -26)

33. (9, -50) and (8, -44)

34. (-9, -20) and (10, 37)

35. (-8, -60) and (-1, -11)

36. (-8, -37) and (-4, -17)

37. (-7, 13) and (7, -1)

38. (2, -17) and (6, -45)

39. (1, -4) and (9, 12)

40. (6, -11) and (-4, -1)

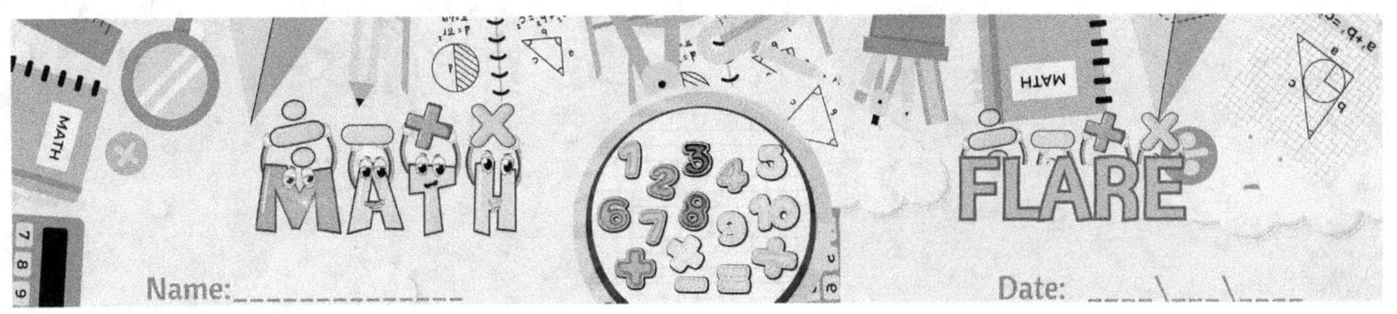

41. (5, 17) and (9, 33)

42. (-10, -53) and (8, 37)

43. (3, -6) and (5, -8)

44. (-7, -14) and (-6, -12)

45. (9, 32) and (-1, 2)

46. (0, -5) and (0, -5)

47. (7, 13) and (7, 13)

48. (-5, -25) and (5, 35)

49. (-1, -11) and (7, 21)

50. (4, -12) and (6, -14)

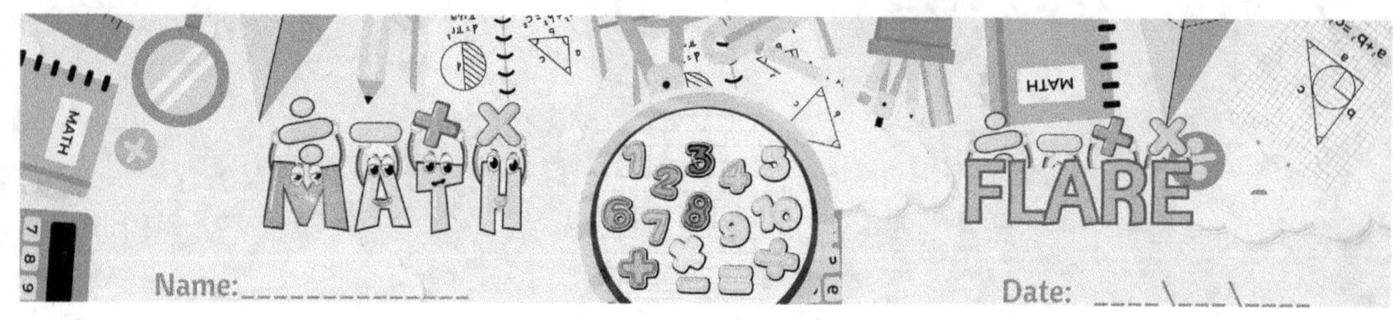

51. (-7, 25) and (-5, 15)

52. (0, 9) and (-6, -45)

53. (-2, -25) and (6, 39)

54. (-9, -47) and (-7, -35)

55. (1, 16) and (-9, -74)

56. (-5, -39) and (10, 81)

57. (-10, -27) and (8, 9)

58. (-4, -5) and (-5, -4)

59. (0, -3) and (3, -6)

60. (2, -8) and (1, 0)

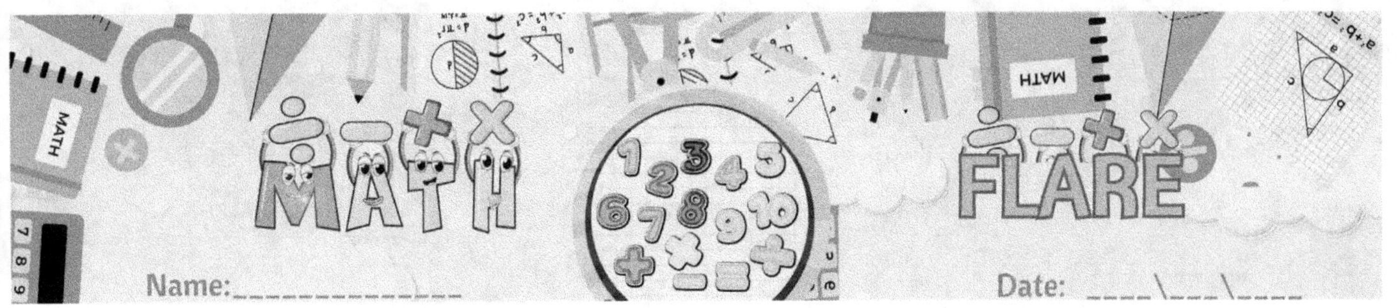

61. (-2, -8) and (8, -8)

66. (4, 26) and (9, 61)

62. (4, -16) and (1, -7)

67. (-7, 21) and (2, 3)

63. (-6, 22) and (6, -14)

68. (3, 33) and (8, 83)

64. (-8, -65) and (-1, -2)

69. (-5, -18) and (-2, -3)

65. (-8, 25) and (0, 1)

70. (6, 4) and (-5, -18)

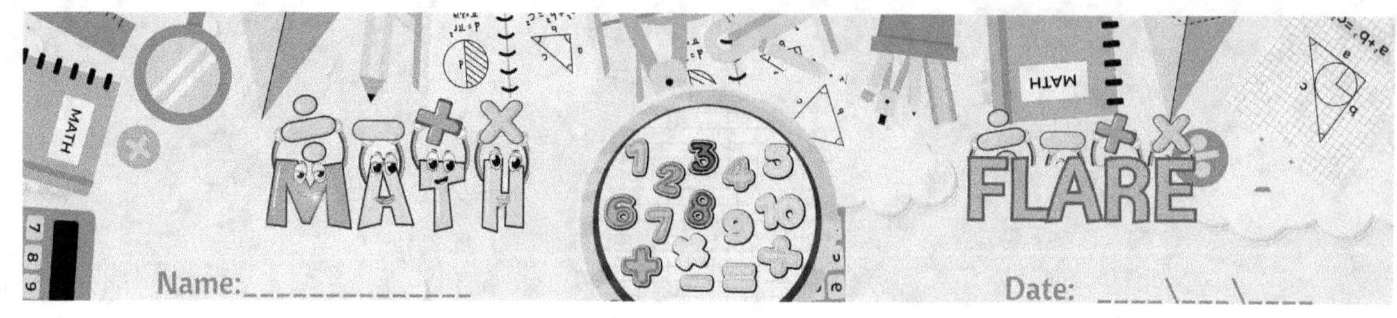

71. (-2, 12) and (2, -24)

72. (3, -17) and (10, -66)

73. (-2, -21) and (-7, -56)

74. (10, 10) and (7, 4)

75. (-6, -6) and (5, -6)

76. (1, 0) and (9, 48)

77. (8, -17) and (-3, 5)

78. (5, -46) and (-10, 89)

79. (9, 57) and (-2, -20)

80. (-1, 7) and (4, 17)

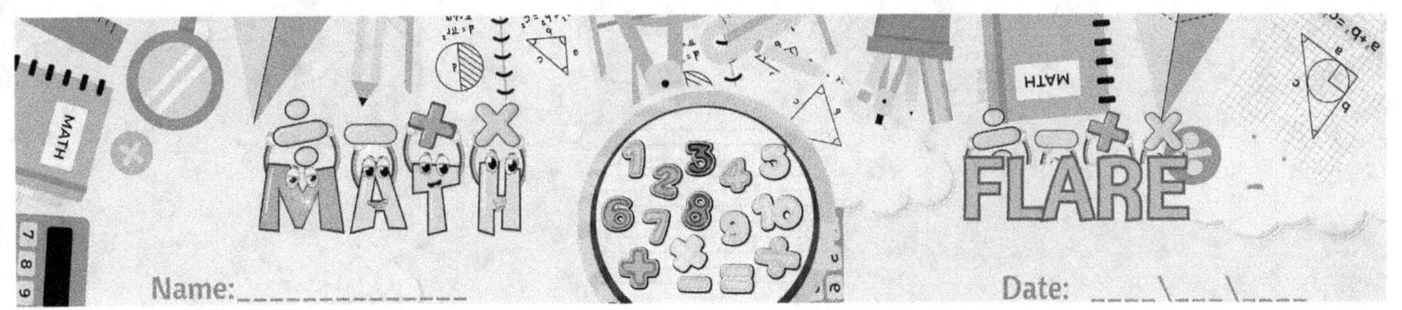

81. (1, 7) and (-6, -21)

82. (0, 0) and (-7, 42)

83. (4, 36) and (-7, -63)

84. (0, -9) and (3, -3)

85. (-8, -23) and (10, 31)

86. (-9, 5) and (-2, 5)

87. (3, -19) and (3, -19)

88. (-4, -15) and (-5, -17)

89. (-6, -5) and (-1, 0)

90. (-6, 6) and (10, 6)

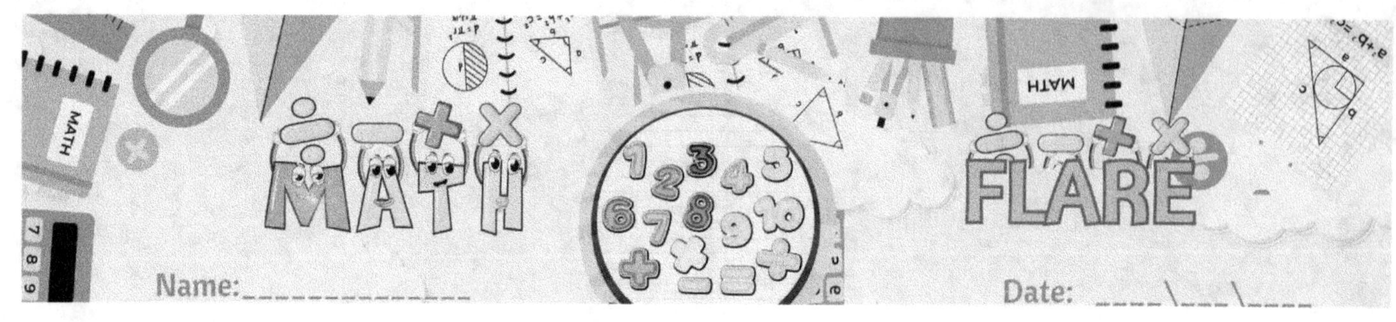

91. (8, 82) and (7, 72)

92. (10, 43) and (-2, -17)

93. (3, -16) and (-9, 44)

94. (3, 15) and (-10, -24)

95. (5, 35) and (-7, -73)

96. (9, 20) and (-4, -6)

97. (6, -32) and (-5, 34)

98. (0, 9) and (-9, 9)

99. (-7, -48) and (1, 16)

100.   (2, -18) and (5, -39)

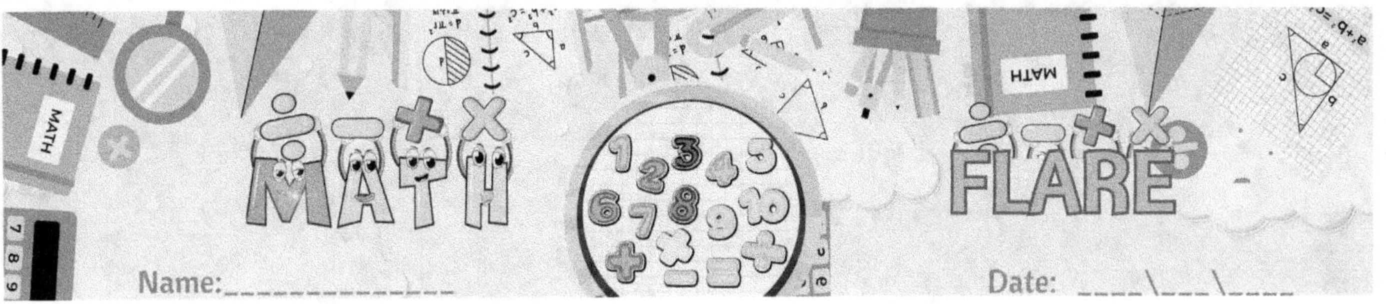

Plotting Lines

Plot and draw the lines.

1.

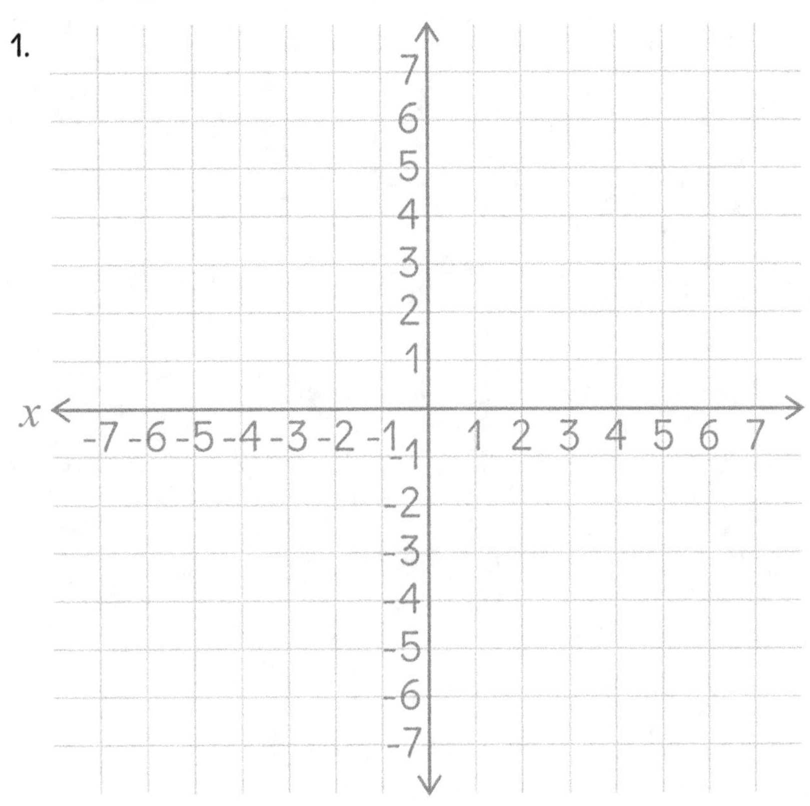

A = (2, -4)   B = (-4, -7)

C = (-2, -6)   D = (0, -5)

E = (4, -3)   F = (6, -2)

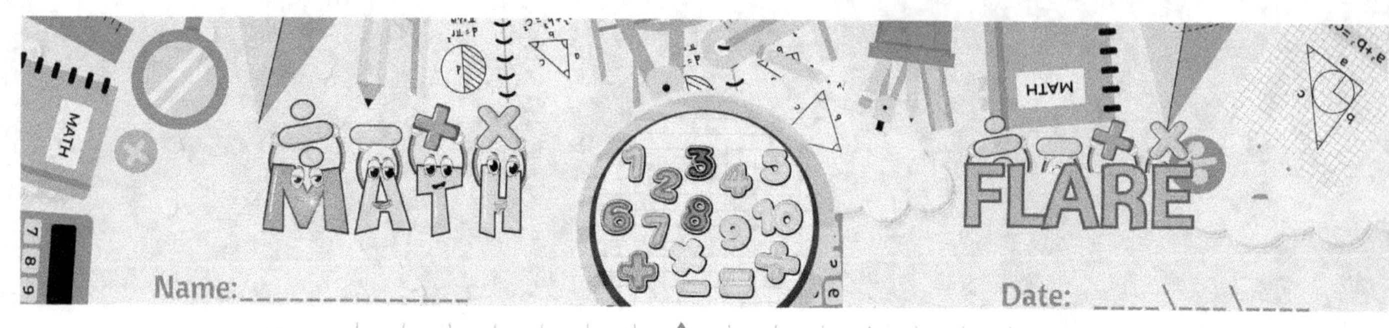

2.

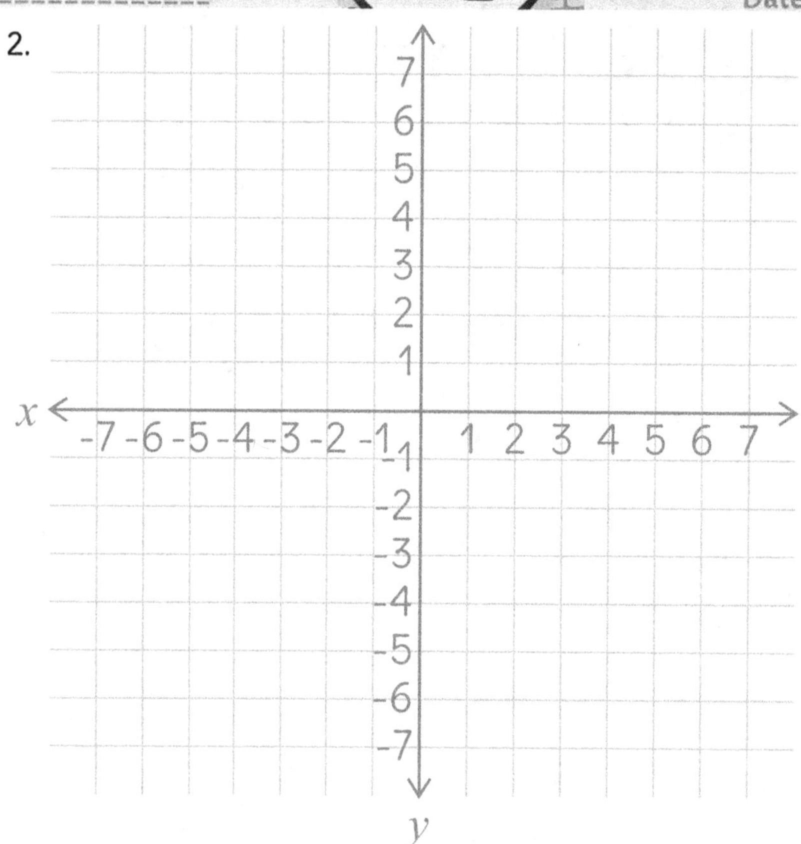

A = (1, -6)   B = (-2, -6)

C = (4, -6)   D = (-1, -6)

E = (-7, -6)   F = (-6, -6)

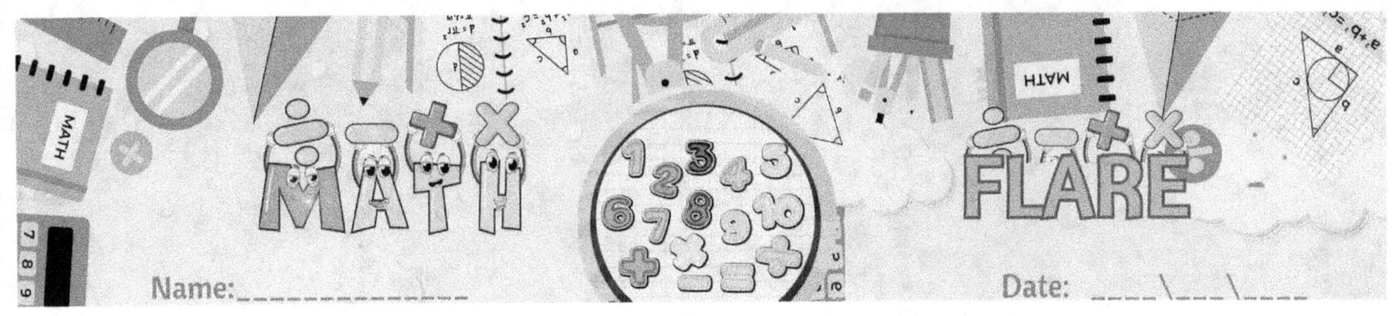

3.

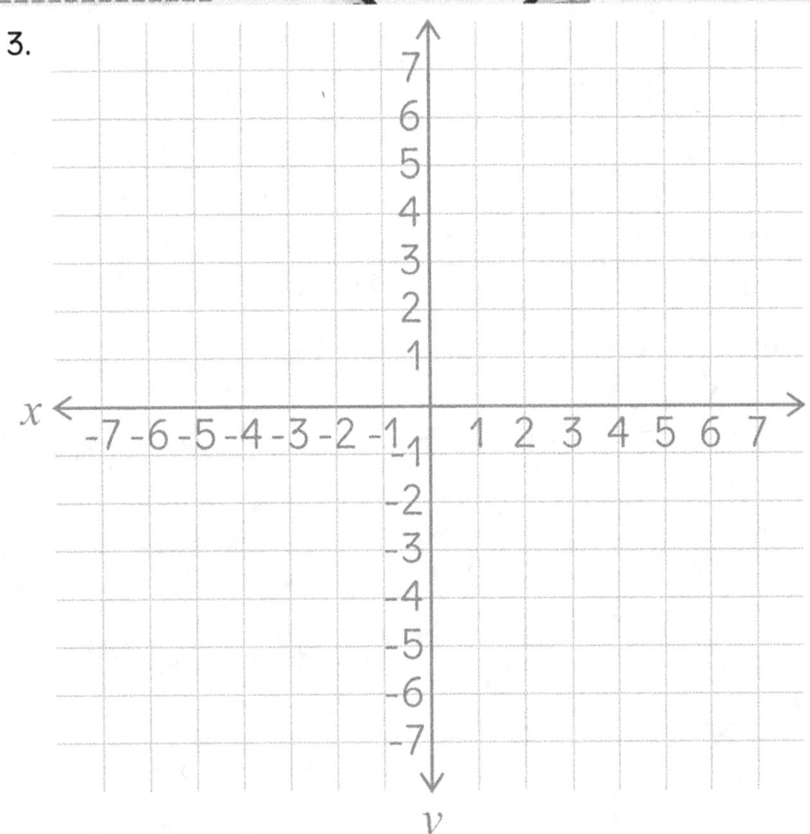

A = (-1, -1)   B = (1, -1)

C = (-6, -1)   D = (3, -1)

E = (5, -1)   F = (-2, -1)

4.

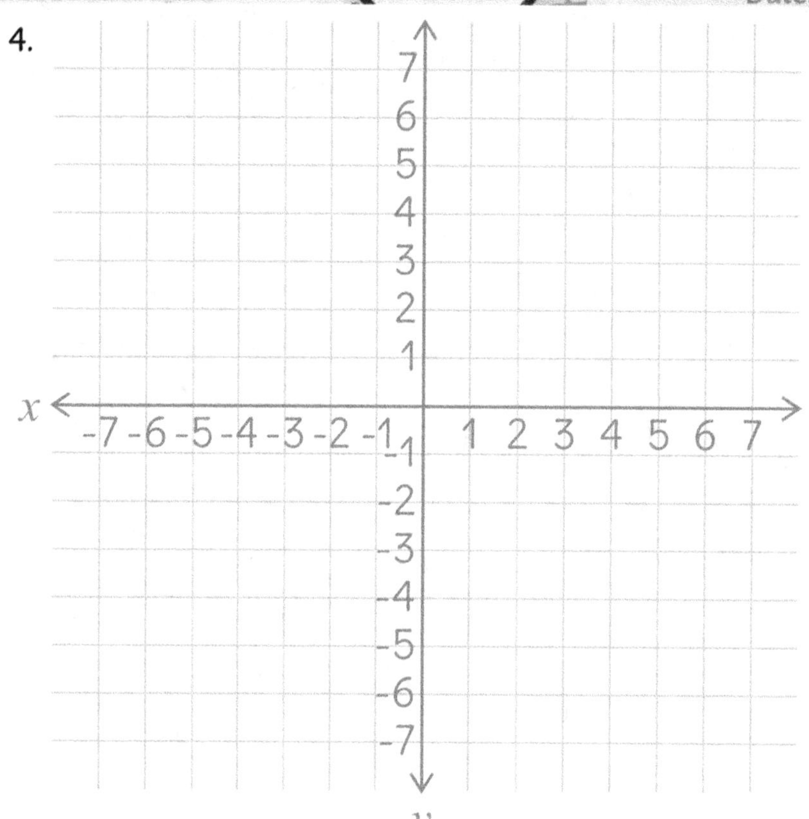

A = (6, -2)   B = (5, -1)

C = (1, 3)   D = (2, 2)

E = (-3, 7)   F = (-1, 5)

5.

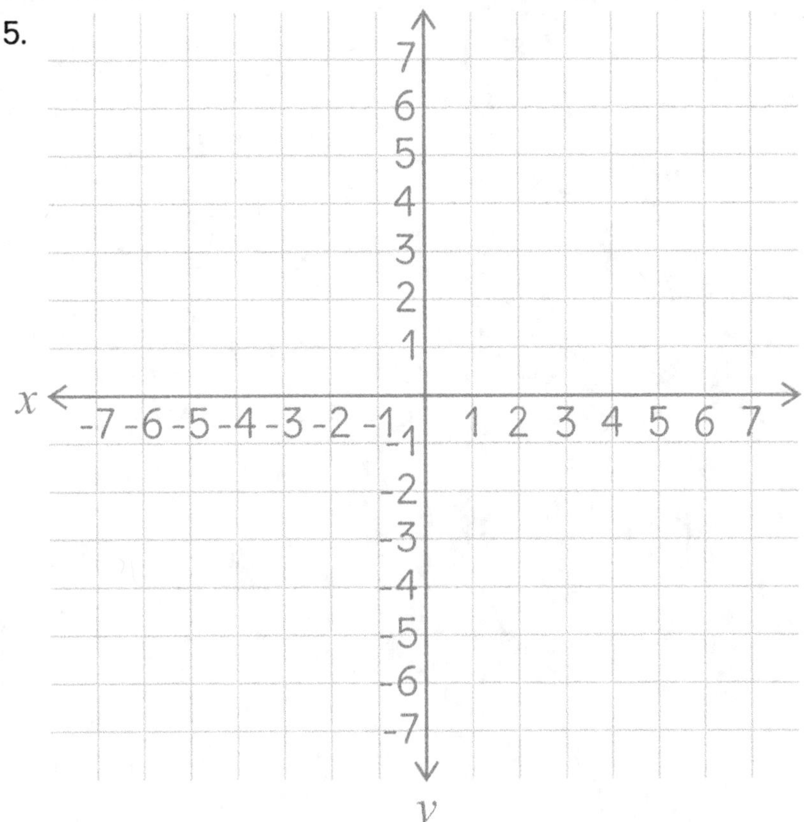

A = (-2, 1)   B = (-5, 1)

C = (2, 1)   D = (6, 1)

E = (-7, 1)   F = (3, 1)

6.

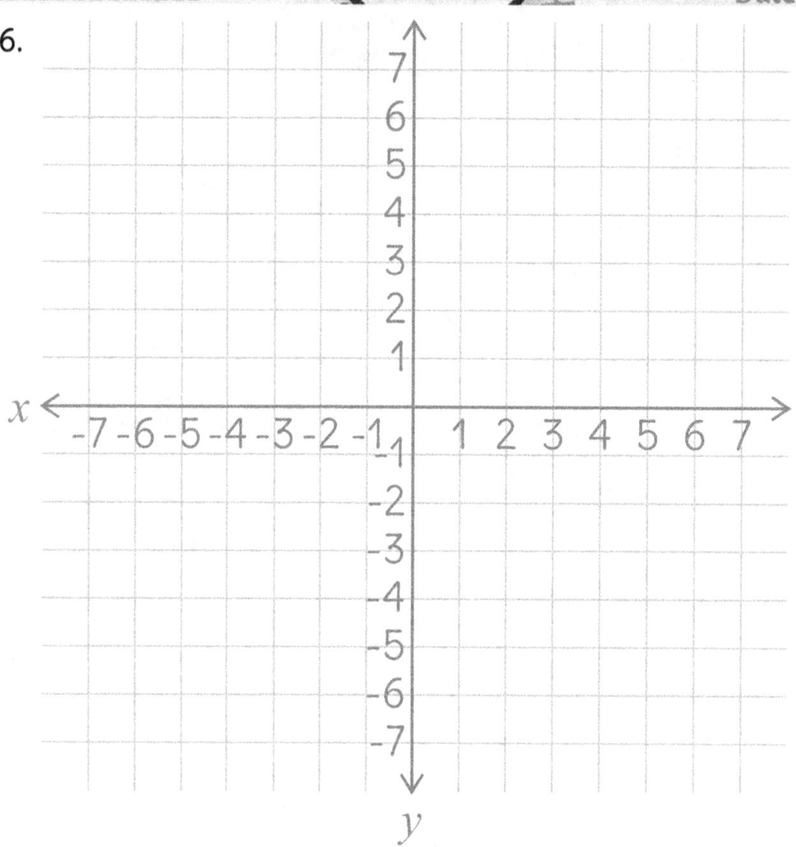

A = (0, 1)   B = (7, 1)

C = (-3, 1)   D = (4, 1)

E = (-1, 1)   F = (-2, 1)

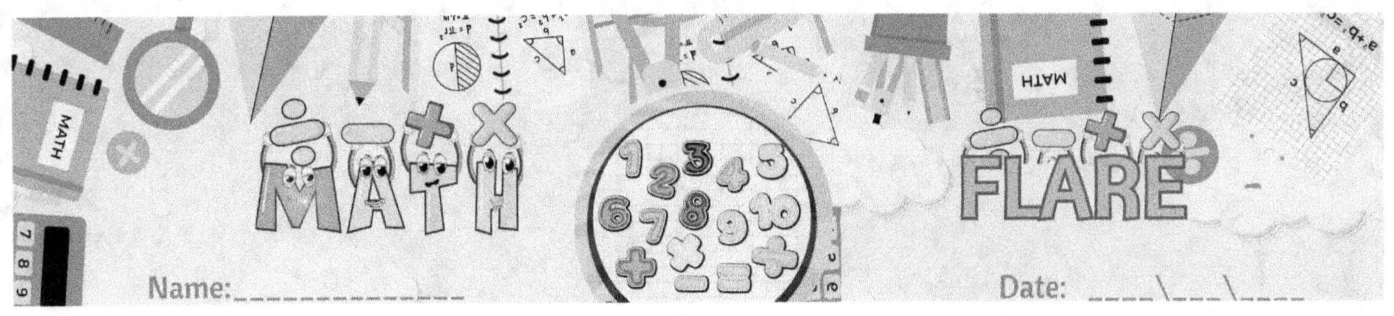

7.

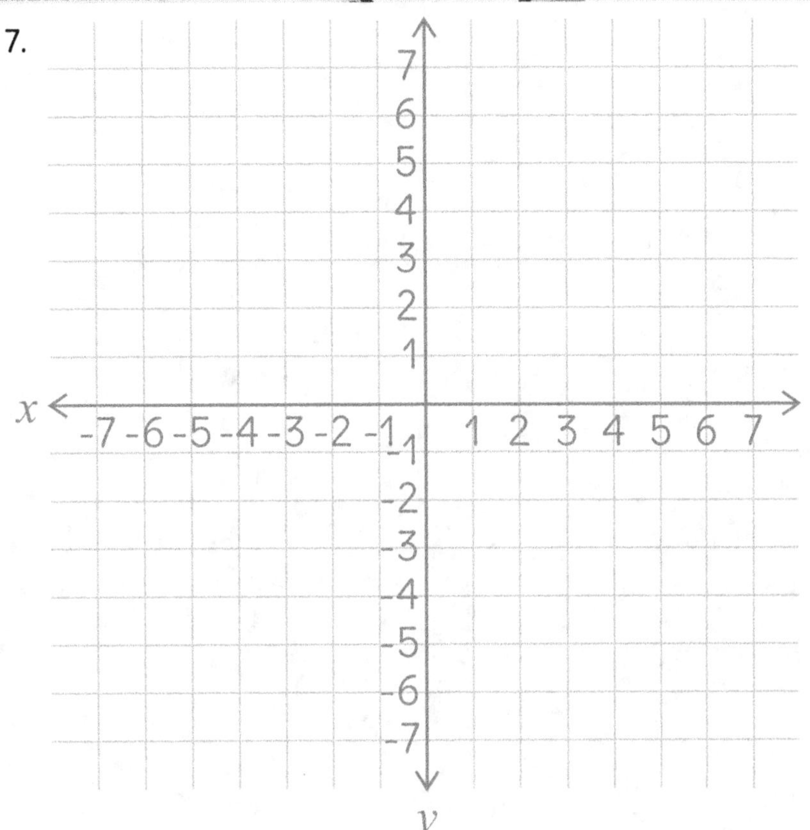

A = (-3, -1)   B = (0, -7)

C = (-2, -3)   D = (-4, 1)

E = (-7, 7)   F = (-1, -5)

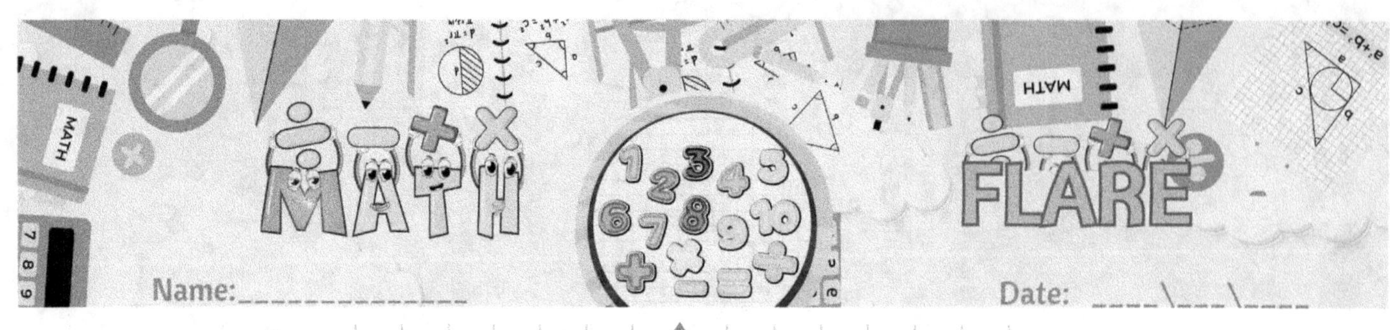

8.

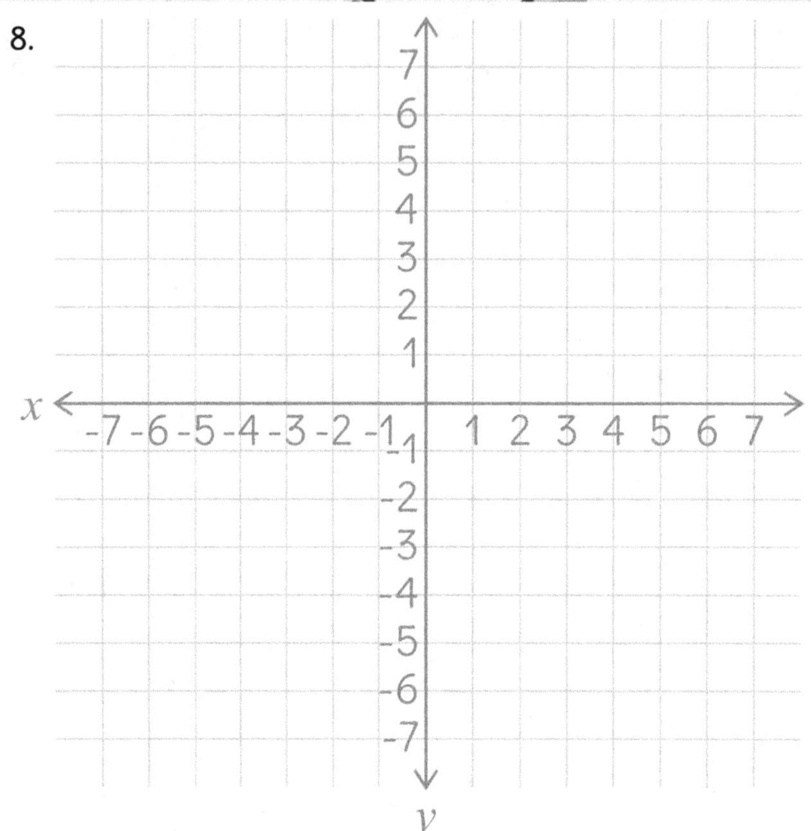

A = (0, 3)   B = (-1, 5)

C = (4, -5)   D = (2, -1)

E = (3, -3)   F = (1, 1)

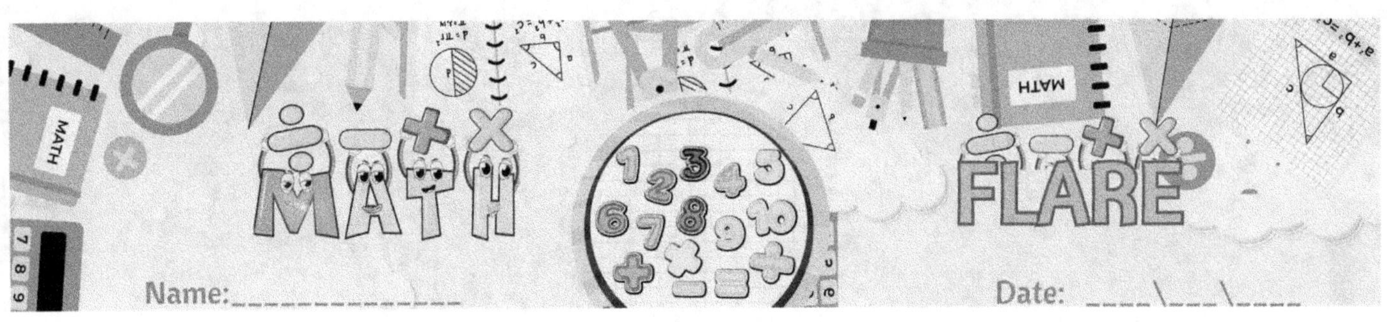

9.

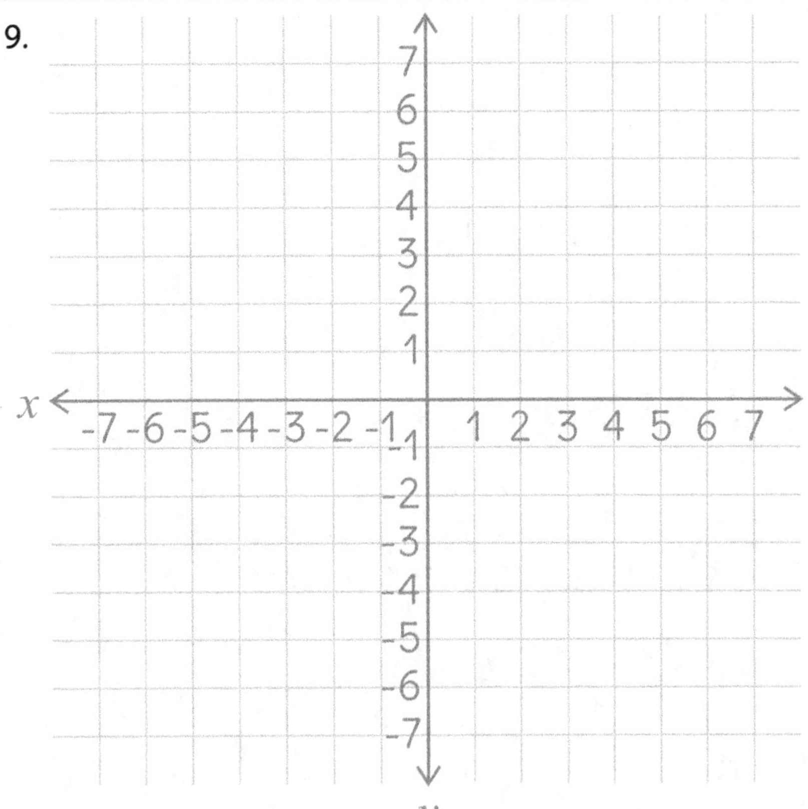

A = (-3, 3)   B = (-2, 1)

C = (-1, -1)   D = (2, -7)

E = (1, -5)   F = (0, -3)

10.

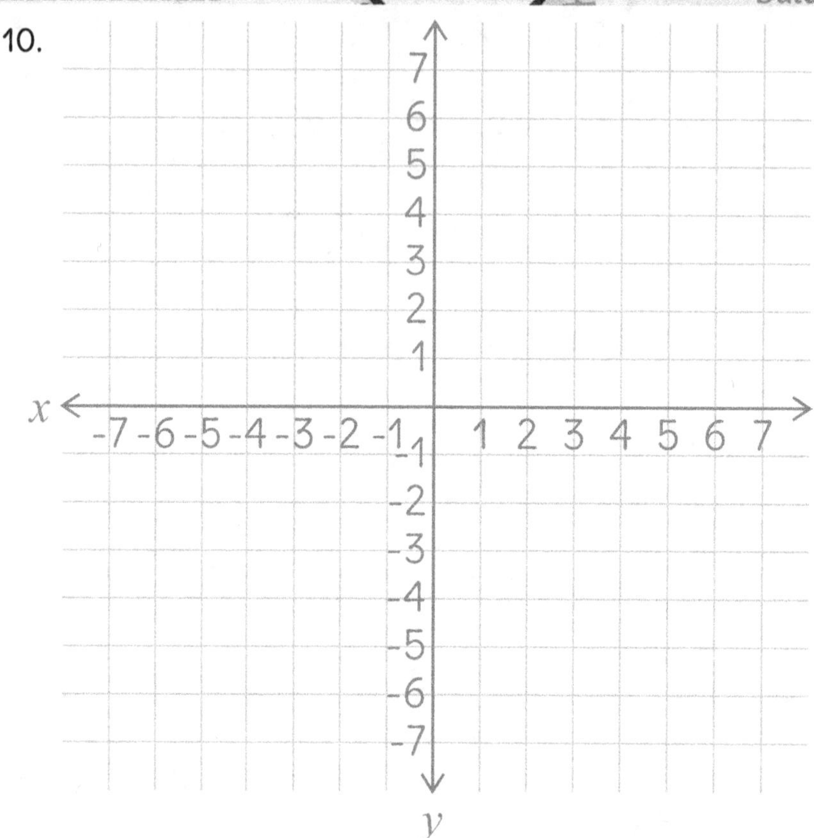

A = (7, 4)   B = (-1, 4)

C = (-4, 4)   D = (6, 4)

E = (2, 4)   F = (0, 4)

Graphing Linear Equations

1.
$$y = \frac{-3}{4}x + 4$$

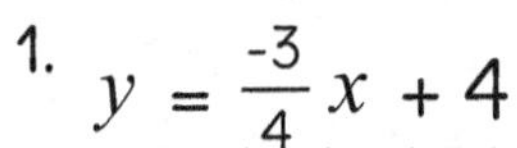

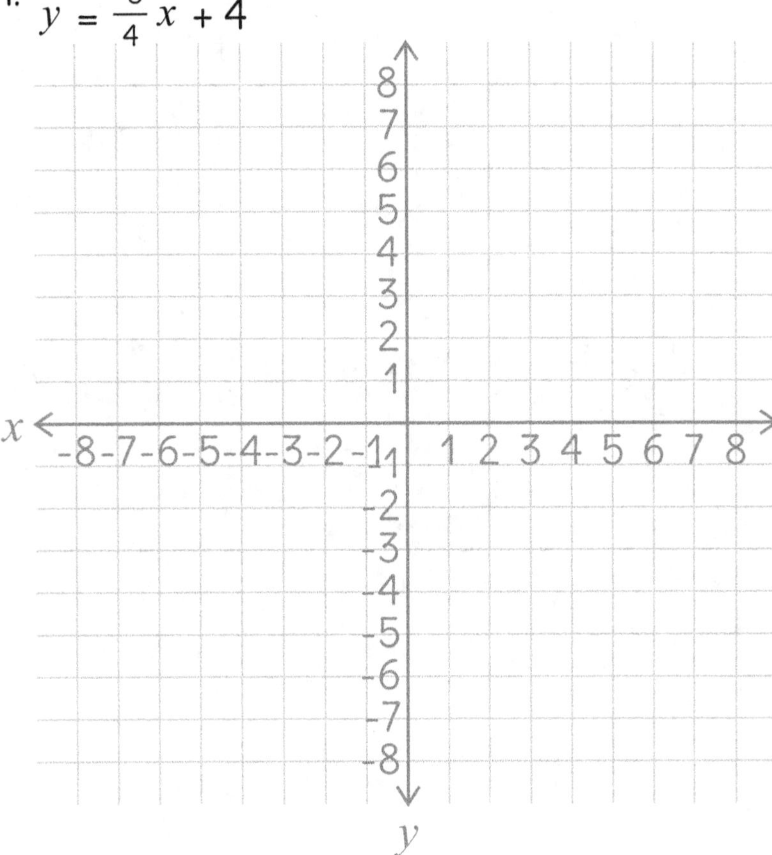

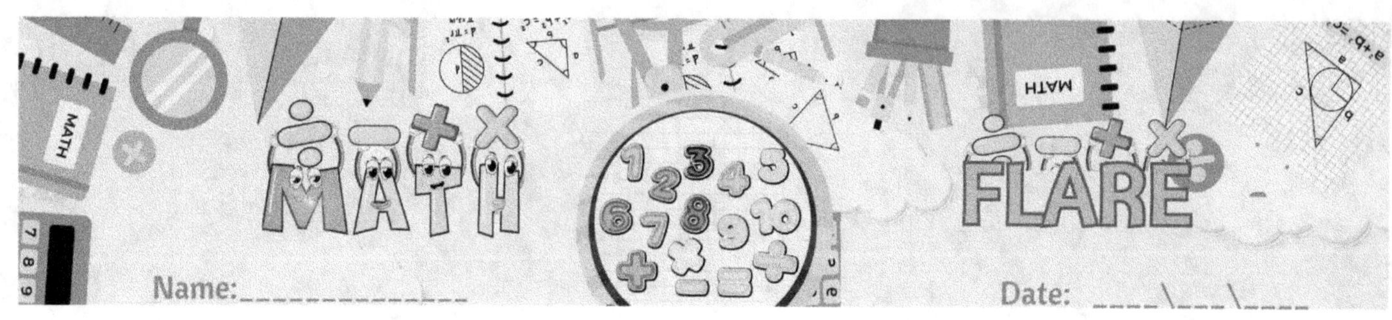

2. $y = \dfrac{-5}{4} x - 5$

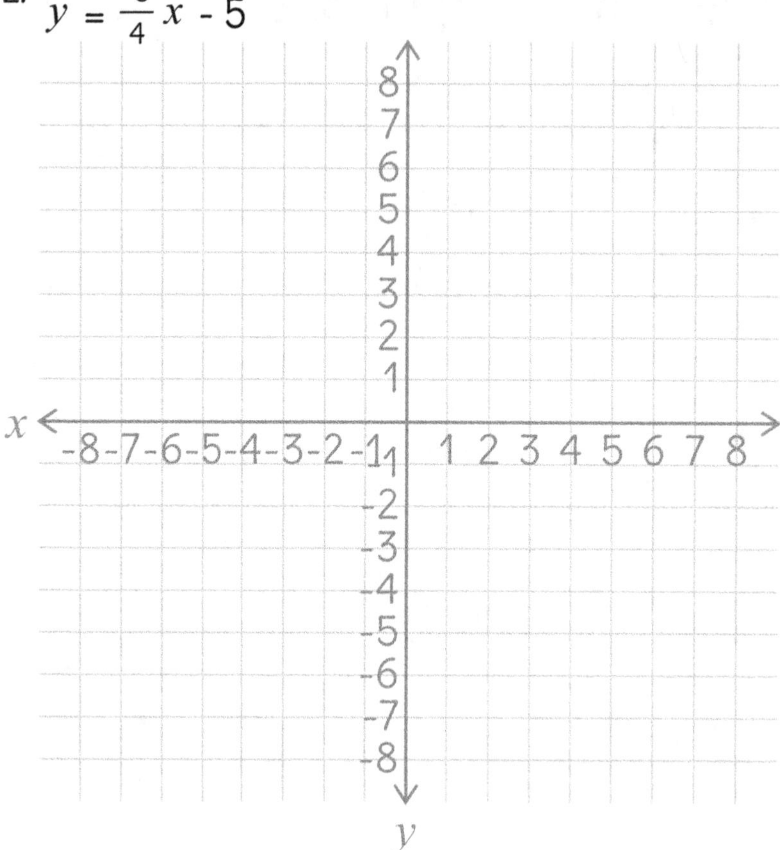

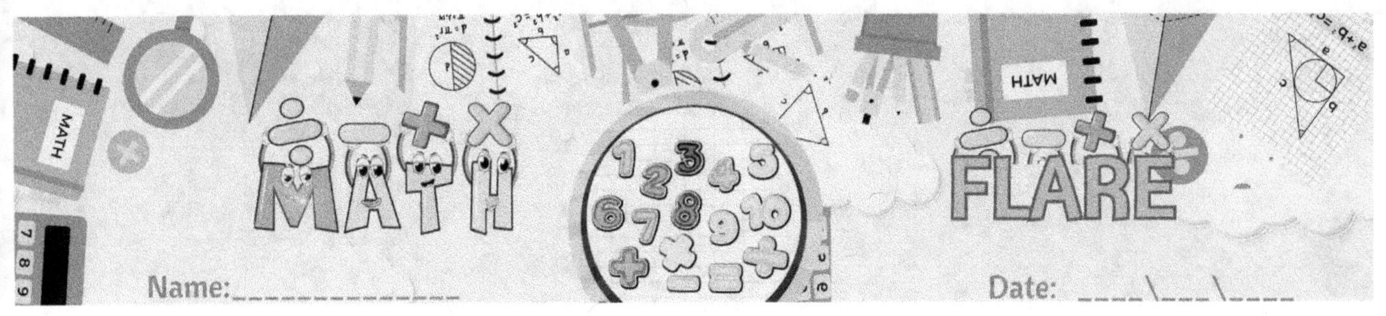

3.

$$y = 2x + 7$$

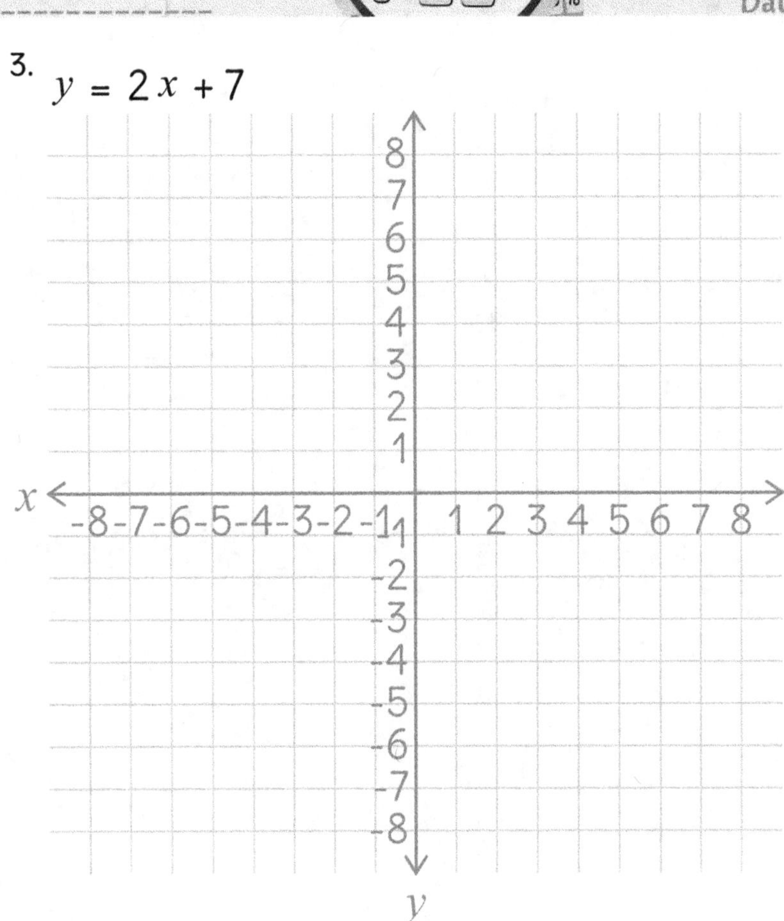

4. $y = x - 7$

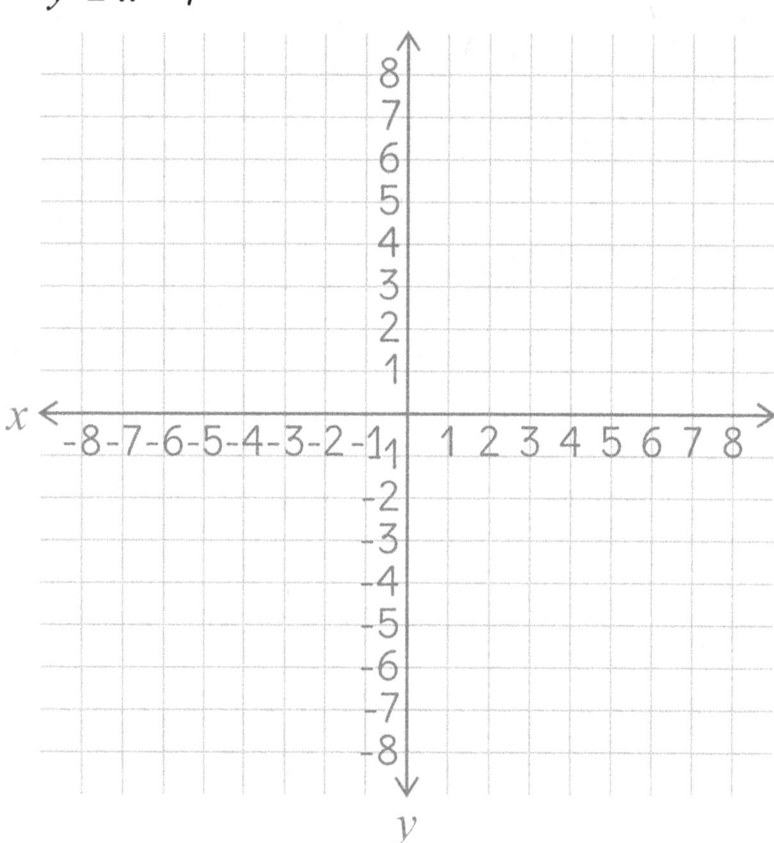

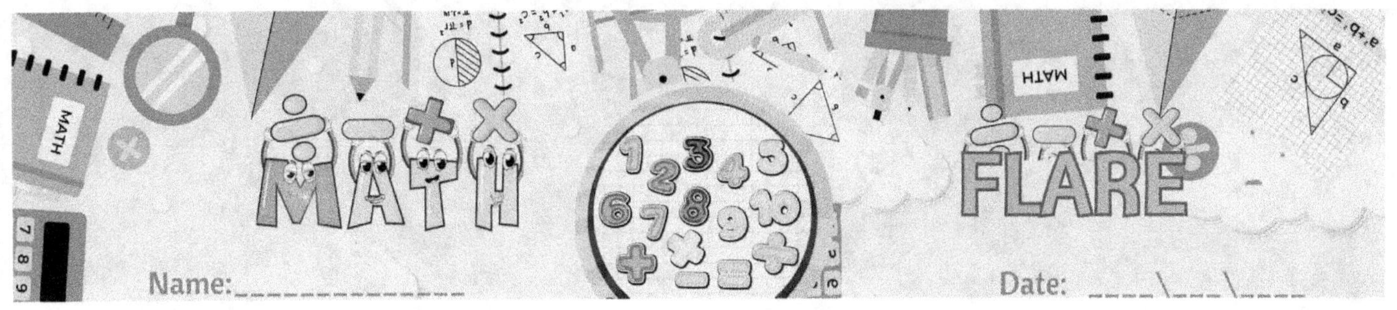

5. $y = \dfrac{11}{4}x + 4$

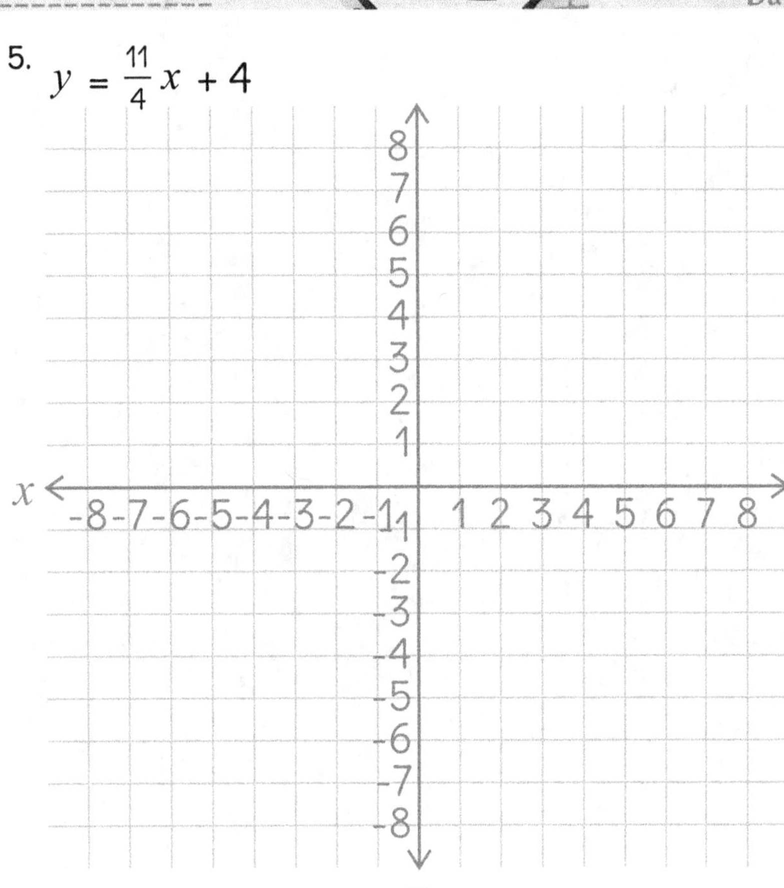

6. $y = \dfrac{1}{2}x - 6$

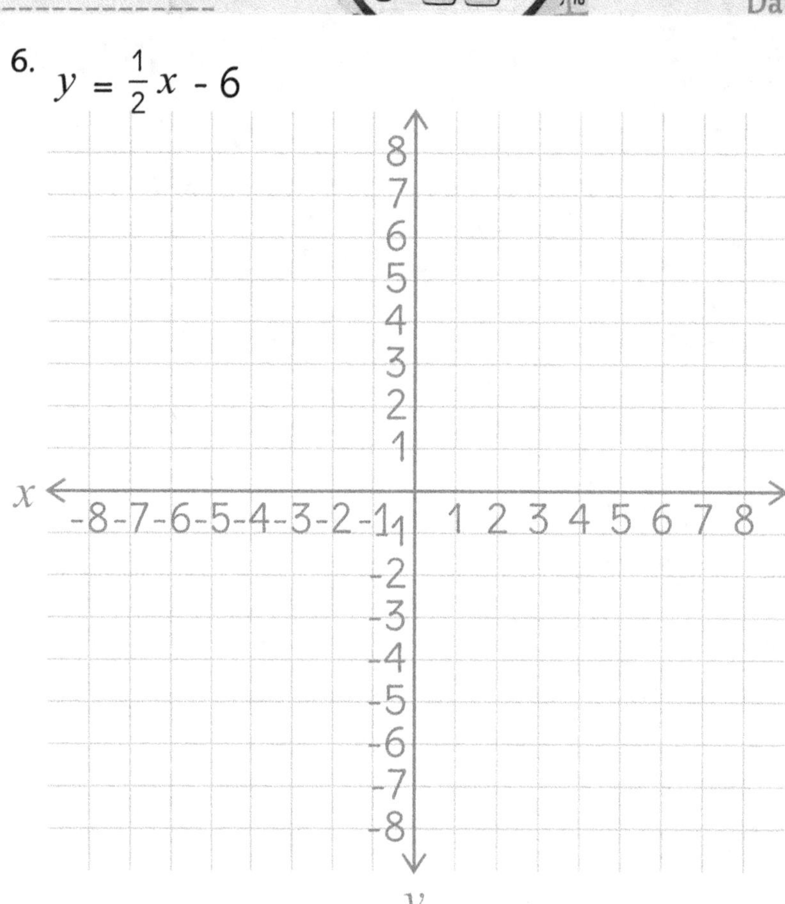

MATH
FLARE
Name:
Date:

7. $y = -x + 5$

x
y
8 7 6 5 4 3 2 1
-8 -7 -6 -5 -4 -3 -2 -1
1 2 3 4 5 6 7 8
-1 -2 -3 -4 -5 -6 -7 -8

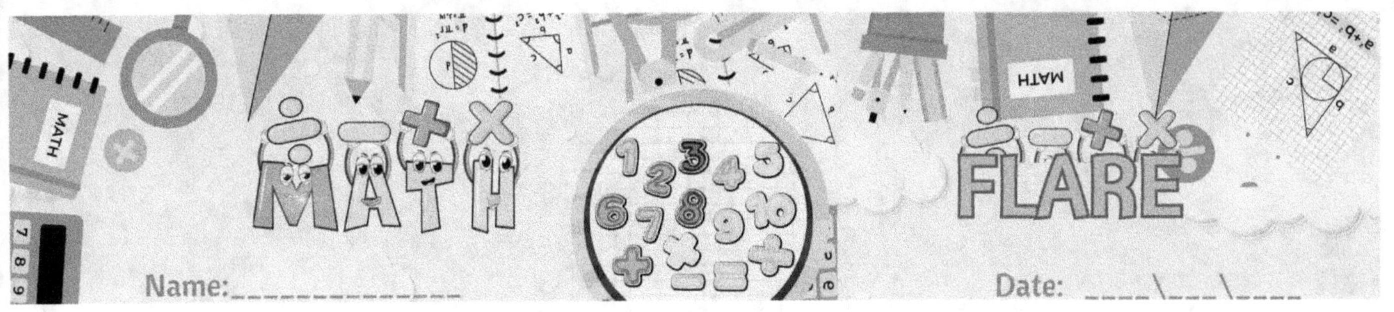

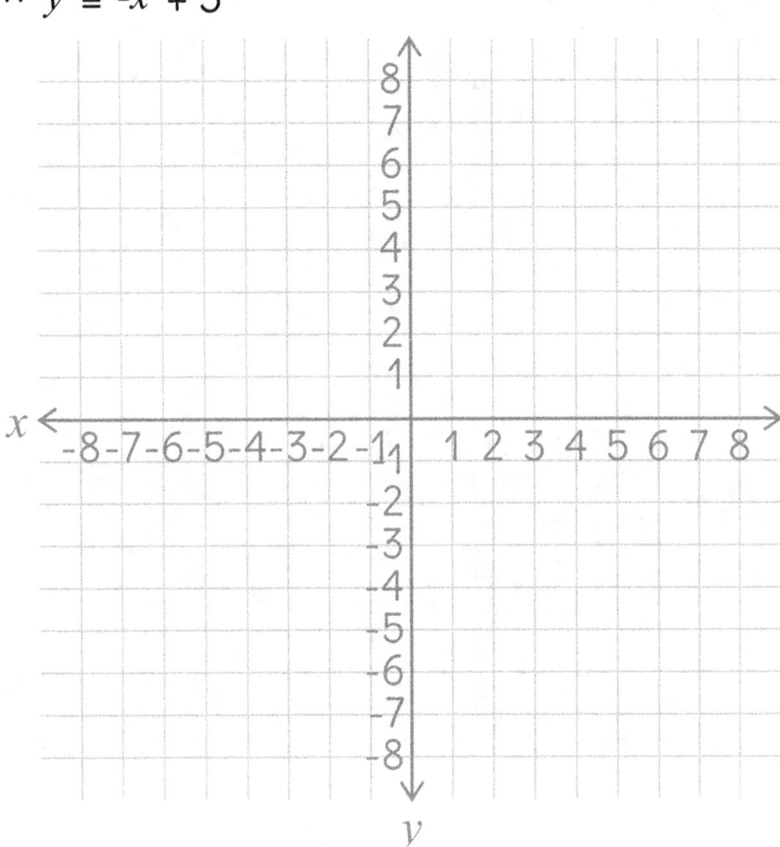

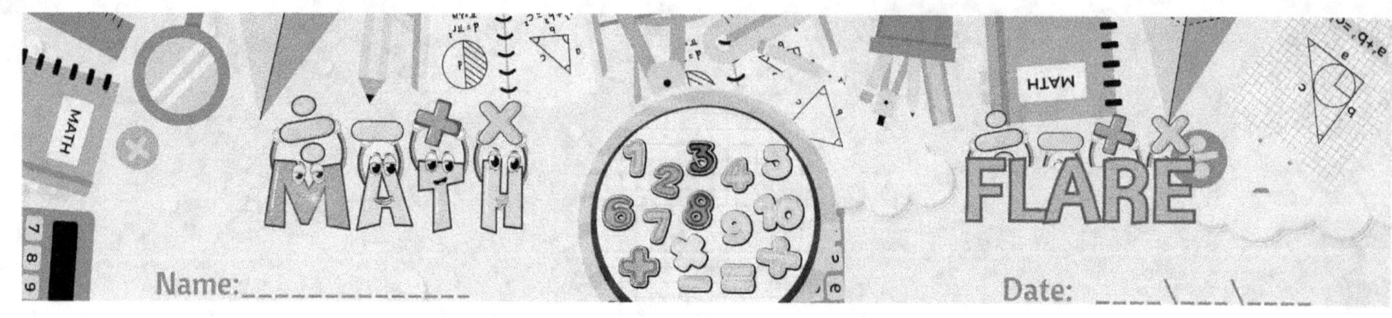

8. $y = \dfrac{9}{4}x + 6$

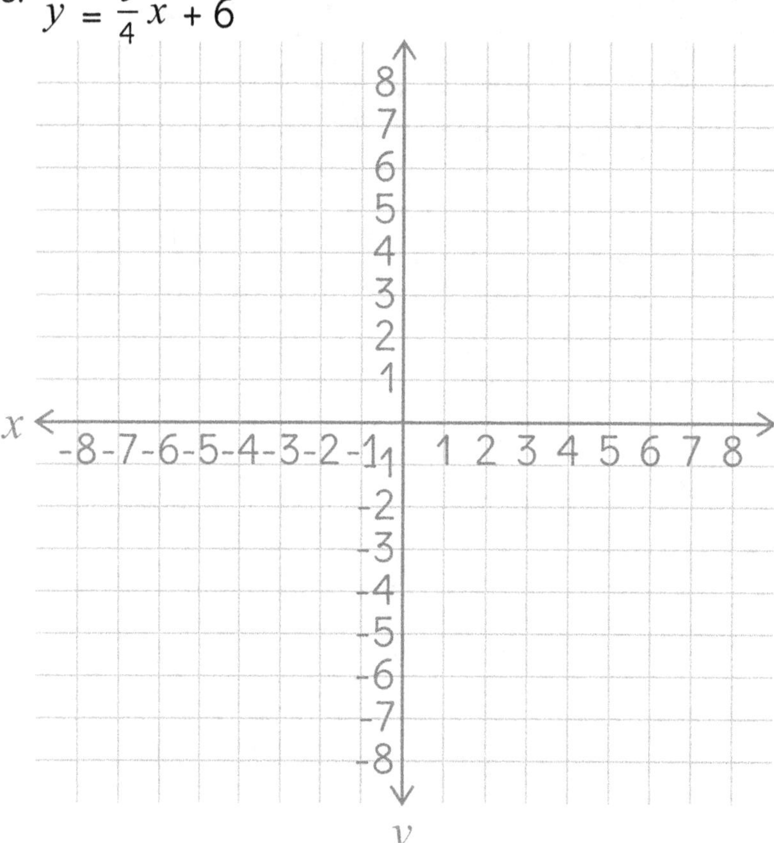

9. $y = 2x + 4$

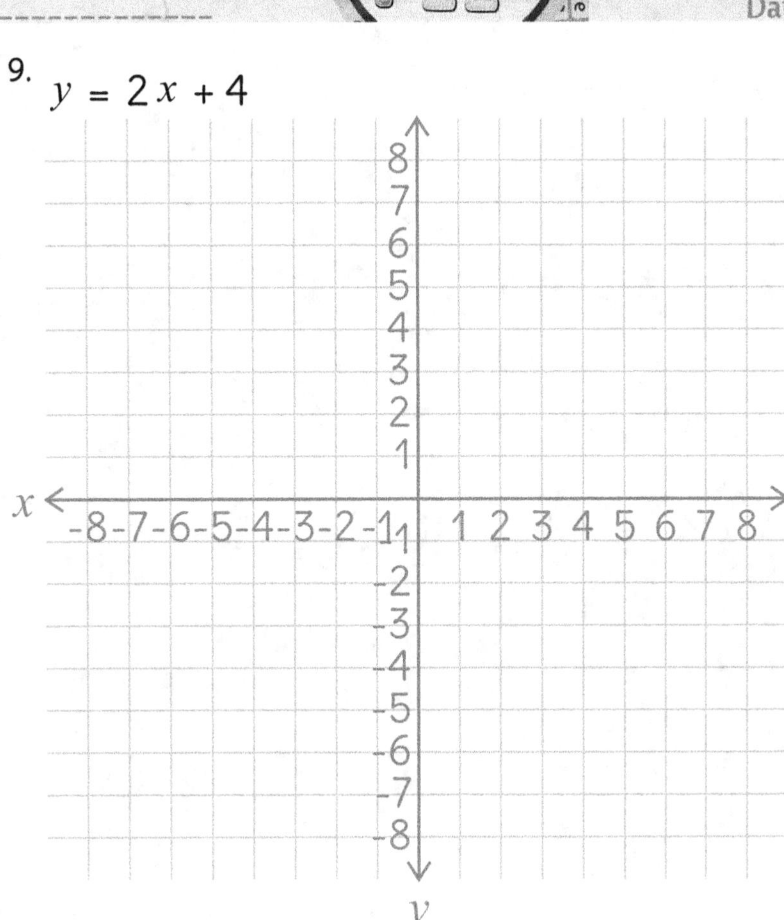

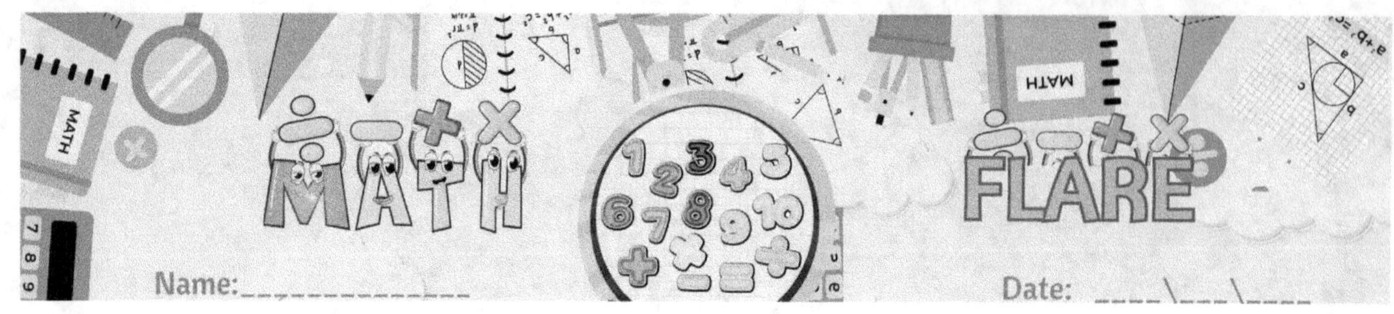

10. $y = \dfrac{5}{2}x - 1$

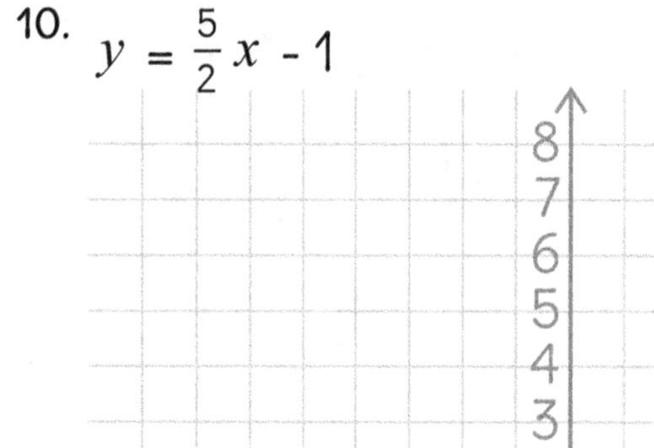

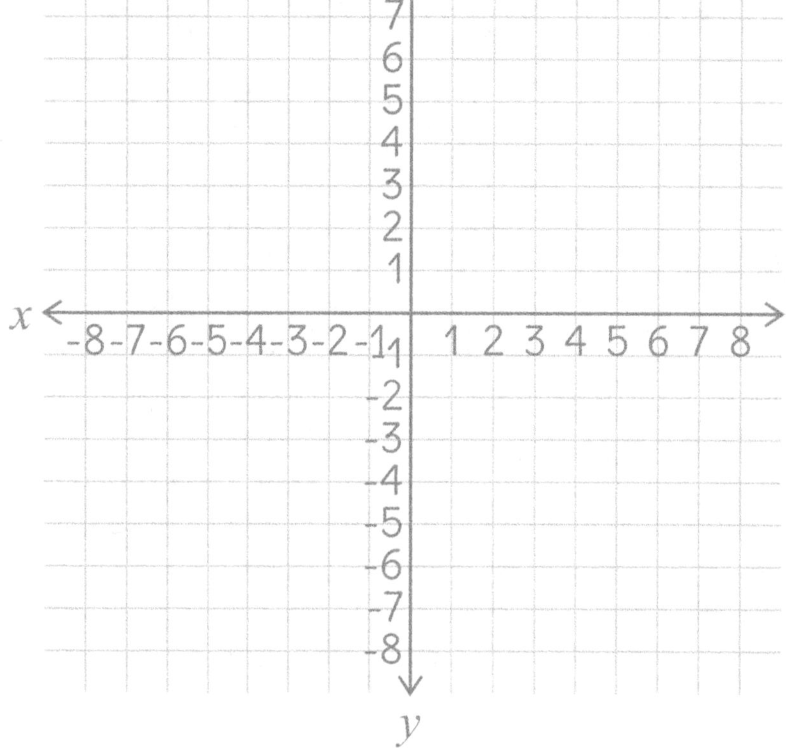

Chapter. 03

System of Equations

A system of equations is a collection of two or more equations involving the same set of variables. The solution to a system of equations is the set of values for the variables that satisfy all the equations simultaneously.

Solving by Elimination:

To solve a system of equations by elimination, we manipulate the equations to eliminate one of the variables.

Given the system:

$$4x + 5y = 6$$

$$10x + 6y = 8$$

Step 1: Multiply each equation by a constant such that the coefficients of one of the variables become equal or multiples of each other.

Let's try to eliminate the variable x.

- Multiply the first equation by 5 and the second equation by -2:

$$20x + 25y = 30$$

$$-20x - 12y = -16$$

Step 2: Add the two equations together to eliminate the variable x.

$$(20x - 20x) + (25y - 12y) = 30 - 16$$

$$13y = 14$$

Step 3: Solve for *y:*

$$y = \frac{14}{13} = 1.077$$

Step 4: Substitute the value of y into one of the original equations to solve for x. Let's use the first equation:

$$4x + 5\left(\frac{14}{13}\right) = 6$$

$$4x + \frac{70}{13} = 6$$

$$4x = 6 - \frac{70}{13}$$

$$4x = \frac{78 - 70}{13}$$

$$4x = \frac{8}{13}$$

$$x = \frac{2}{13} = 0.154$$

the solution to the system of equations is x = 0.154 and y = 1.077.

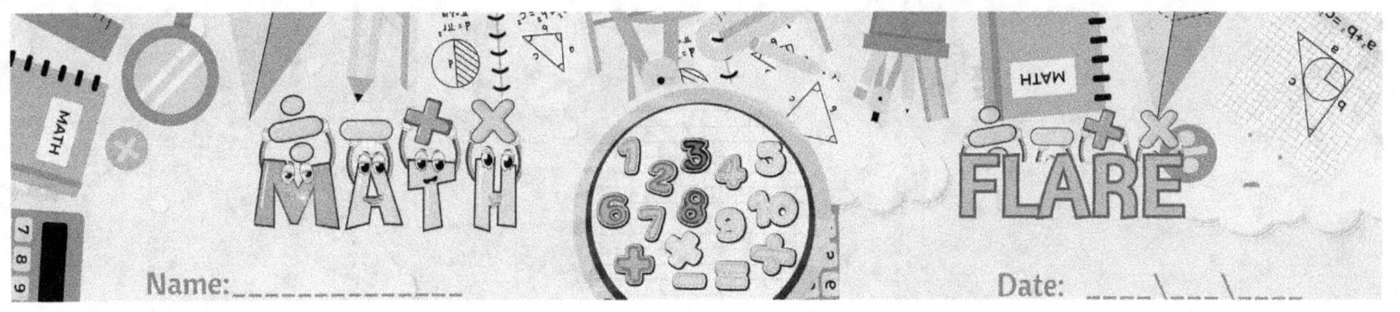

System of Equations

1. $1x + 2y = 3$

   $10x + 5y = 1$

2. $7x + 5y = 1$

   $2x + 10y = 5$

3. $9x + 4y = 5$

   $6x + 5y = 10$

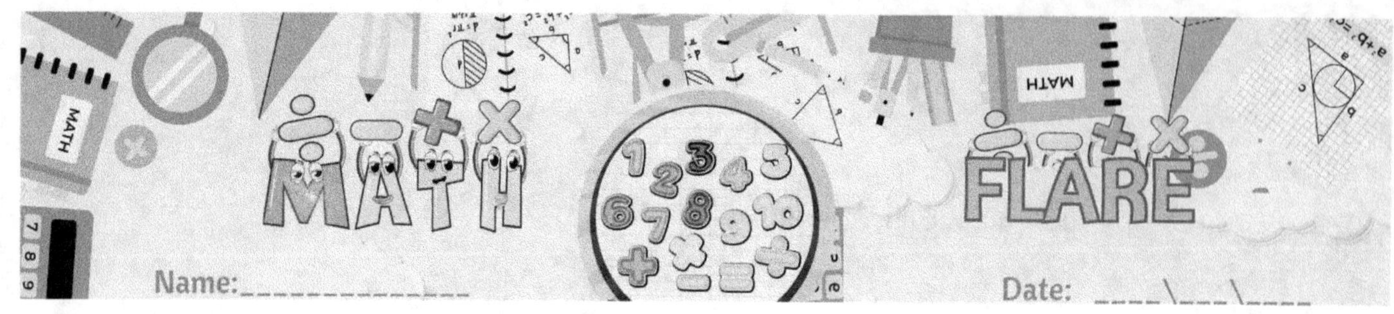

4. $3x + 9y = 1$

   $10x + 4y = 6$

5. $8x + 1y = 8$

   $10x + 10y = 1$

6. $6x + 4y = 10$

   $3x + 6y = 3$

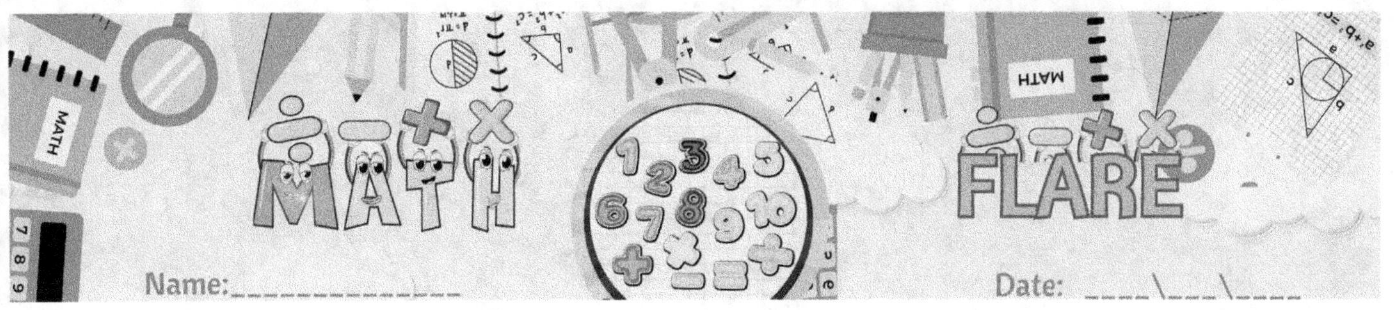

7. $6x + 9y = 3$

   $4x + 9y = 9$

8. $1x + 8y = 3$

   $8x + 8y = 3$

9. $3x + 5y = 1$

   $4x + 9y = 4$

10. $8x + 3y = 7$

$7x + 9y = 7$

11. $6x + 9y = 6$

$2x + 8y = 7$

12. $7x + 5y = 10$

$2x + 1y = 9$

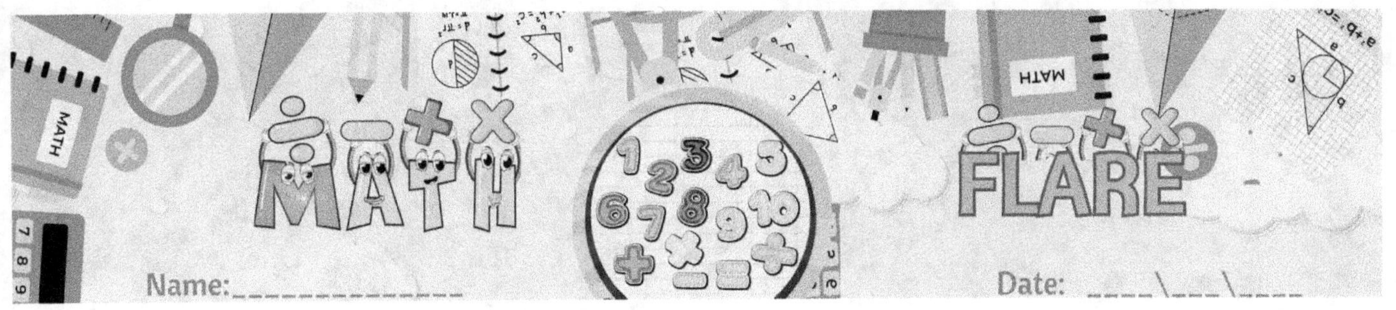

13. $2x + 4y = 10$

$2x + 8y = 3$

14. $3x + 8y = 4$

$2x + 4y = 5$

15. $10x + 1y = 9$

$4x + 5y = 6$

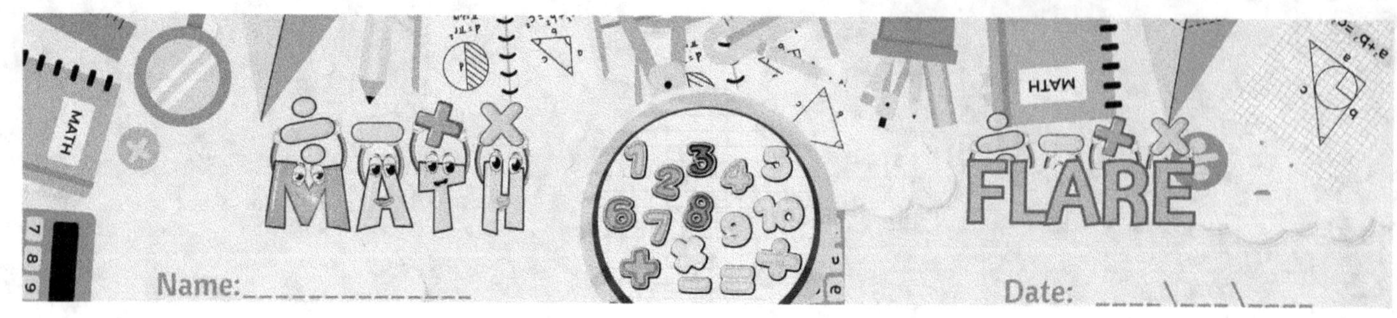

16. 6x + 3y = 1

    4x + 4y = 8

17. 5x + 1y = 7

    5x + 7y = 8

18. 8x + 3y = 2

    9x + 4y = 4

19. 1x + 9y = 1

    5x + 6y = 5

20. 9x + 7y = 2

    2x + 5y = 10

21. 9x + 5y = 4

    5x + 4y = 2

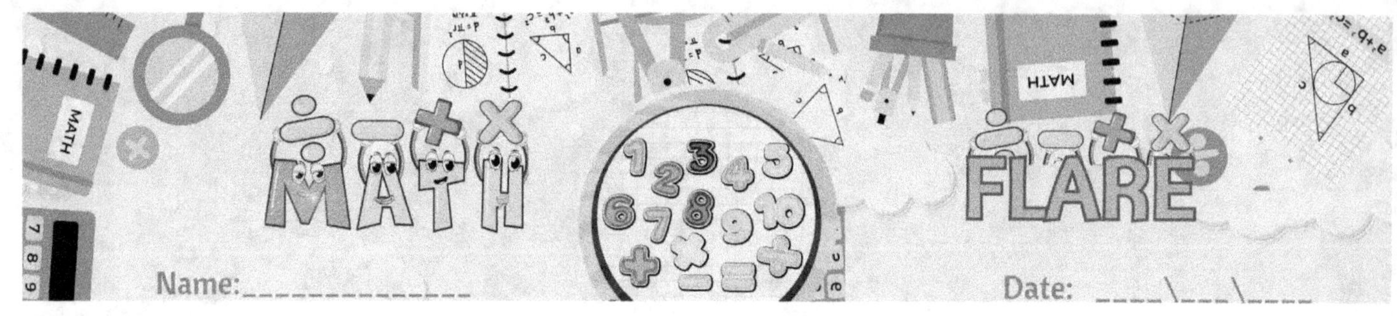

22. $9x + 4y = 8$

$4x + 9y = 6$

23. $5x + 7y = 5$

$8x + 4y = 5$

24. $2x + 6y = 4$

$10x + 8y = 6$

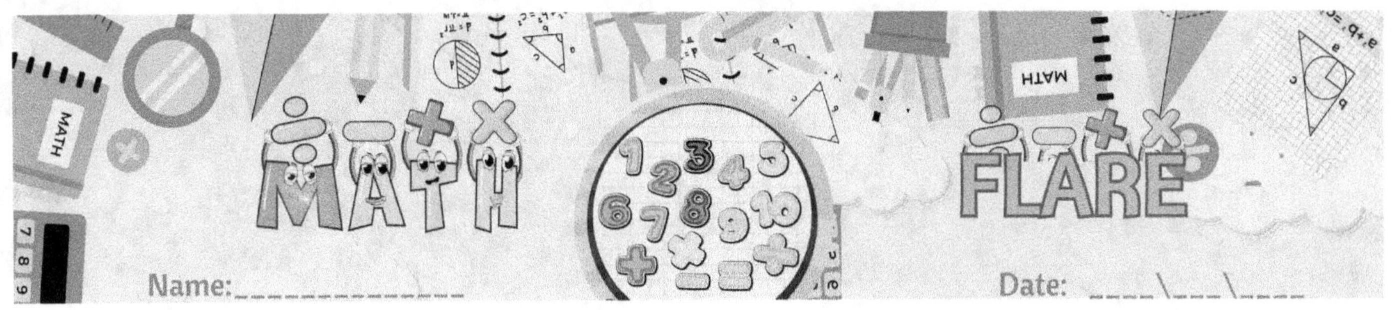

25. 6x + 7y = 6

3x + 10y = 9

26. 7x + 9y = 3

3x + 8y = 1

27. 2x + 7y = 3

1x + 2y = 4

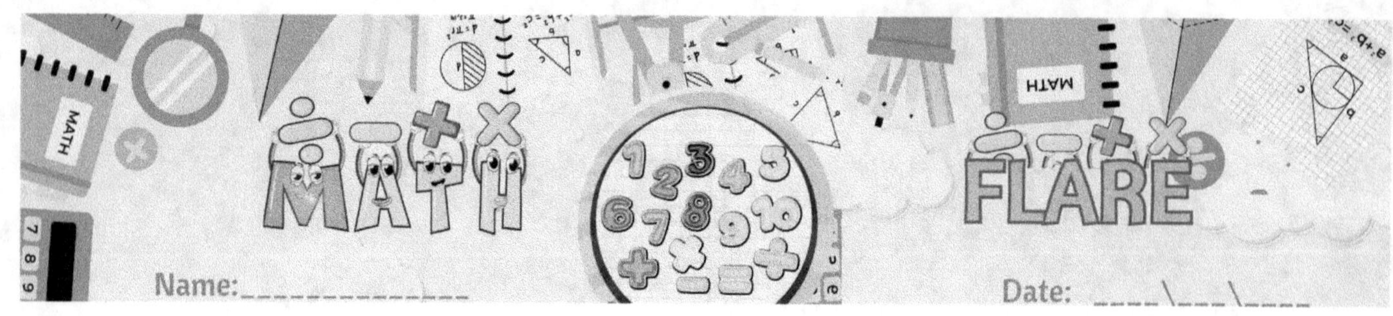

28. 1x + 3y = 10

   9x + 10y = 9

29. 6x + 7y = 6

   1x + 3y = 2

30. 6x + 9y = 7

   6x + 10y = 2

31. $4x + 10y = 7$

   $6x + 3y = 7$

32. $10x + 3y = 4$

   $9x + 4y = 10$

33. $2x + 6y = 6$

   $8x + 8y = 10$

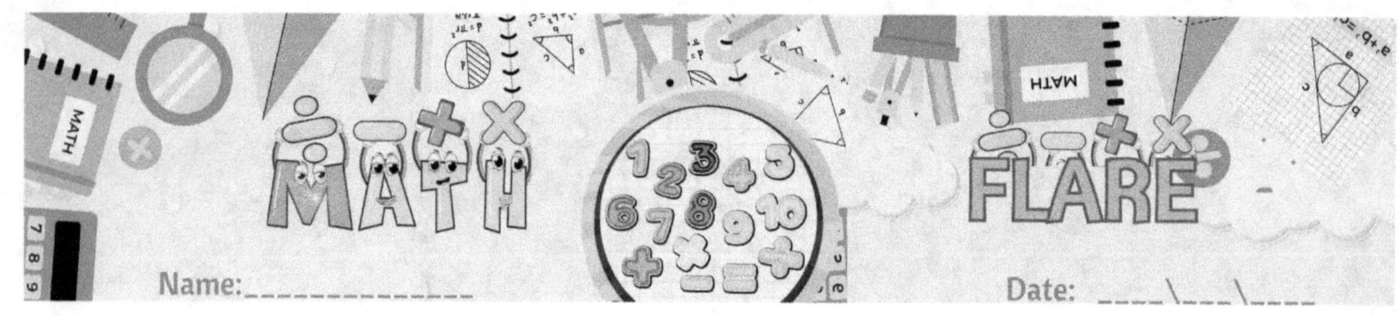

34. $1x + 9y = 9$

    $6x + 2y = 9$

35. $7x + 6y = 10$

    $8x + 6y = 7$

36. $10x + 2y = 3$

    $9x + 9y = 10$

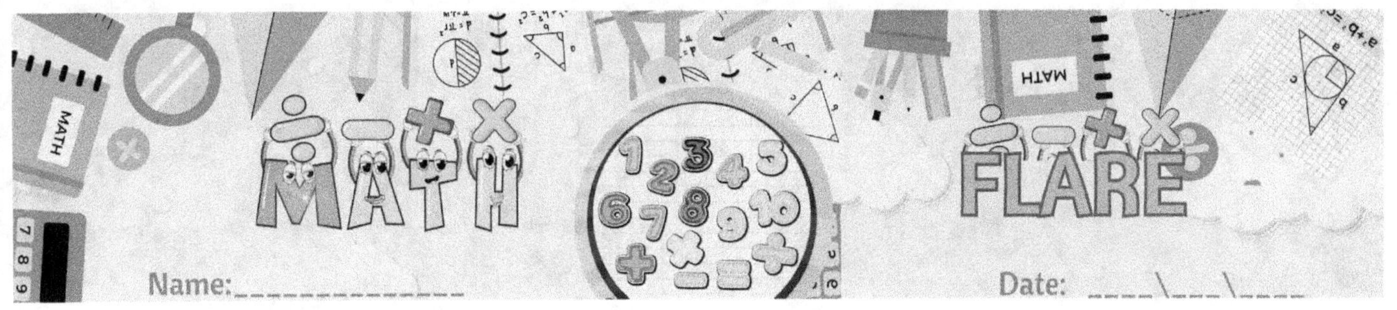

37. $3x + 3y = 8$

$5x + 9y = 3$

38. $10x + 10y = 5$

$1x + 9y = 1$

39. $7x + 9y = 7$

$6x + 2y = 9$

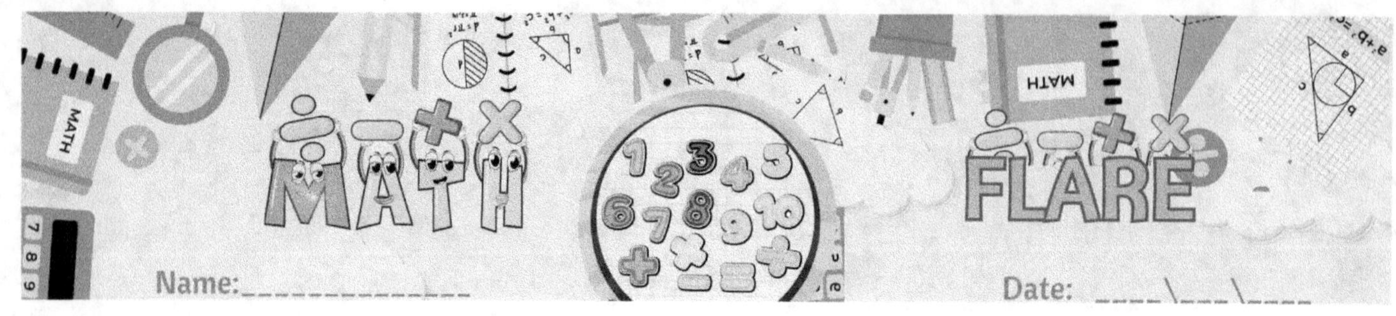

40. 8x + 8y = 1

7x + 5y = 9

41. 1x + 7y = 8

1x + 5y = 6

42. 1x + 8y = 5

4x + 8y = 5

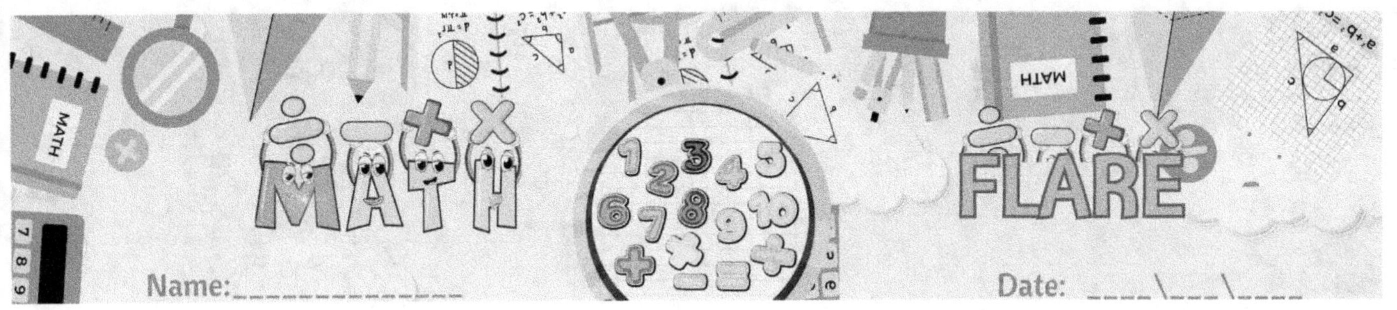

43. $5x + 1y = 8$

   $5x + 10y = 3$

44. $10x + 10y = 9$

   $7x + 2y = 7$

45. $2x + 4y = 8$

   $5x + 1y = 7$

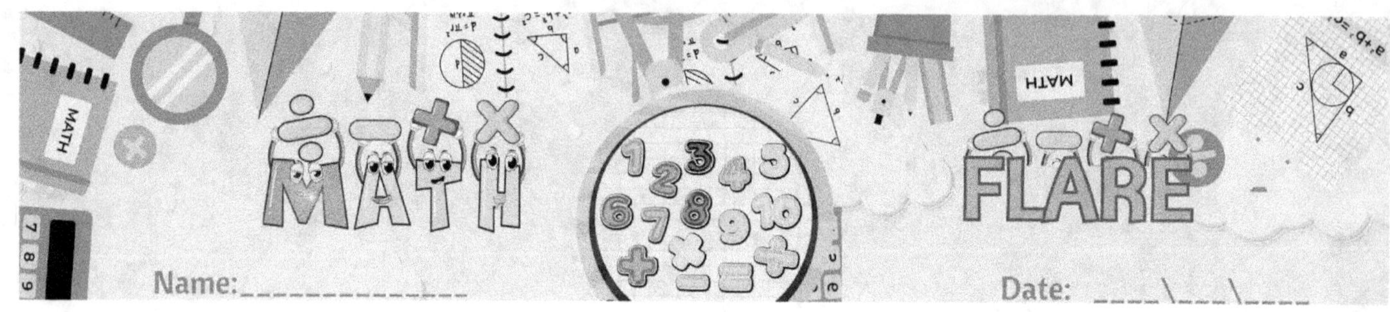

46. 4x + 3y = 10

   7x + 7y = 7

47. 3x + 1y = 6

   6x + 4y = 8

48. 2x + 6y = 7

   8x + 7y = 8

49. $5x + 3y = 9$

$7x + 9y = 1$

50. $7x + 6y = 3$

$9x + 7y = 7$

Chapter. 04

Quadratic Equations

A quadratic equation is a polynomial equation of the second degree, meaning it can be written in the form:

$$ax^2 + bx + c = 0$$

where a, b, and c are constants, and x is the variable being solved for. The solutions to a quadratic equation are the values of x that make the equation true.

Now, let's solve the quadratic equation $11x^2 - 1 = 0$ and understand it step by step using quadratic formula.

1. **Identify the coefficients:**

   In the equation $11x^2 - 1 = 0$,

   $$a=11, b=0, \text{ and } c=-1.$$

2. **Apply the quadratic formula:**

   The quadratic formula states that for an equation $ax^2 + bx + c = 0$, the solutions for x are given by:

   $$x = \frac{-b \pm \sqrt{b^2 - 4ac}}{2a}$$

   Plugging in the values a=11, b=0, and c=−1 into the quadratic formula, we get:

   $$x = \frac{-0 \pm \sqrt{0 - 4(11)(-1)}}{2(11)}$$

3. Simplify inside the square root:

$$0^2 - 4(11)(-1) = 0 - (-44) = 44$$

4. Plug in the simplified values:

$$X = \frac{\pm \sqrt{44}}{22}$$

5. Simplify the square root:

Since 44 is not a perfect square, we can write it as $\sqrt[2]{11}$

$$X = \frac{\pm \sqrt[2]{11}}{22}$$

6. Simplify further if possible:

We can simplify $\sqrt[2]{11}$ to $\sqrt{11}$ by canceling out the common factor:

$$X = \frac{\pm \sqrt{11}}{11}$$

7. Final solution:

So, the solutions to the equation are:

$$X = \frac{\sqrt{11}}{11} \text{ and } X = \frac{-\sqrt{11}}{11}$$

or

$$(x = 0.302, \text{ and } x = -0.302)$$

These are the roots of the quadratic equation. They represent the points where the graph of the quadratic equation intersects the x-axis.

Let's solve another equation:

$$-4p^2 + 6p - 6 = 0$$

$$p = \frac{-b \pm \sqrt{b^2 - 4ac}}{2a}$$

where $a = -4$, $b = 6$, and $c = -6$.

Let's plug these values into the quadratic formula:

$$p = \frac{-6 \pm \sqrt{6^2 - 4(-4)(-6)}}{2(-4)}$$

First, let's simplify inside the square root:

$$6^2 - 4(-4)(-6)$$

$$= 36 - 96 = -60$$

So, we have:

$$p = \frac{-6 \pm \sqrt{-60}}{-8}$$

We can simplify the square root of -60 by factoring out -1:

$$\sqrt{-60}$$

$$= \sqrt{-1 \times 60}$$

$$= \sqrt{-1} \times \sqrt{60}$$

$$= i\sqrt{60}$$

So, we have:

$$p = \frac{-6 \pm i\sqrt{60}}{-8}$$

Simplify:

$$\sqrt{60} \text{ to } \sqrt{4 \times 15} = 2\sqrt{15}$$

$$p = \frac{-6 \pm i \times 2\sqrt{15}}{-8}$$

Now, divide both the numerator and denominator by −2 to simplify:

$$p = \frac{3 \pm i\sqrt{15}}{4}$$

So, the solutions to the equation are:

$$p = \frac{3 + i\sqrt{15}}{4} \text{ and } p = \frac{3 - i\sqrt{15}}{4}$$

This equation -4p² + 6p - 6 = 0 has no real solutions.

When a quadratic equation has no real solutions, it means that the solutions are not real numbers, but rather complex numbers. In this case, the solutions involve the imaginary unit i because the discriminant ($b^2 - 4ac$) is negative, which results in taking the square root of a negative number when applying the quadratic formula.

In mathematics, such equations are said to have "no real roots" or "no real solutions." They are also sometimes referred to as having "complex roots" or "complex solutions." Complex numbers include a real part and an imaginary part, and they are often written in the form $a + bi$, where a and b are real numbers and i is the imaginary unit, defined as $i = \sqrt{-1}$.

Let's solve another equation:

$$12x^2 + 6x - 2 = 0$$

$$x = \frac{-b \pm \sqrt{b^2 - 4ac}}{2a}$$

where $a = 12$, $b = 6$, and $c = -2$.

Let's plug these values into the quadratic formula:

$$x = \frac{-6 \pm \sqrt{6^2 - 4(12)(-2)}}{2(12)}$$

First, let's simplify inside the square root:

$$6^2 - 4(12)(-2)$$

$$= 36 - (-96)$$

$$= 36 + 96$$

$$= 132$$

So, we have:

$$x = \frac{-6 \pm \sqrt{132}}{24}$$

Now, let's simplify the square root of 132:

$$x = \frac{-6 \pm \sqrt{4 \times 33}}{24}$$

$$x = \frac{-6 \pm 2\sqrt{33}}{24}$$

$$x = \frac{-6 \pm \sqrt{33}}{12}$$

So, the solutions to the equation are:

$$X = \frac{-6+\sqrt{33}}{12} \text{ and } X = \frac{-6-\sqrt{33}}{12}$$

or (x = 0.229, and x = -0.729)

Let's solve a Quadratic Equation where the right side is a number instead of 0.

$$-8n^2 + 6n + 30 = 7$$

To solve the equation, we first need to bring all terms to one side to set the equation equal to zero:

$$-8n^2 + 6n + 30 - 7 = 0$$

Simplify:

$$-8n^2 + 6n + 23 = 0$$

Now, to solve for n, we can use the quadratic formula:

$$n = \frac{-b \pm \sqrt{b^2 - 4ac}}{2a}$$

where $a = -8$, $b = 6$, and $c = 23$.

Plugging these values into the formula, we get:

$$n = \frac{-6 \pm \sqrt{6^2 - 4(-8)(23)}}{2(-8)}$$

$$n = \frac{-6 \pm \sqrt{36 + 736}}{-16}$$

$$n = \frac{-6 \pm \sqrt{772}}{-16}$$

Now, let's simplify the square root of 772. We can factor out 4:

$$\sqrt{772} = \sqrt{4 \times 193} = 2\sqrt{193}$$

So, our equation becomes:

$$n = \frac{-6 \pm 2\sqrt{193}}{-8}$$

So, the solutions to the equation are:

$$n = \frac{-3+\sqrt{193}}{-8} \text{ and } n = \frac{-3-\sqrt{193}}{-8}$$

or

$$(n = -1.362, \text{ and } n = 2.112)$$

Quadratic Equations

1. $11x^2 - 1 = 0$

2. $-4p^2 + 6p - 6 = 0$

3. $12x^2 + 6x - 2 = 0$

4. $4v^2 - 49 = 0$

5. $-3a^2 + 18 = 0$

6. $-7x^2 + 2x + 21 = 0$

7. $3n^2 - n - 30 = 0$

8. $4x^2 - 81 = 0$

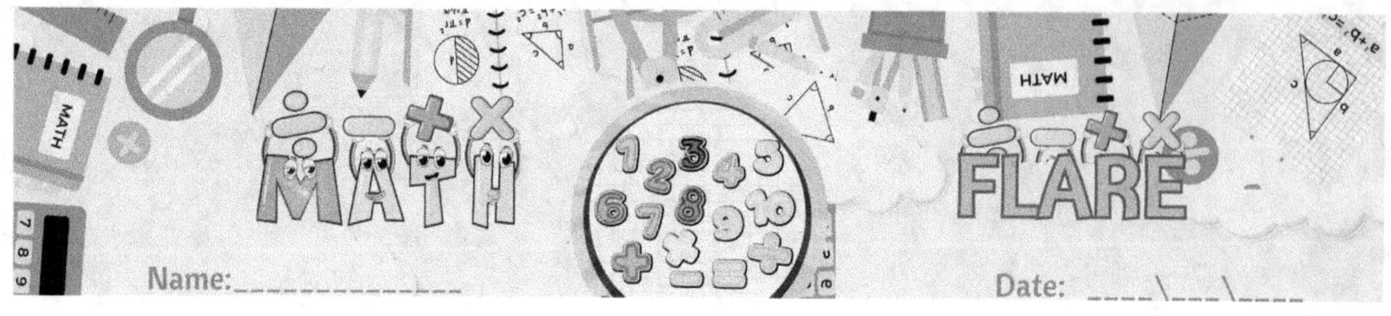

9. $-5n^2 - 4n + 33 = 0$

13. $-m^2 + 9m + 52 = 0$

10. $-9v^2 - v + 21 = 0$

14. $-4n^2 + 4 = 0$

11. $-6m^2 - 5m - 11 = 0$

15. $-2m^2 - 8m + 2 = 0$

12. $-12x^2 + 9x - 1 = 0$

16. $-2x^2 - 10x + 132 = 0$

17. $12x^2 - 22 = 0$

21. $x^2 + 9x - 36 = 0$

18. $-11k^2 + 11k - 8 = 0$

22. $4x^2 + 12x + 8 = 0$

19. $-6m^2 + m + 92 = 0$

23. $3x^2 + 12x - 63 = 0$

20. $5m^2 - 6m - 32 = 0$

24. $4n^2 - 3n - 14 = 0$

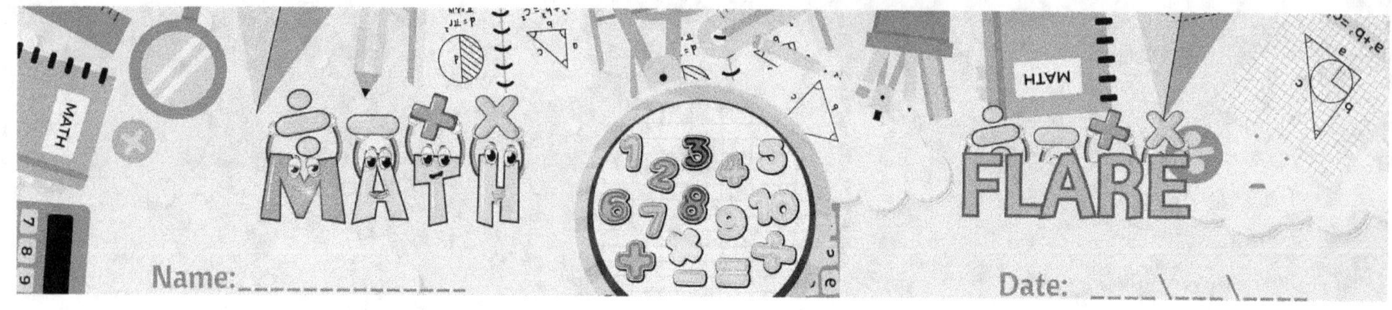

25. $9n^2 + n + 10 = 0$

29. $4b^2 + 9b + 5 = 0$

26. $-12x^2 - 12x + 11 = 0$

30. $5n^2 + 3n - 140 = 0$

27. $6n^2 - 4n - 42 = 0$

31. $2x^2 - 9x = 10$

28. $r^2 + 11r + 12 = 0$

32. $12b^2 - 11b + 5 = -3$

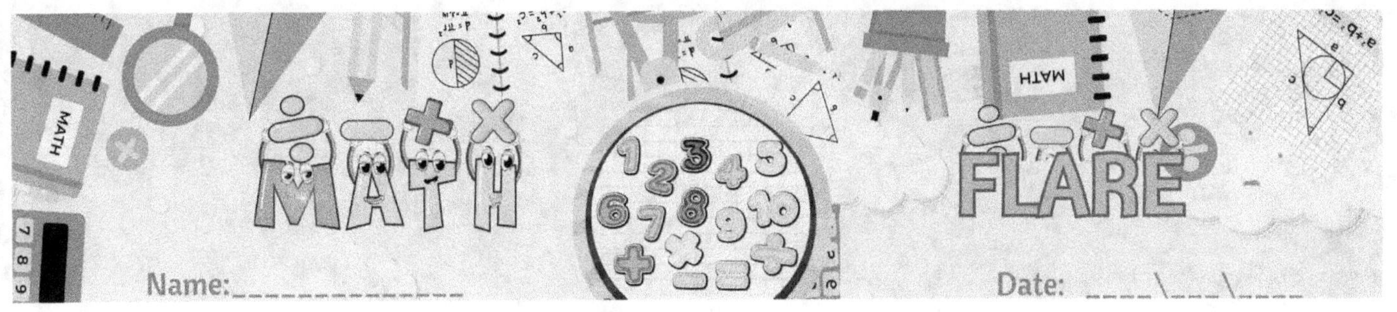

Name:_______________ Date: ____________

33. $5b^2 - 9b - 27 = 11$

37. $10x^2 + 2x - 5 = 2$

34. $2k^2 - k - 12 = -11$

38. $6x^2 + 7x - 100 = -10$

35. $-6p^2 - 6p + 23 = 3$

39. $4x^2 + 11x - 9 = 3$

36. $-5a^2 + 2a + 10 = -12$

40. $2a^2 - 7a - 9 = -10$

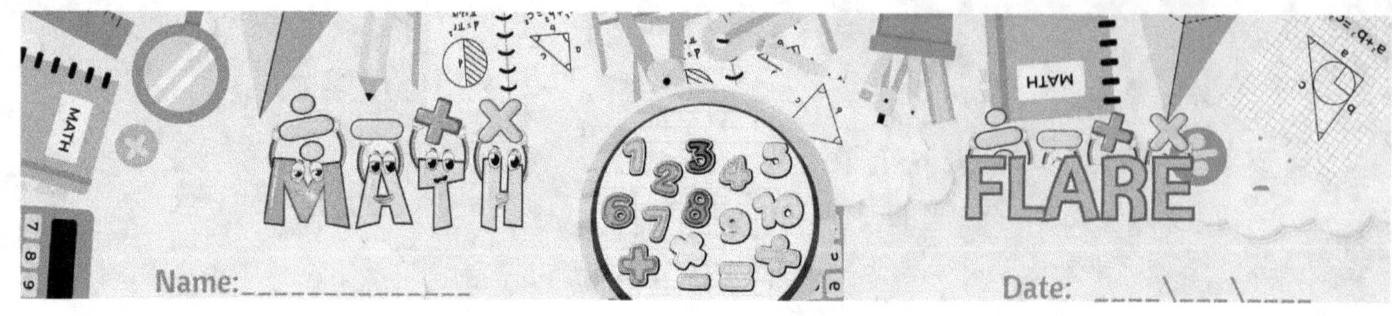

41. $n^2 = 11$

45. $9p^2 + 5p - 20 = -8$

42. $2v^2 - 3 = -10$

46. $x^2 - 103 = -3$

43. $8x^2 + 5x + 1 = 9$

47. $10n^2 - 14 = 8$

44. $-11r^2 - 10r + 11 = -3$

48. $-2x^2 - 3x - 7 = 3$

Name: _______________   Date: ____________

49. $6n^2 + 9 = 11$

53. $12x^2 - 7x + 11 = 3$

50. $10m^2 + 10m + 11 = 2$

54. $-5b^2 + 10 = 5$

51. $5n^2 + 12n - 28 = -4$

55. $3b^2 - 5b - 14 = -12$

52. $v^2 + 3 = -7$

56. $-8n^2 + 6n + 30 = 7$

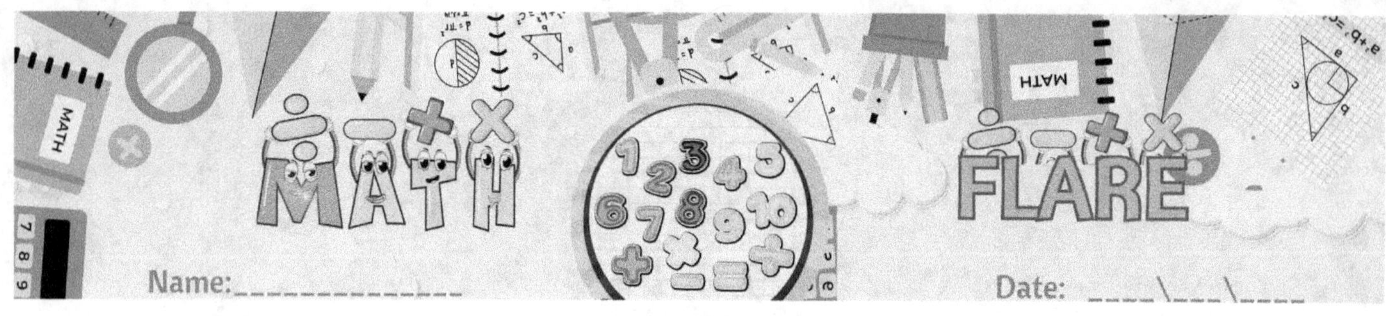

57. $-7p^2 + p + 32 = 9$

58. $-4m^2 + m - 17 = -5$

59. $-2b^2 + 4b + 7 = 6$

60. $-8n^2 + n + 33 = 10$

Chapter. 05

Geometry

Area and Perimeter

The area of a shape represents the amount of space it occupies. The perimeter of a shape is the total distance around its outer edge.

Area of Rectangle

For a square, since all four sides are equal, we only need to know the length of one side to find its area. We can calculate the area of a square by multiplying the length of one side by itself (squared). So, if the length of one side of the square is 's', then the area (A) is given by:

$$A = s \times s$$

4 in

4 in

$$A = 4 \times 4$$

$$A = 16$$

Perimeter of Rectangle

For a square, since all four sides are equal, we can find the perimeter by adding up the lengths of all four sides. If 's' represents the length of one side, then the perimeter (P) is given by:

$$P = 4 \times s$$

$$P = 4 \times 4$$

$$P = 16$$

Area of Triangle:

The area of a triangle represents the amount of space enclosed within its three sides. The formula for calculating the area of a triangle depends on the type of triangle. For a general triangle, we use the formula:

$$A = \frac{1}{2} \times \text{base} \times \text{height}$$

Where:

- A represents the area of the triangle.

- The base is the length of any one side of the triangle.

- The height is the perpendicular distance from the base to the opposite vertex.

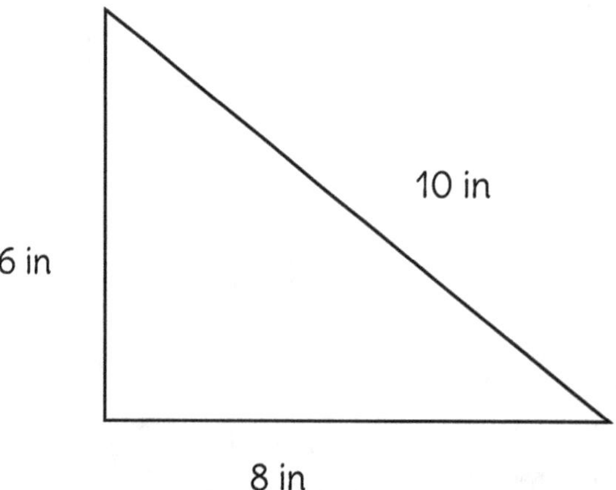

$$A = \frac{1}{2} \times \text{base} \times \text{height}$$

$$A = \frac{1}{2} \times 6 \times 8$$

$$A = \frac{1}{2} \times 48$$

$$A = 24$$

Perimeter of Triangle:

The perimeter of a triangle is the total length of its three sides. To find the perimeter, we simply add the lengths of all three sides together:

$$P = \text{side1} + \text{side2} + \text{side3}$$

$$P = 6 + 8 + 10$$

$$P = 24$$

Equilateral Triangle

An equilateral triangle is a triangle in which all three sides are equal in length. To find the area and perimeter of an equilateral triangle, we can use the following formulas:

- Area (A): $\frac{\sqrt{3}}{4} \times a^2$ where a is the length of one side of the equilateral triangle.

- Perimeter (P): $P = 3a$ where a is the length of one side of the equilateral triangle.

Let's solve a problem:

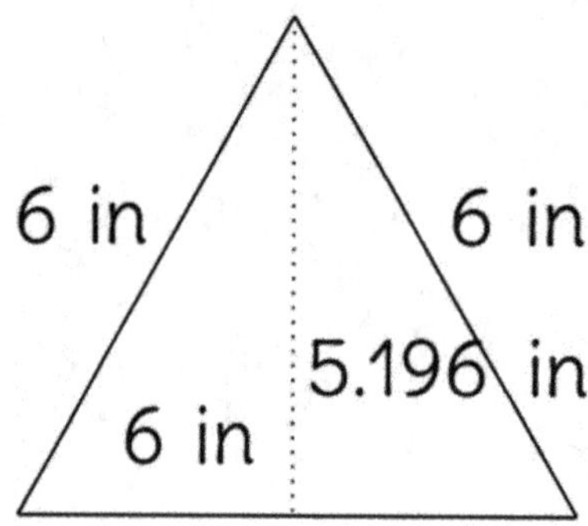

Area of Equilateral Triangle:

$$\text{Area (A): } \frac{\sqrt{3}}{4} \times (6)^2$$

$$\text{Area (A): } \frac{\sqrt{3}}{4} \times 36$$

$$\text{Area (A): } \frac{36\sqrt{3}}{4}$$

$$\text{Area (A): } \frac{36(1.73)}{4}$$

$$\text{Area (A): } \frac{62.35}{4}$$

$$\text{Area (A): } 15.59 \text{ in}^2$$

Perimeter of Equilateral Triangle:

$$P = 3a$$

$$P = 3(6) = 18$$

Isosceles Triangle

An isosceles triangle is a triangle with at least two sides of equal length. The angles opposite the equal sides are also equal.

Area of Isosceles Triangle

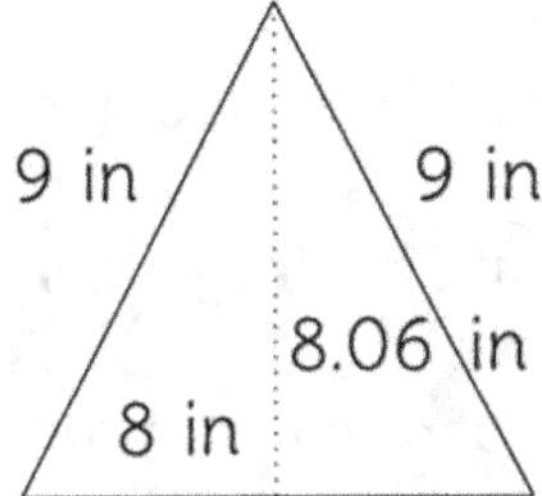

$$A = \frac{1}{2} \times base \times height$$

$$A = \frac{1}{2} \times 8 \times 8$$

$$A = \frac{1}{2} \times 64$$

$$A = 32$$

Perimeter of Isosceles Triangle

The perimeter of a triangle is the total length of its three sides. To find the perimeter, we simply add the lengths of all three sides together:

$$P = side1 + side2 + side3$$

$$P = 9 + 9 + 8$$

$$P = 26$$

Scalene Triangle

A scalene triangle is a triangle with no equal sides and no equal angles. The formula for finding various properties of a scalene triangle is as follows:

Area (A): The area of a scalene triangle can be calculated using Heron's formula, which is given by:

$$A = \sqrt{s(s-a)(s-b)(s-c)}$$

where s is the semi-perimeter of the triangle,

and a, b, and c are the lengths of its three sides.

Perimeter (P): The perimeter of a scalene triangle is the sum of the lengths of its three sides.

$$P = side1 + side2 + side3$$

Let's find the Area and Perimeter of a Scalene Triangle:

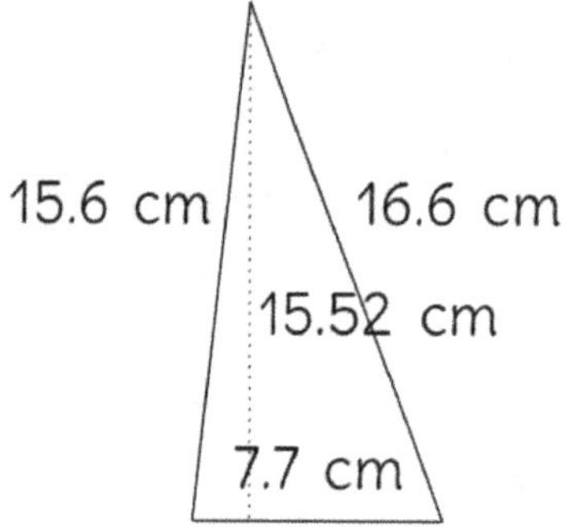

Area (A): First, we calculate the semi-perimeter (s):

$$S = \frac{a + b + c}{2} = \frac{15.6 + 16.6 + 7.7}{2} = \frac{39.8}{2} = 19.9 \text{ cm}$$

Heron's formula to find the area:

$$A = \sqrt{s(s-a)(s-b)(s-c)}$$

$$A = \sqrt{19.9\,(19.9 - 15.6)\,(19.9 - 16.6)\,(19.9 - 7.7)}$$

$$A = \sqrt{19.9 \times 4.3 \times 3.3 \times 12.2}$$

$$A = \sqrt{3445} \approx 59$$

Perimeter (P):

$$P = side1 + side2 + side3$$

$$P = 15.6 + 16.6 + 7.7$$

$$P = 39.8$$

Area and Perimeter of an L-shape

The L-shaped figure typically consists of two rectangles joined together to form an L-shape. To find the area and perimeter of an L-shaped figure, we will need to calculate the areas and perimeters of each rectangle and then combine them.

Area=Area of Rectangle 1 + Area of Rectangle 2

Perimeter=Perimeter of Rectangle 1 + Perimeter of Rectangle 2

Let's find the Area and Perimeter of an L-shape:

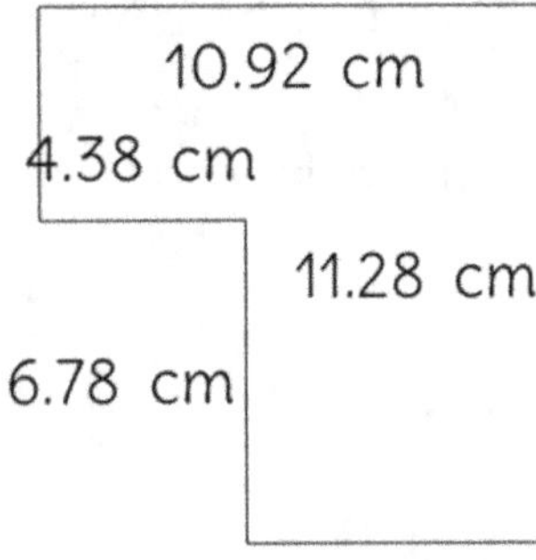

Area of L-Shape

$$\text{Area 1} = 4.38 \times 4.5 = 19.7 \text{ cm}^2$$

$$\text{Area 2} = 11.28 \times 6.54 = 73.7 \text{ cm}^2$$

$$\text{Area} = 19.7 + 73.7$$

$$\text{Area} = 93.481 \text{ cm}^2$$

Perimeter of L-Shape

$$P = 11.28 + 6.54 + 6.78 + 4.38 + 4.5 + 10.92$$

$$P = 44.4 \text{ cm}$$

Area and Perimeter of U-shape

U-shape is basically composed of three rectangles, we'll need to calculate the area and perimeter of each rectangle separately and then sum them up.

Area of the U-shape:

The total area (A) of the U-shape is the sum of the areas of the three rectangles:

$$A = A1 + A2 + A3$$

Perimeter of the U-shape: The total perimeter (P) of the U-shape is the sum of the perimeters of the three rectangles:

$$P = P1 + P2 + P3$$

Let's find the area and perimeter of the following U-shape:

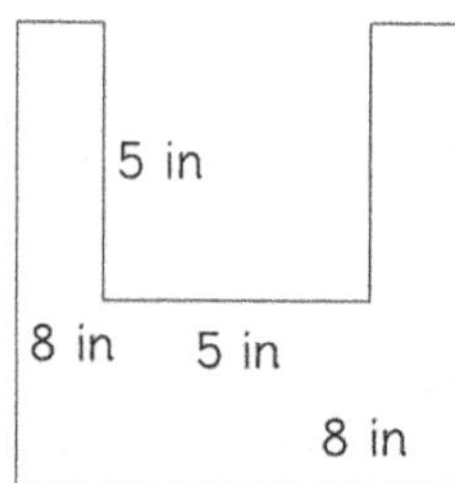

Area:

$$A_1 = 8 \times 1.5 = 12 + A_2 = 3 \times 5 = 15 + A_3 = 8 \times 1.5 = 12$$

$$= 12 + 15 + 12$$

$$= 39 \text{ in}^2$$

Perimeter:

$$2 \times 8 + 2 \times 5 + 2 \times 8$$

$$= 16 + 10 + 16$$

$$= 42$$

Area and Perimeter of T-shape

The T-shape consists of two rectangles joined together to form a T-like structure.

Area of the T-shape:

To find the total area of the T-shape, we need to calculate the areas of both rectangles and then add them together.

$$\text{Area of Rectangle 1} = \text{Length} \times \text{Width}$$

$$\text{Area of Rectangle 2} = \text{Length} \times \text{Width}$$

$$\text{Total Area} = \text{Area of Rectangle 1} + \text{Area of Rectangle 2}$$

The perimeter of the T-shape is the sum of the perimeters of the two rectangles, minus the length of the overlapping side:

$$\text{Perimeter} = 2(l_1+w_1) + 2(l_2+w_2) - (w_1-w_2)$$

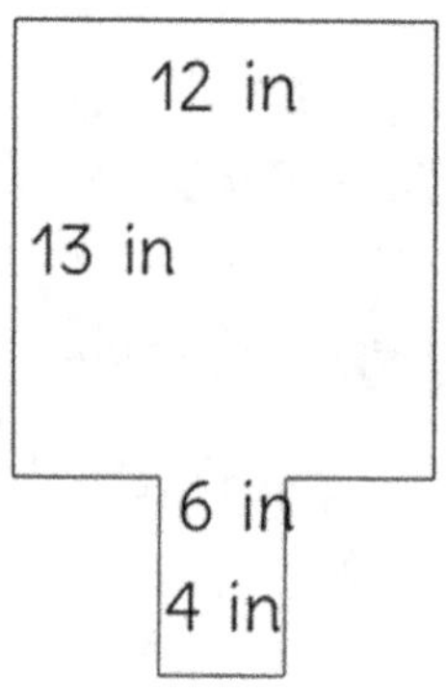

Area= 12 × 13 + 6 × 4

Area= 156 + 24

Area= 180 in²

Perimeter= 2(12+13) +2(6+4) – (12-4)

Perimeter=2(25) + 2(10) – 8

Perimeter= 50 + 20 – 8

Perimeter= 62 in²

Area and Perimeter of Parallelogram

A parallelogram is a four-sided polygon with opposite sides that are parallel and equal in length. To find the area and perimeter of a parallelogram, we use specific formulas based on its dimensions.

For example:

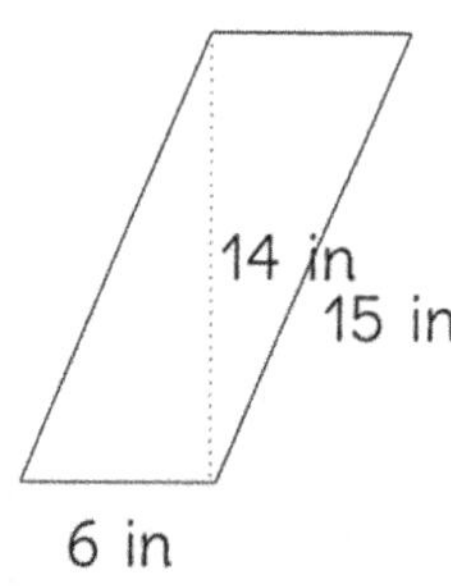

Let's denote:

- The length of one side of the parallelogram as $a = 15$.

- The length of an adjacent side (parallel to a) $b = 6$.

- The height of the parallelogram (perpendicular distance between the two parallel sides) as $h=14$

Area of Parallelogram

$$Area = Base \times Height$$

$$Area = 6 \times 14$$

$$Area = 84$$

Perimeter of Parallelogram

$$2(a + b)$$

$$= 2(15+6)$$

$$= 2(21)$$

$$= 42$$

Area and Perimeter of Trapezoids

A trapezoid is a quadrilateral with at least one pair of parallel sides. To find the area and perimeter of a trapezoid, we use specific formulas based on its dimensions.

For example:

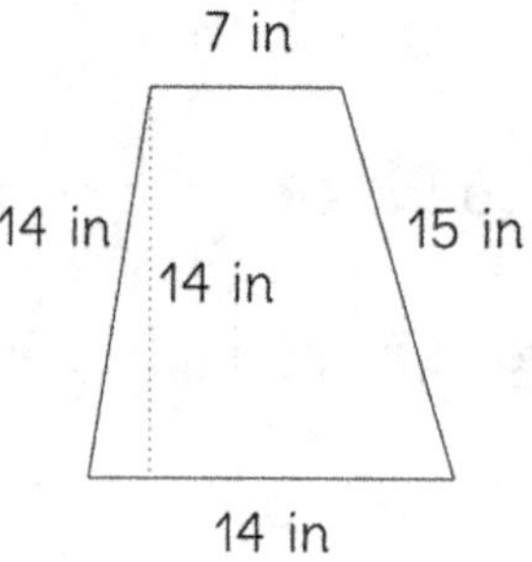

Let's denote:

- The lengths of the parallel sides of the trapezoid as $a = 7$ and $b = 14$.

- The lengths of the non-parallel sides as $c = 14$ and $d = 15$.

- The height of the trapezoid (the perpendicular distance between the parallel sides) as $h=14$.

Area of the Trapezoid:

The area of a trapezoid is given by the formula:

$$\text{Area} = \frac{1}{2} \times \text{Height} \times \text{(Sum of the lengths of the parallel sides)}$$

$$\text{Area} = \frac{1}{2} \times h \times (a + b)$$

$$\text{Area} = \frac{1}{2} \times 14 \times (7 + 14)$$

$$\text{Area} = \frac{1}{2} \times 14 \times 21$$

$$\text{Area} = 147 \text{ in}^2$$

Perimeter of the Trapezoid:

$$\text{Perimeter} = 7 + 14 + 14 + 15$$

$$= 50 \text{ in}^2$$

Pythagorean Theorem

The Pythagorean Theorem is a fundamental principle in geometry that relates the lengths of the sides of a right triangle. It states that in any right triangle, the square of the length of the hypotenuse (the side opposite the right angle) is equal to the sum of the squares of the lengths of the other two sides.

$$a2 + b2 = c2$$

Let's use the Pythagorean Theorem to find the length of the hypotenuse (c) when $a=44$ and $b=78$.

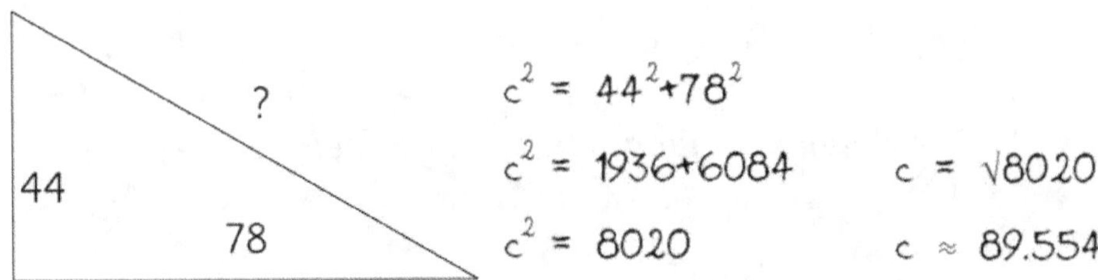

Volume and surface Area

Volume refers to the amount of space occupied by a three-dimensional object. For shapes like cubes or rectangular prisms, we calculate volume by multiplying their length, width, and height.

To find the volume V of a rectangular prism, we use the formula:

$$Volume = length \; x \; width \; x \; height$$

Surface Area represents the total area covering all the faces of a three-dimensional object. For shapes like cubes or rectangular prisms, we find the surface area by summing the areas of all its faces.

The formula for surface area SA of a cube or rectangular prism is:

$$Surface\ Area\ =\ 2lw\ +\ 2lh\ +\ 2wh$$

Where: l is the length, w is the width, and h is the height of the object.

For example: Let's find the Volume and Surface Area of following rectangular prisms:

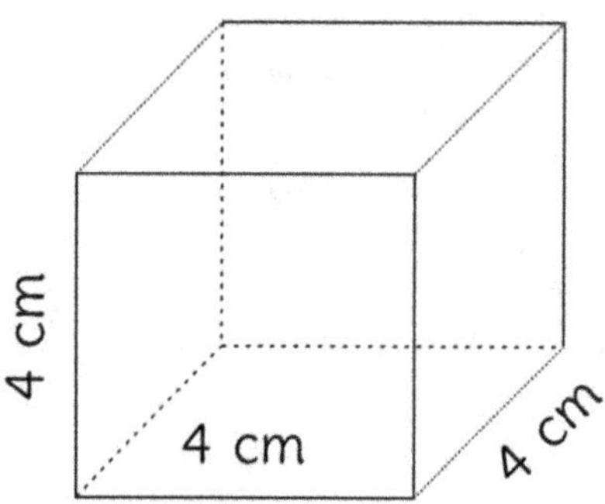

$$Volume\ =\ length\ \times\ width\ \times\ height$$

$$= 4 \times 4 \times 4$$

$$= 64\ cm^2$$

$$Surface\ Area\ =\ 2lw\ +\ 2lh\ +\ 2wh$$

$$= 2(4 \times 4) + 2(4 \times 4) + 2(4 \times 4)$$

$$= 32 + 32 + 32$$

$$= 96\ cm2$$

Different 3D objects have unique formulas for finding their volume and surface area. Here are some common ones:

1. Cube:

    - Volume: $V = s^3$ (where s is the length of one side of the cube)

    - Surface area: $SA = 6s^2$

2. **Sphere:**

   - Volume: $V = \left(\frac{4}{3}\right)\pi r^3$ (where r is the radius of the sphere)

   - Surface area: $SA = 4\pi r^2$

3. **Cone:**

   - Volume: $V = \left(\frac{1}{3}\right)\pi r^2 h$ (where r is the radius of the base and h is the height of the cone)

   - Surface area: $SA = \pi r^2 + \pi r\sqrt{(r^2 + h^2)}$

4. **Cylinder:**

   - Volume: $V = \pi r^2 h$ (where r is the radius of the base and h is the height of the cylinder)

   - Surface area: $SA = 2\pi r^2 + 2\pi rh$

5. **Pyramid:**

   - Volume: $V = \left(\frac{1}{3}\right)Bh$ (where B is the area of the base and h is the height of the pyramid)

   - Surface area: $SA = B + \frac{1}{2}Pl$ (where P is the perimeter of the base and l is the slant height of the pyramid)

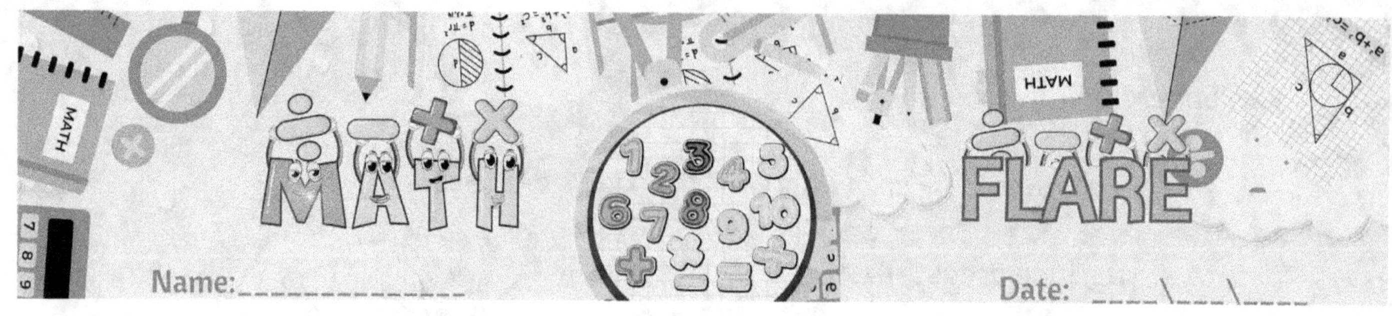

Area and Perimeter

1.

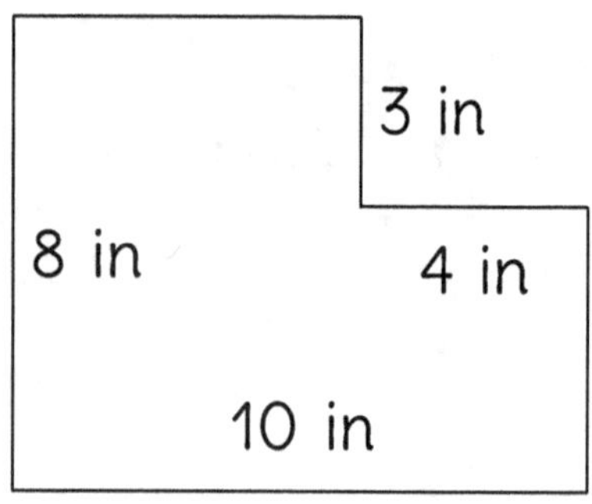

2.

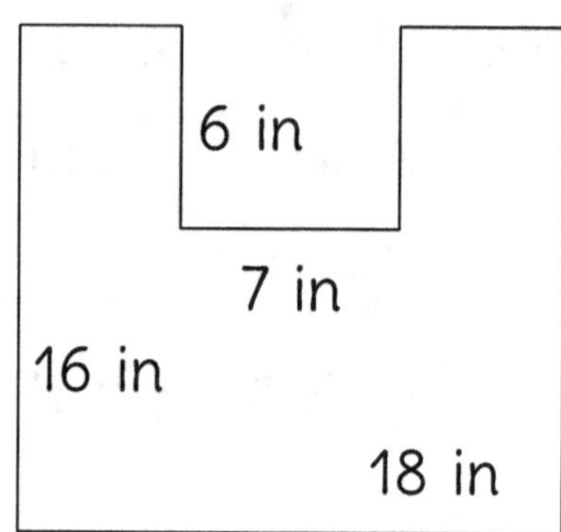

3.

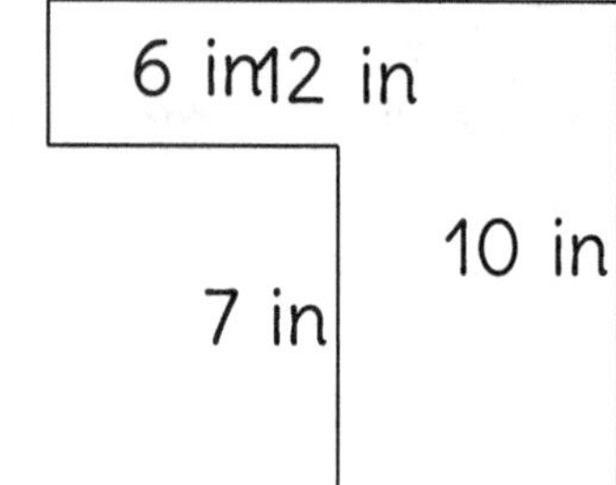

4.

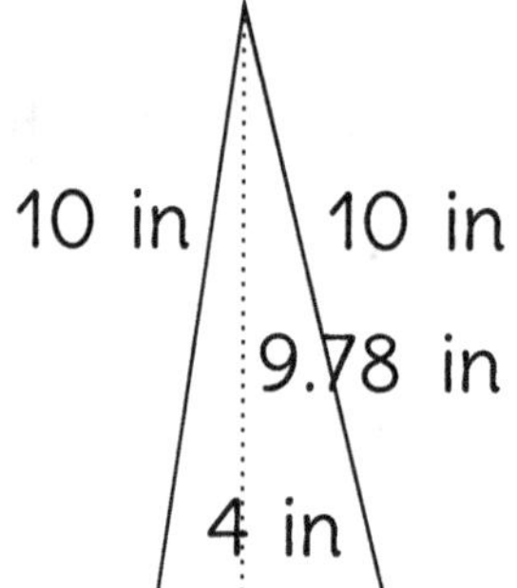

MATH
FLARE
MATH
Name:
Date:

5.

7 in
5 in
5 in
3 in

6.

3 in
7 in   4 in
7 in

7.

9 in
10 in
12 in

8.

5 in   9 in
4.70 in
10 in

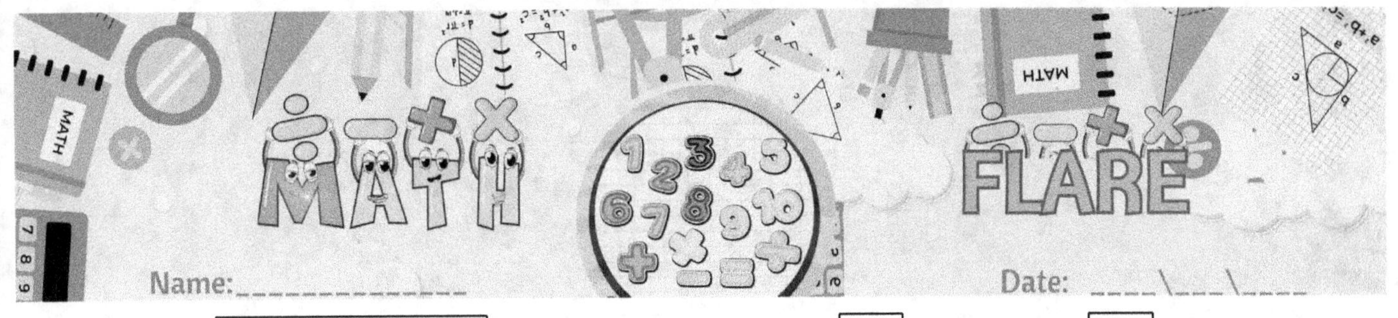

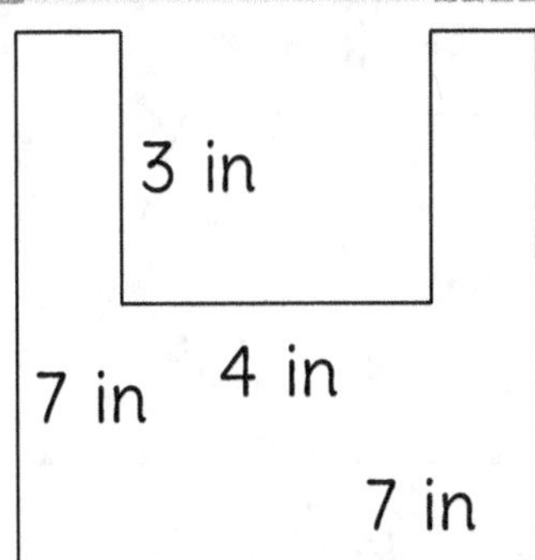

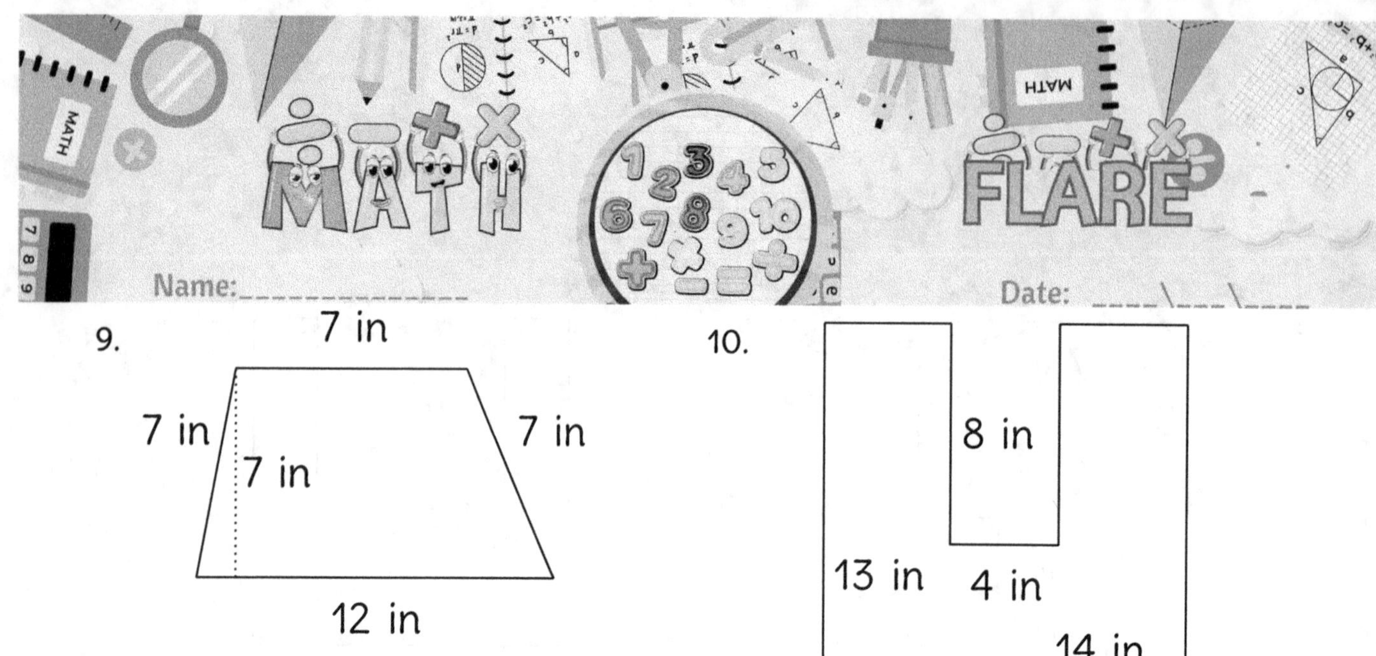

9.

10.

11.

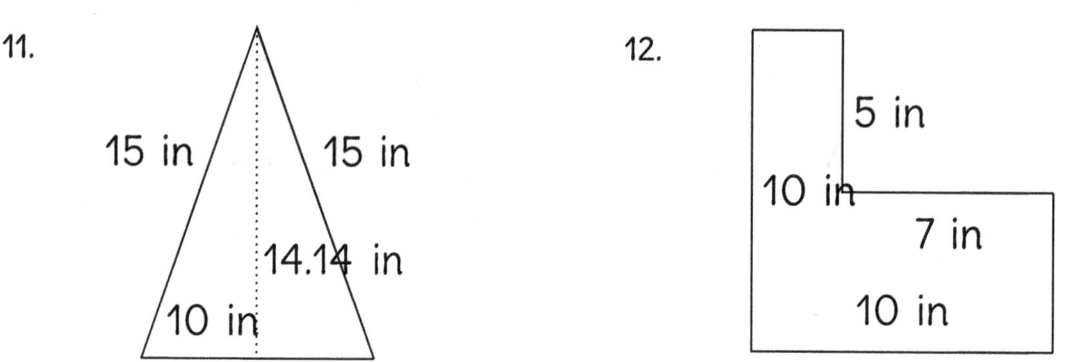

12.

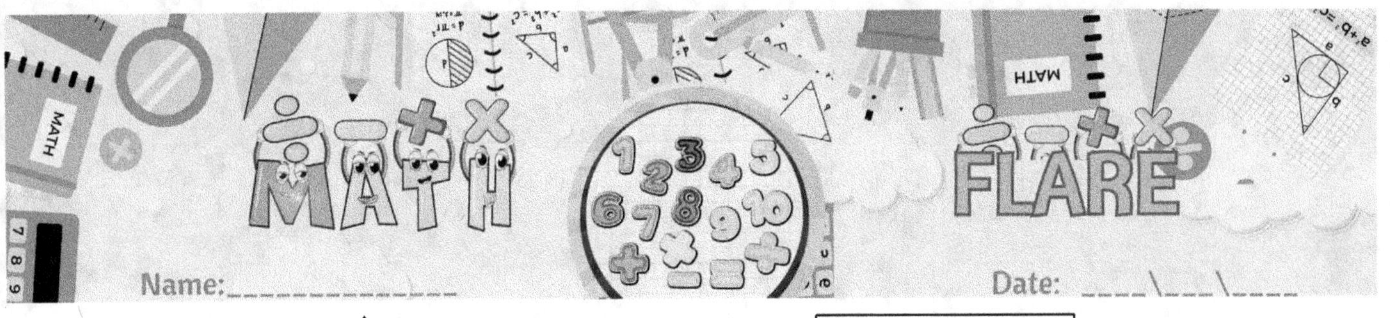

13.

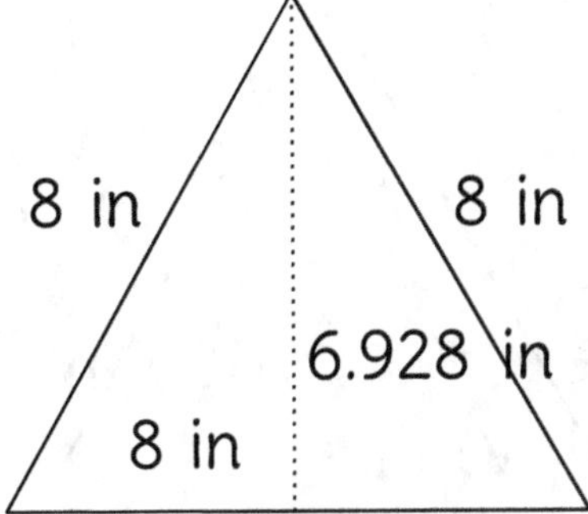

14.

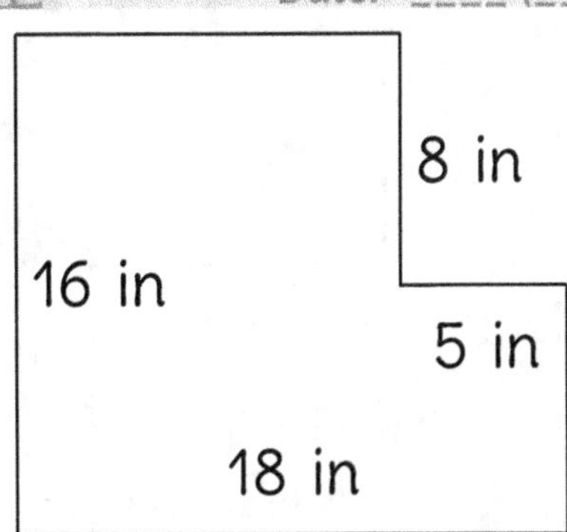

15.

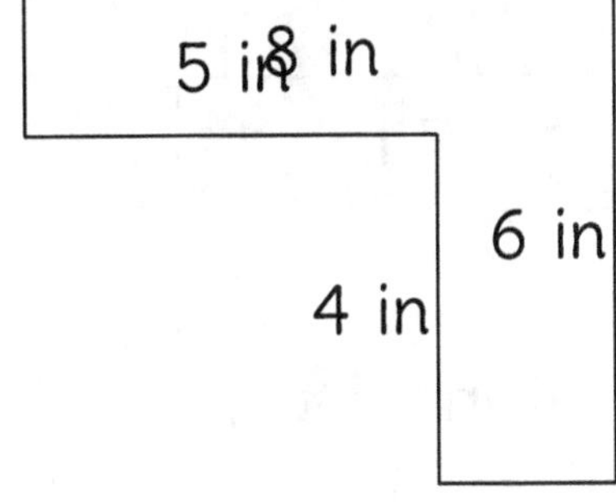

16.

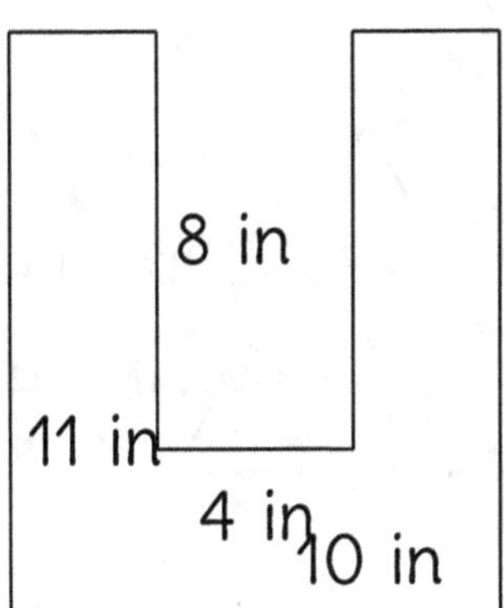

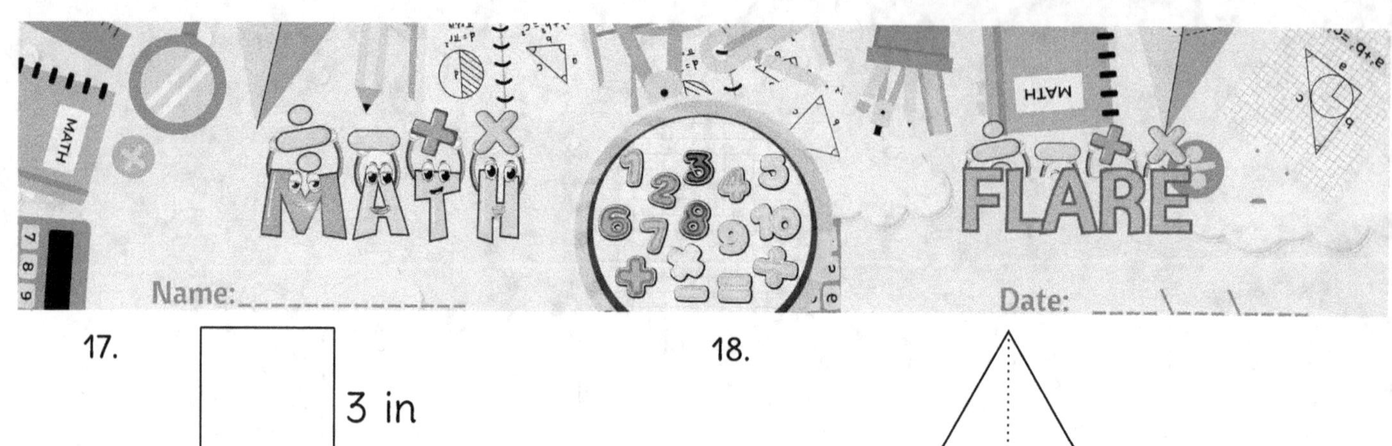

17.

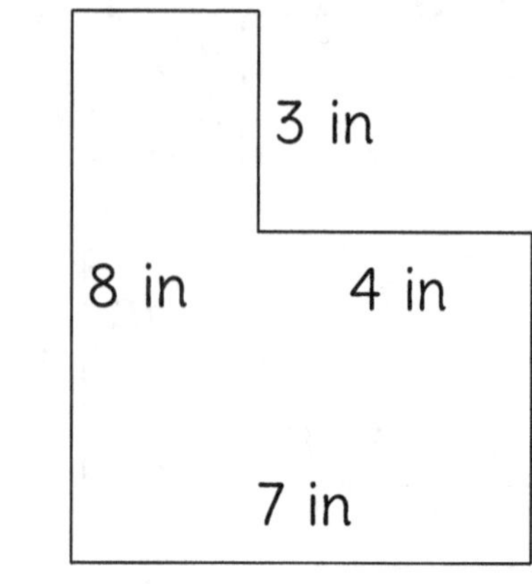

18.

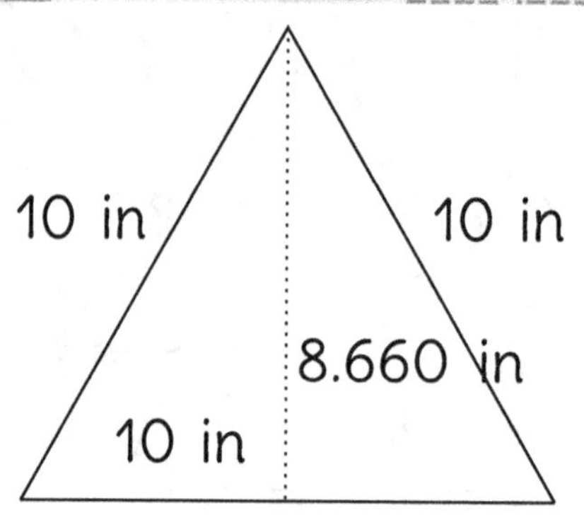

19.

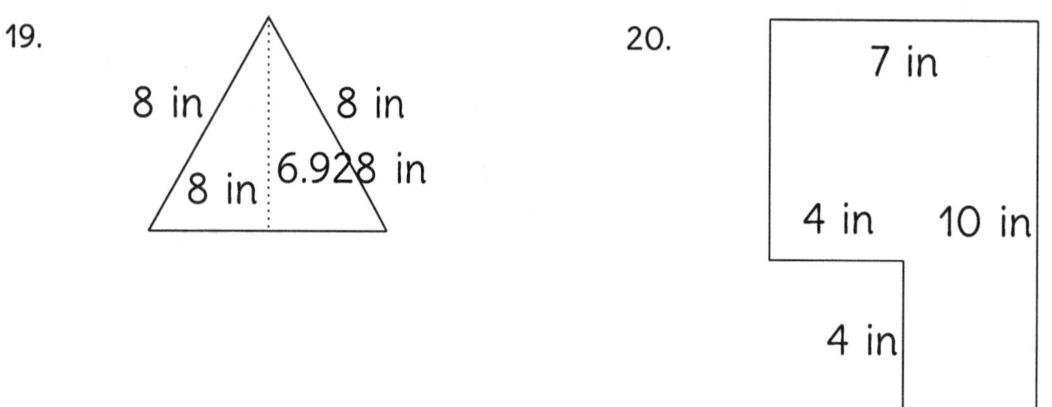

20.

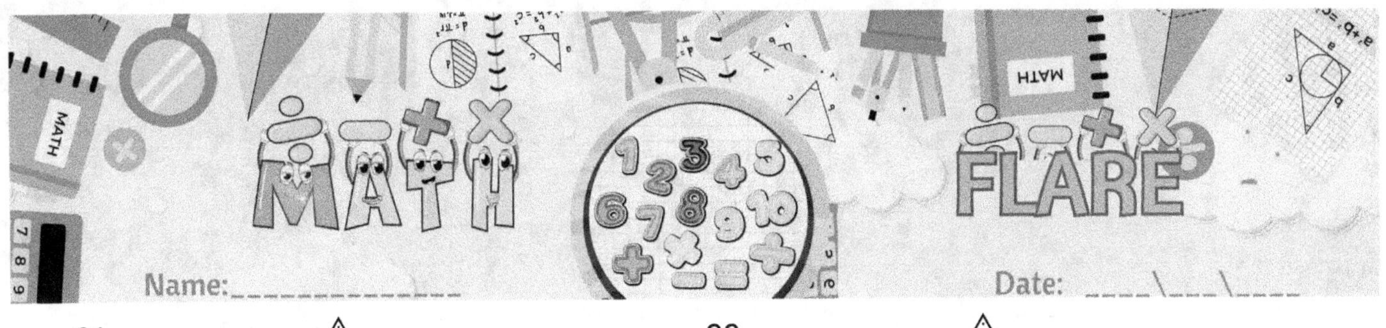

21.

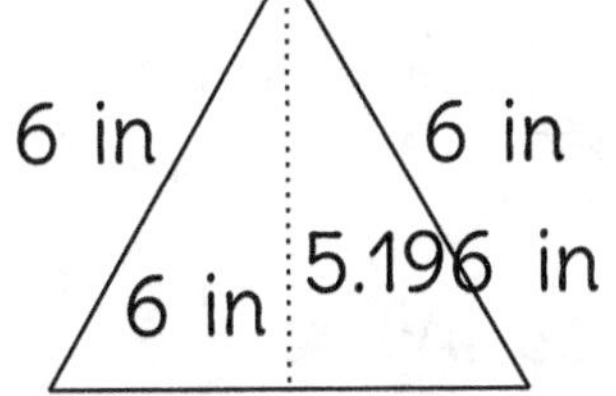

22.

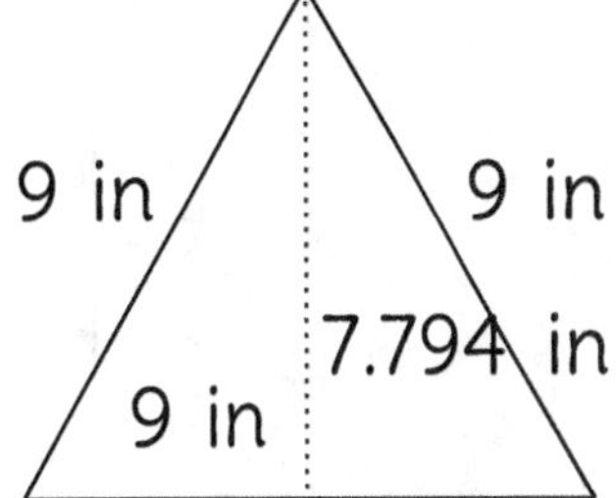

23.

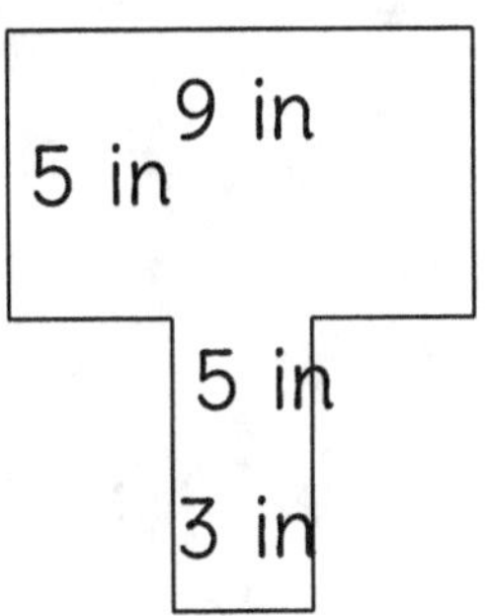

24.

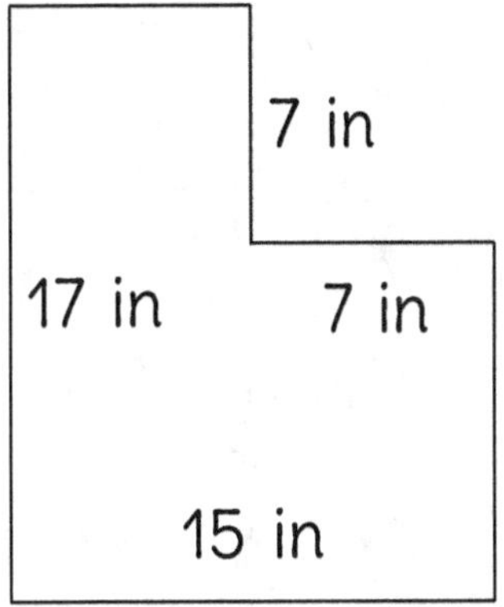

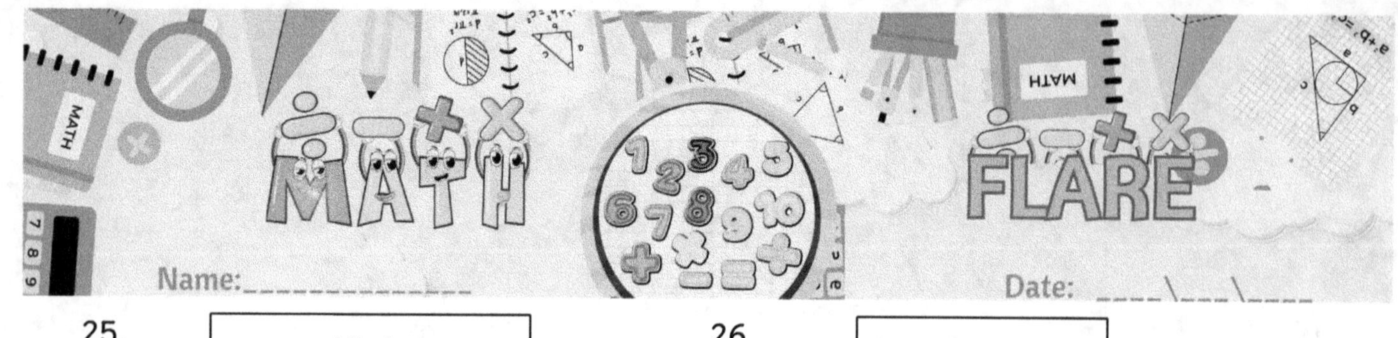

25.

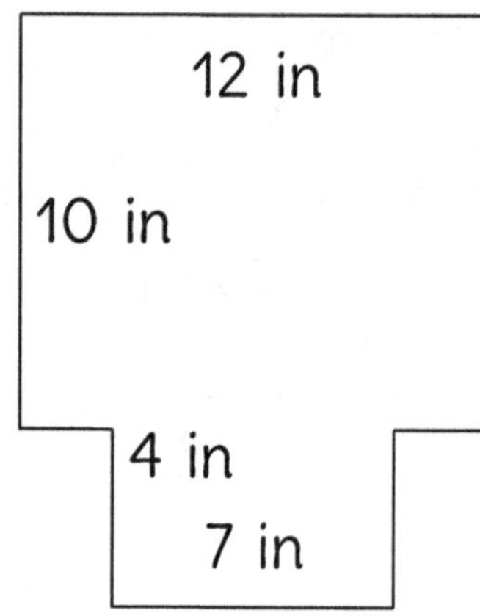

26.

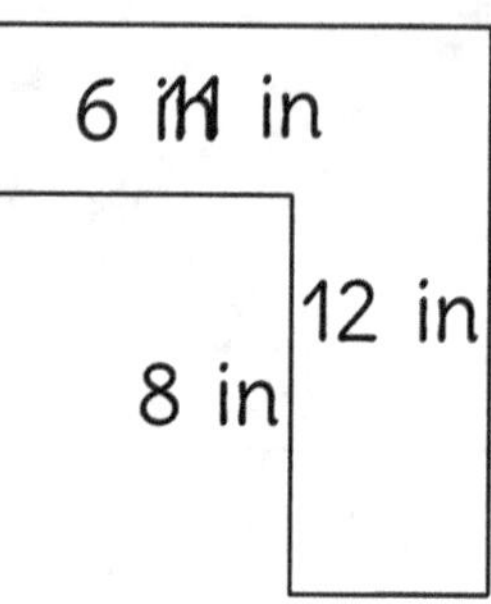

27.

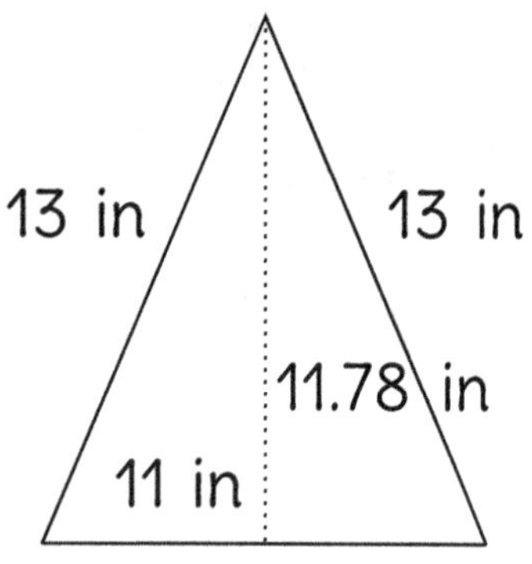

28.

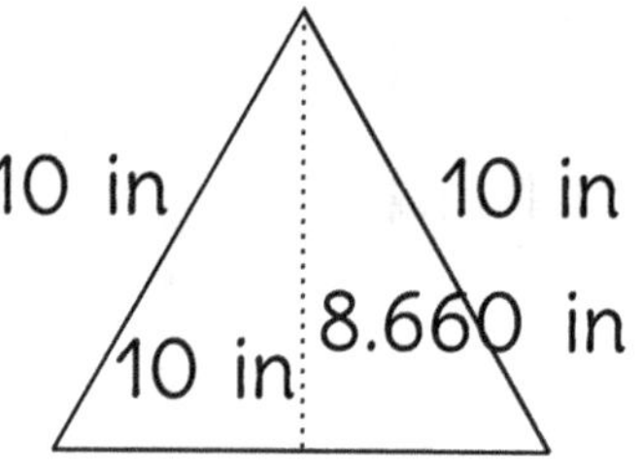

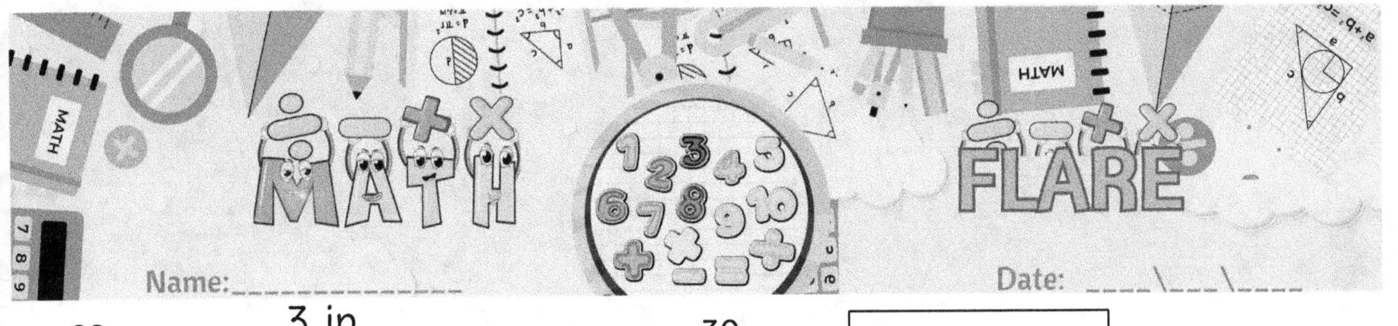

29.

3 in
4 in
5 in
4 in
7 in

30.

10 in
4 in
12 in
7 in

31.

12 in
10 in
6 in
7 in

32.

8 in
5 in
4 in
10 in

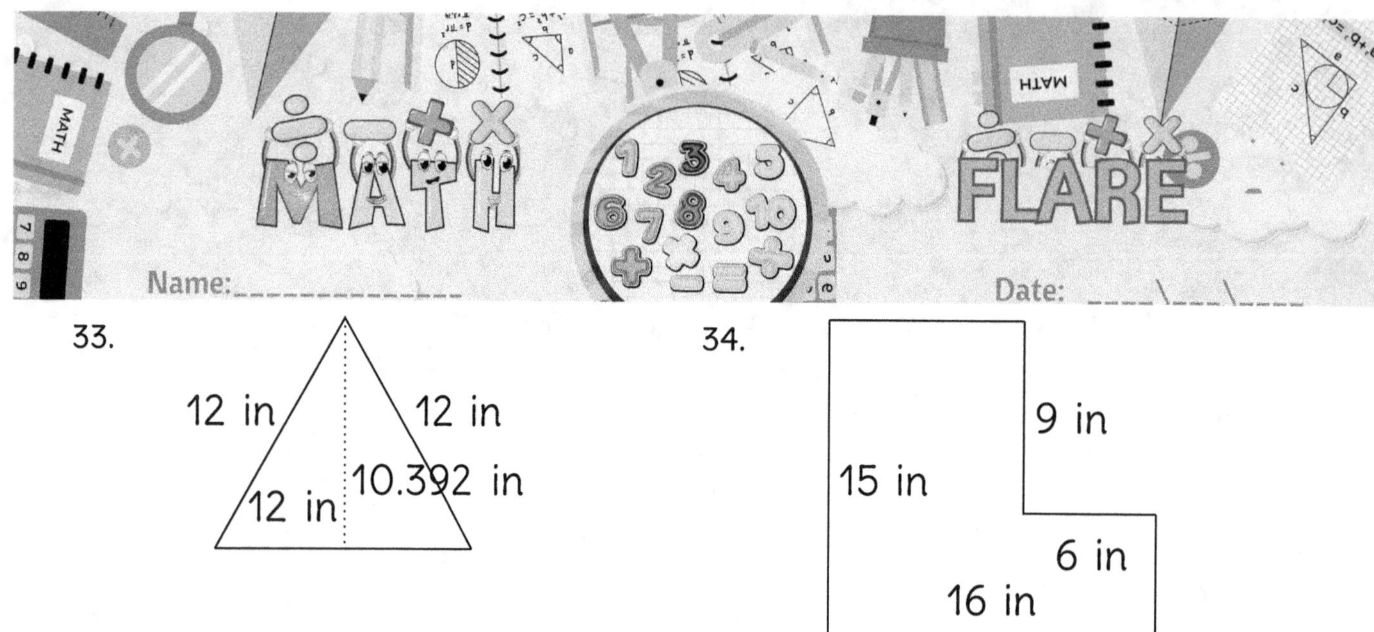

33.

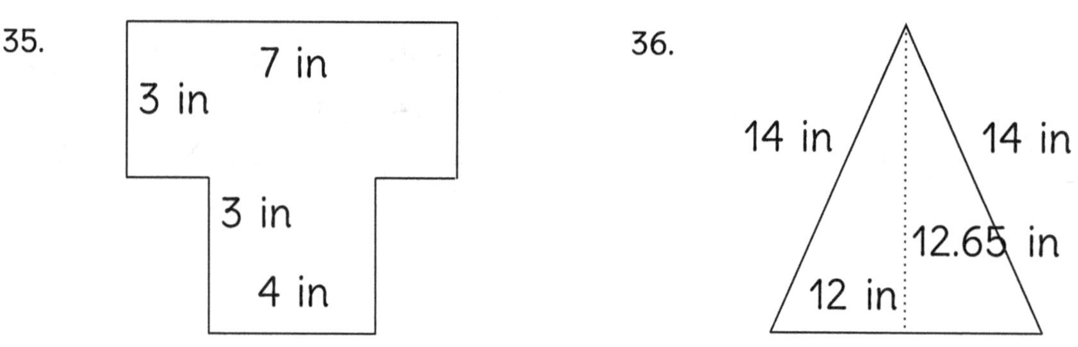

34.

35.

36.

MATH
FLARE
Name: ___________________
Date: _______________

37.

10 in
10 in
8.660 in
10 in

38.

12 in
13 in
10 in

39.

6 in
3 in
4 in
3 in

40.

14 in
10 in
9.45 in
14 in

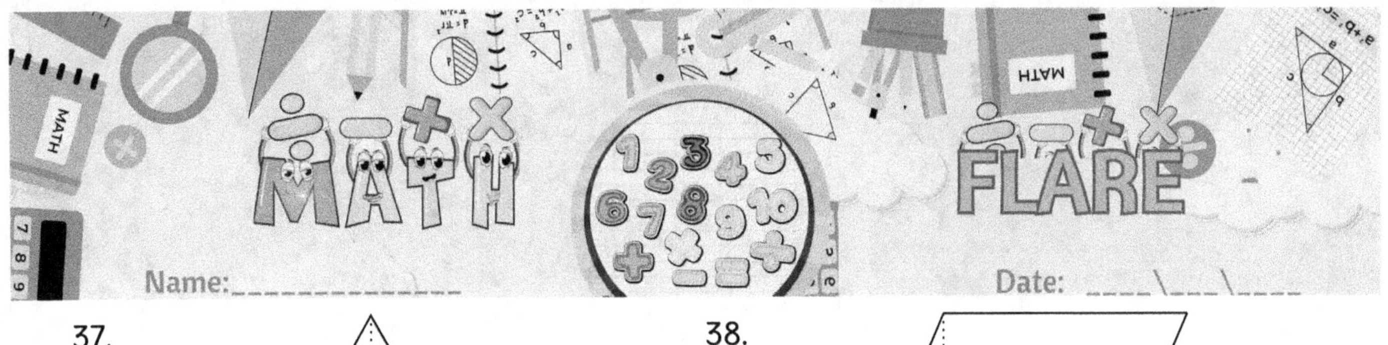

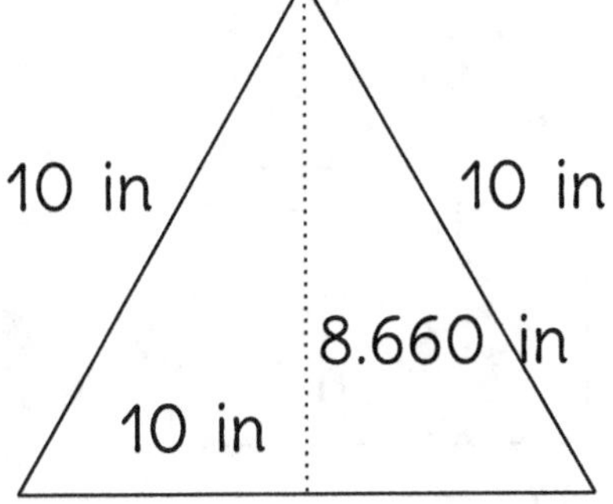

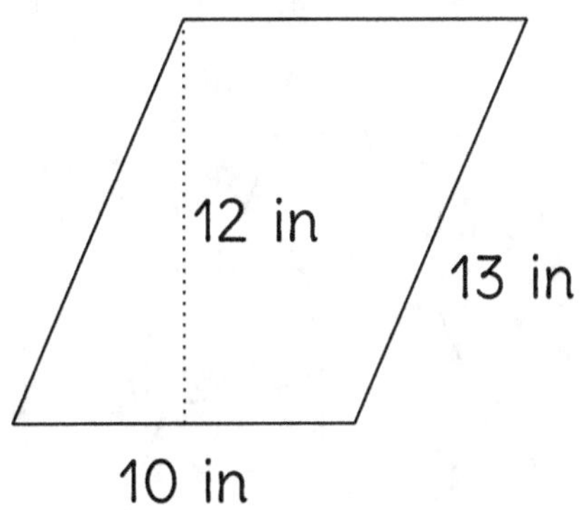

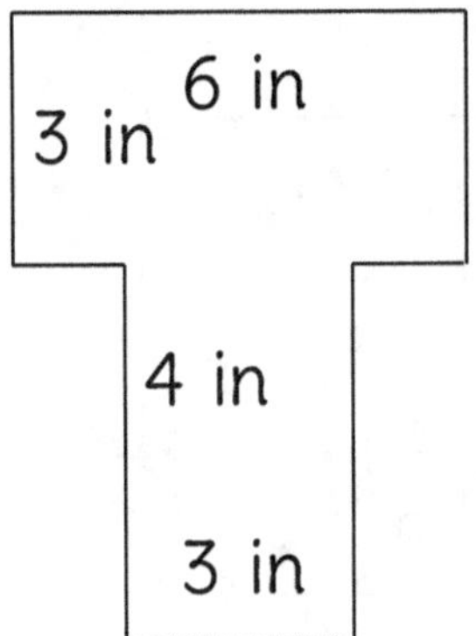

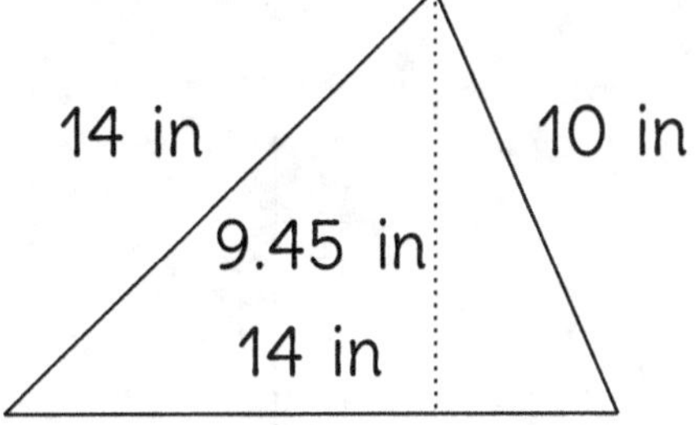

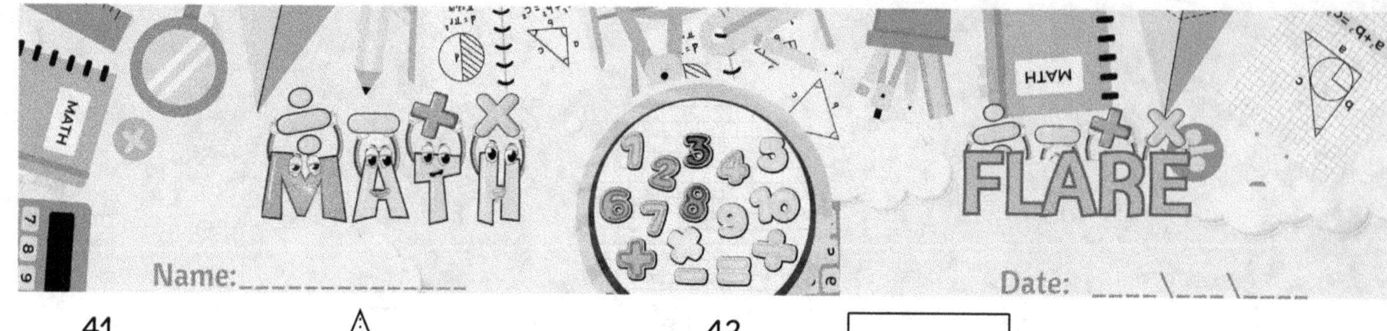

41.

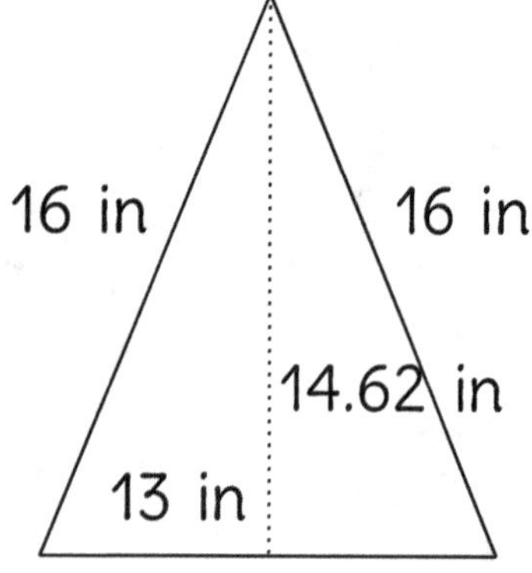

42.

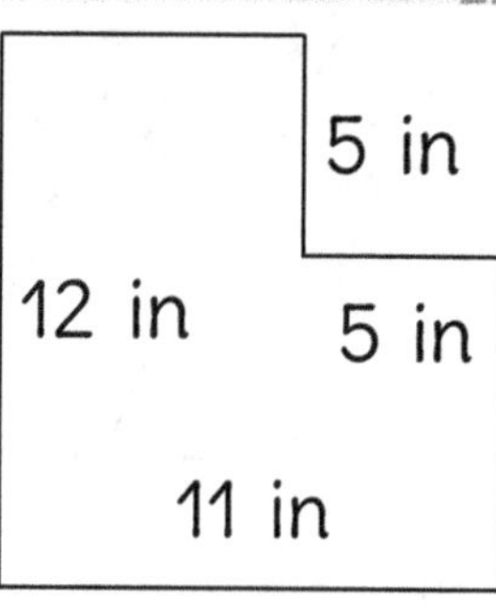

43.

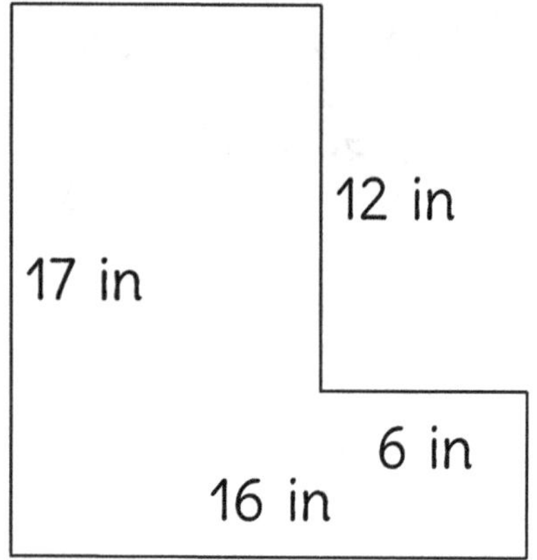

44.

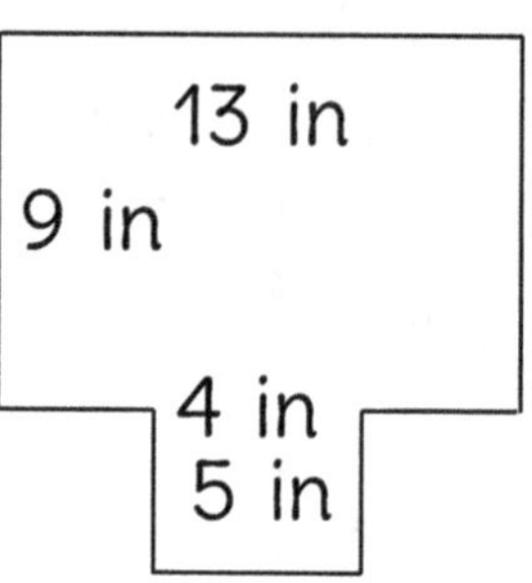

MATH
FLARE
MATH
Name:
Date:

45.

12 in
8 in
17 in
12 in

46.

11 in
11 in
10.04 in
9 in

47.

9 in
4 in
4 in
3 in

48.

6 in
7 in
16 in
13 in

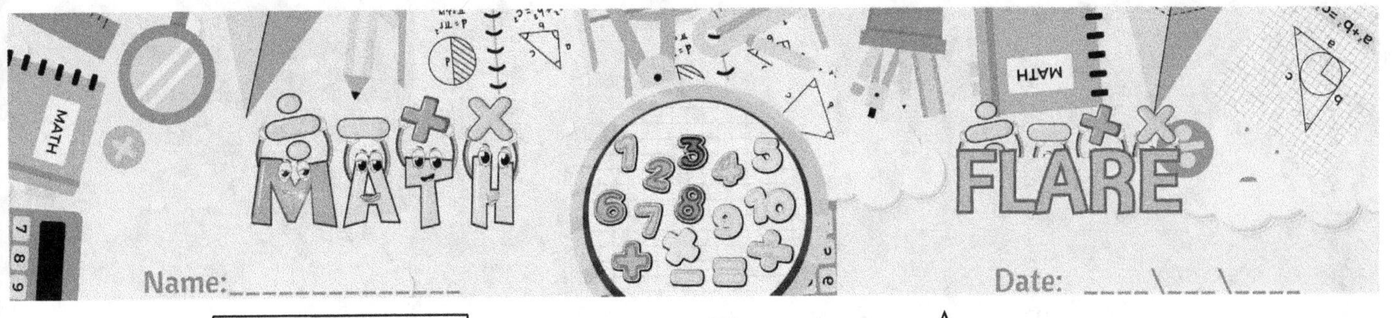

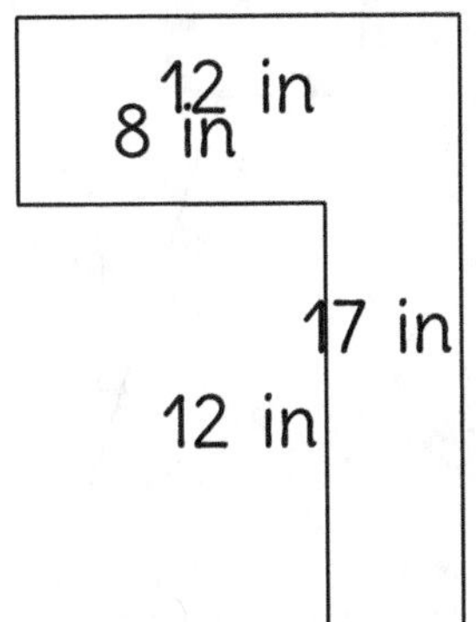

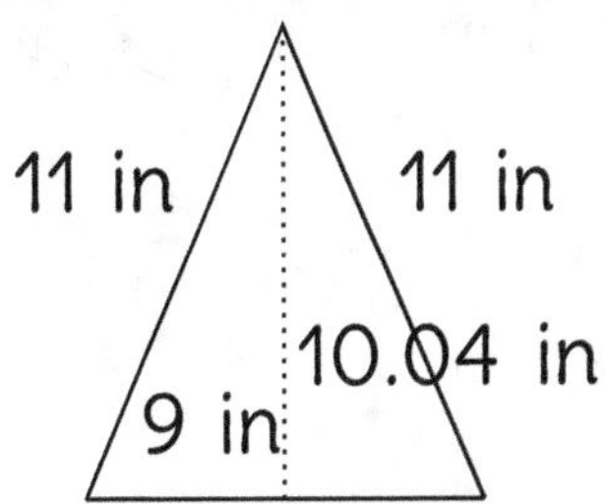

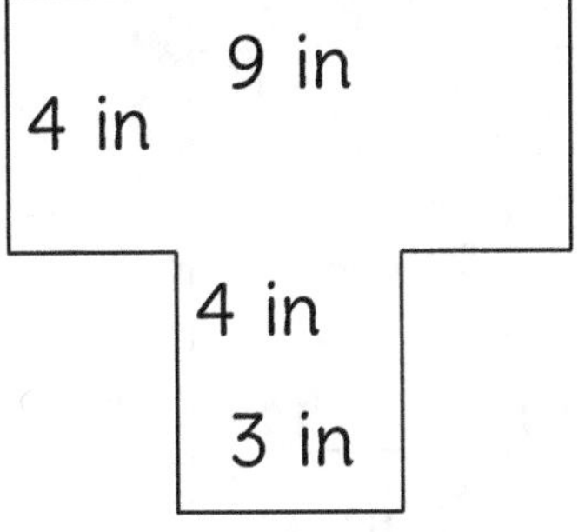

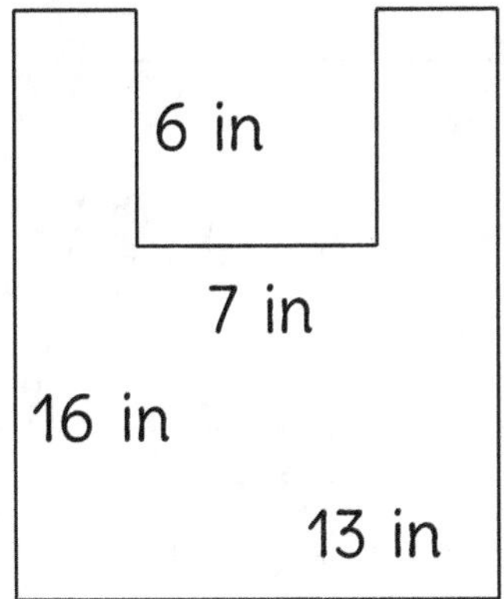

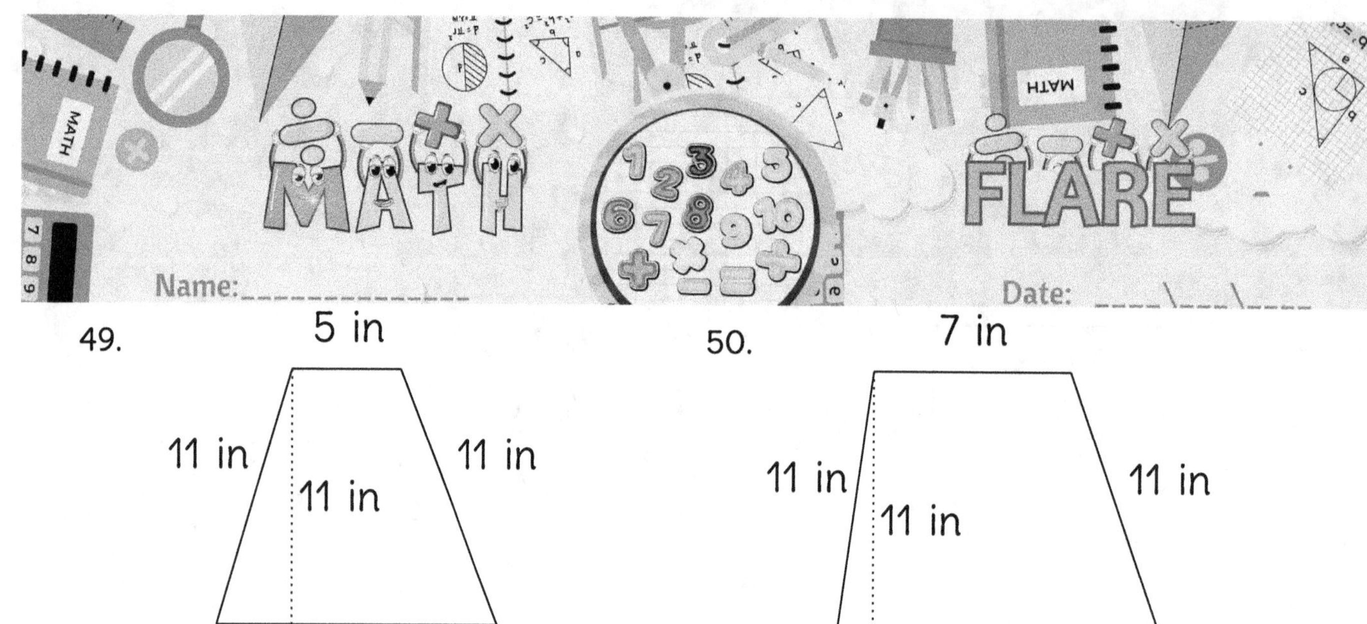

49.

50.

51.

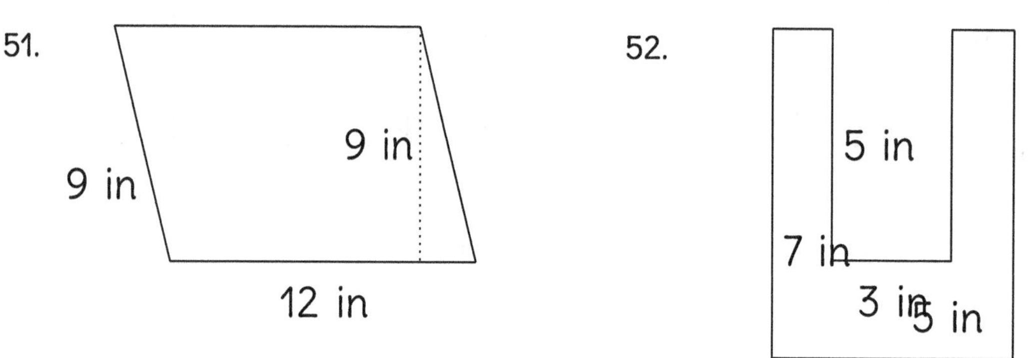

52.

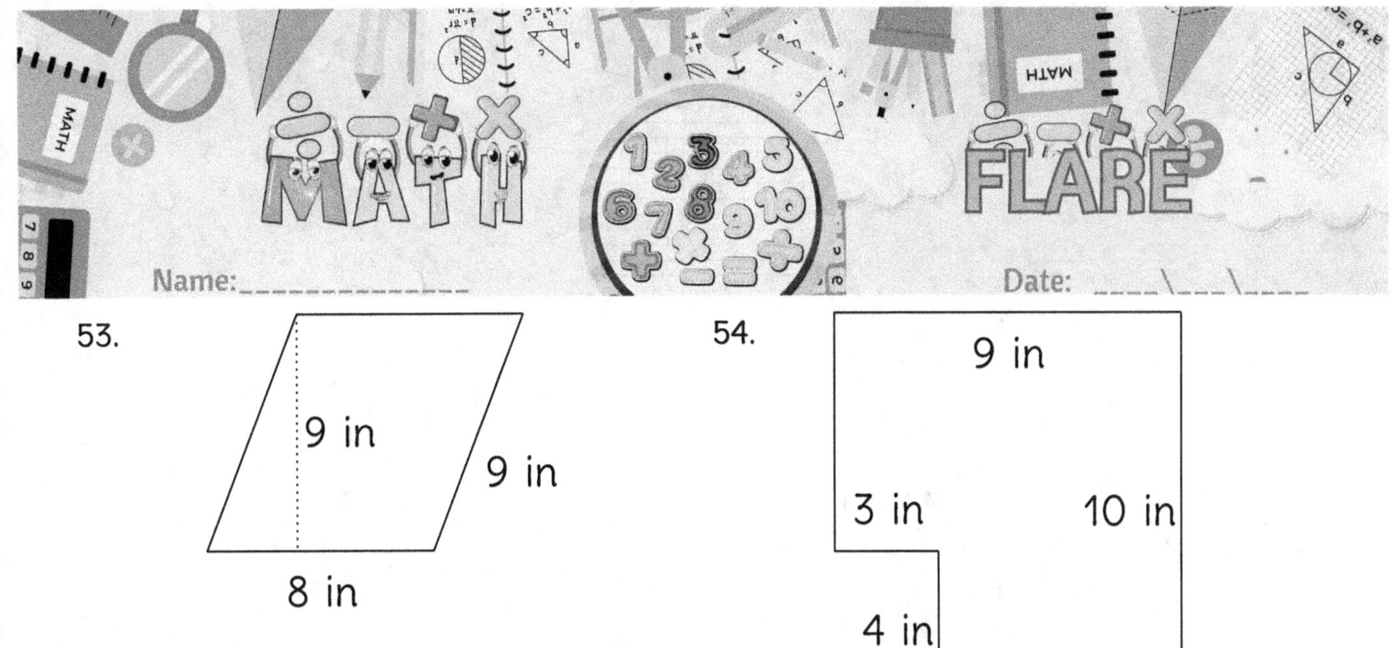

53.

54.

55. 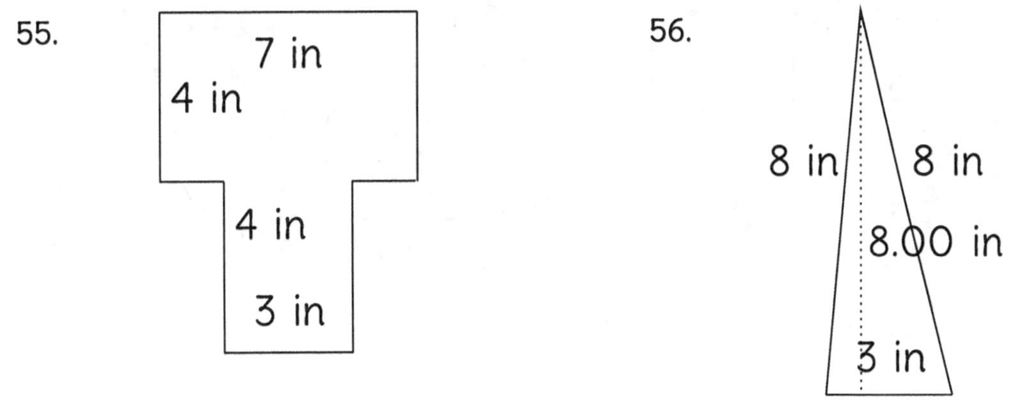

56.

153

Name:
Date:

57.

8 in
4 in
5 in
4 in
2 in

58.

9 in
9 in
8.29 in
7 in

59.

3 in
11 in
8 in
6 in

60.

11 in
11 in
9.80 in
10 in

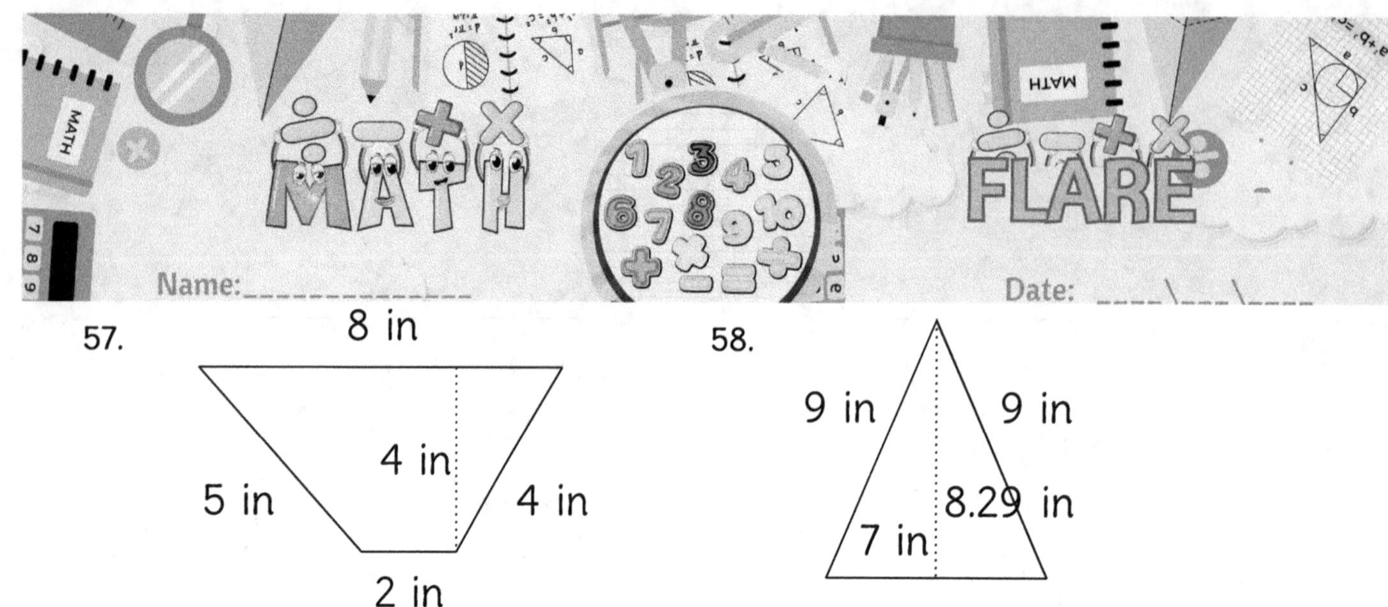

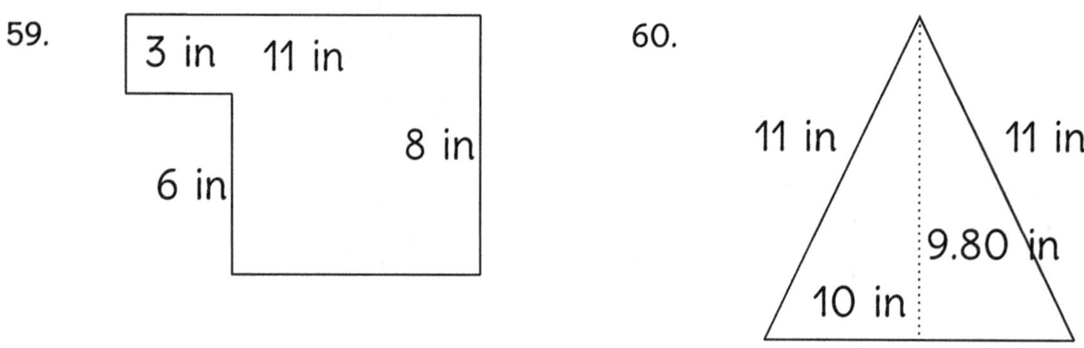

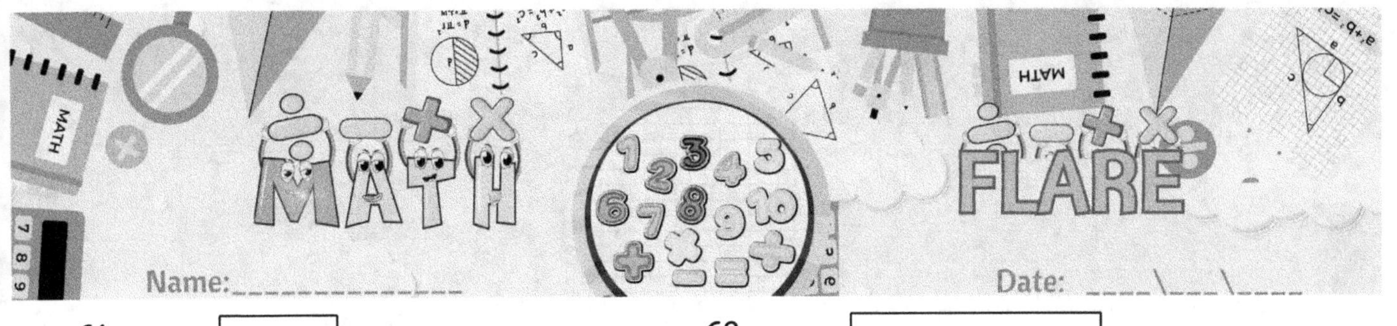

61.

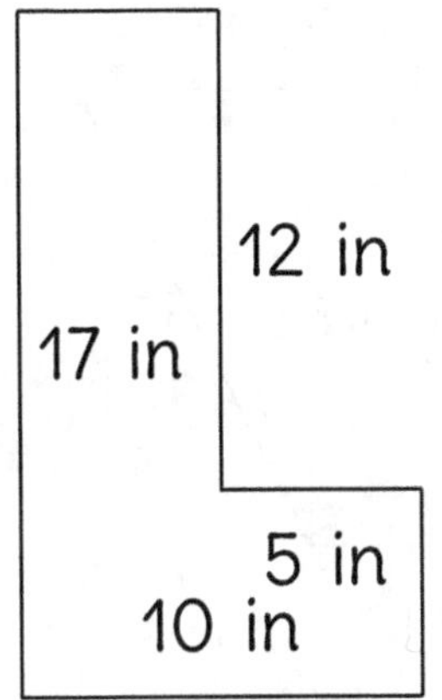

62.

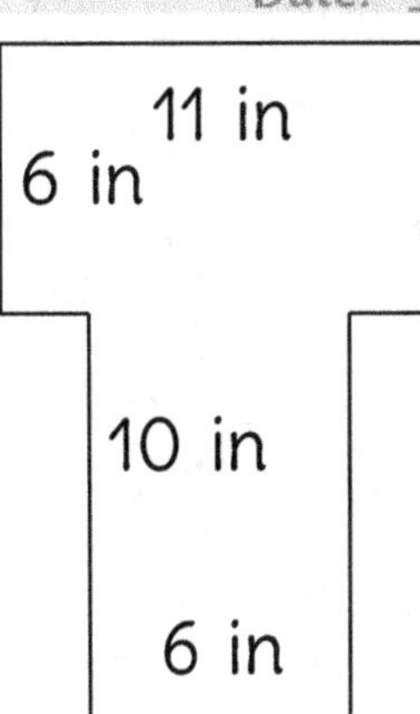

63.

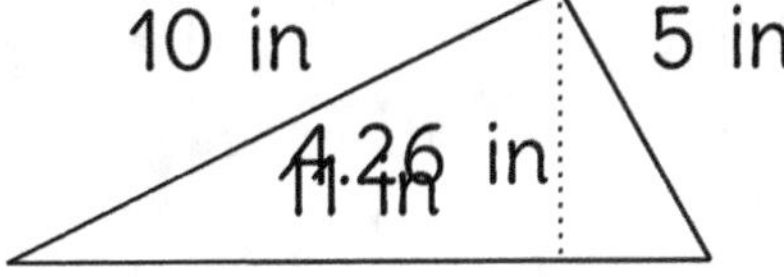

64.

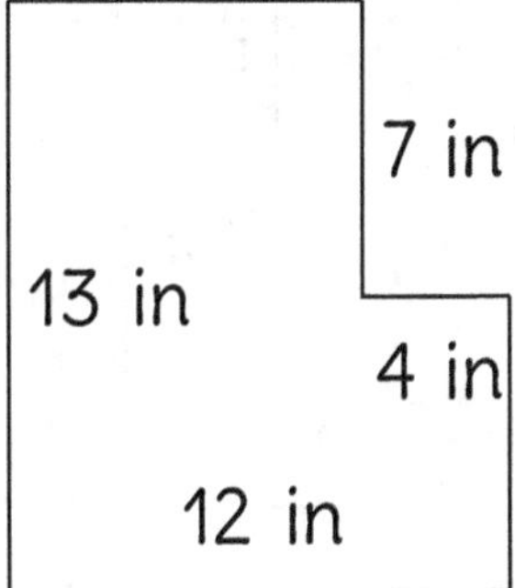

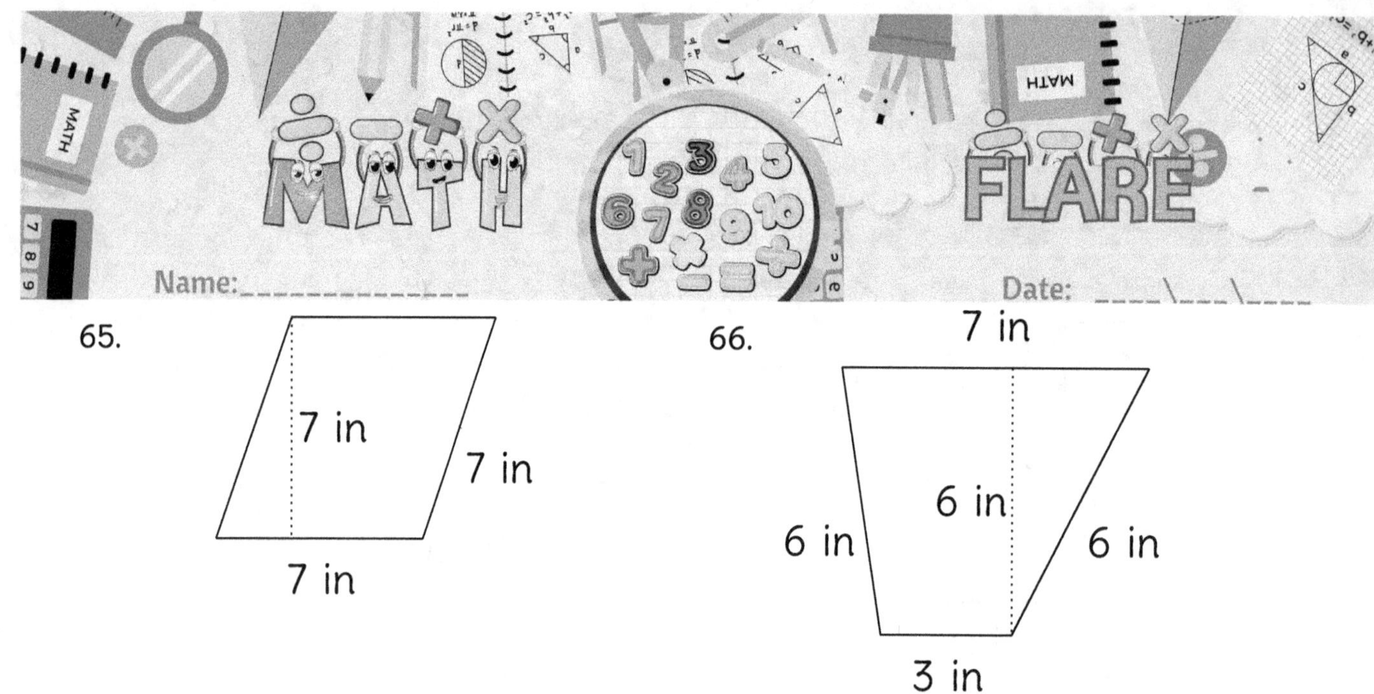

65.

66.

67.

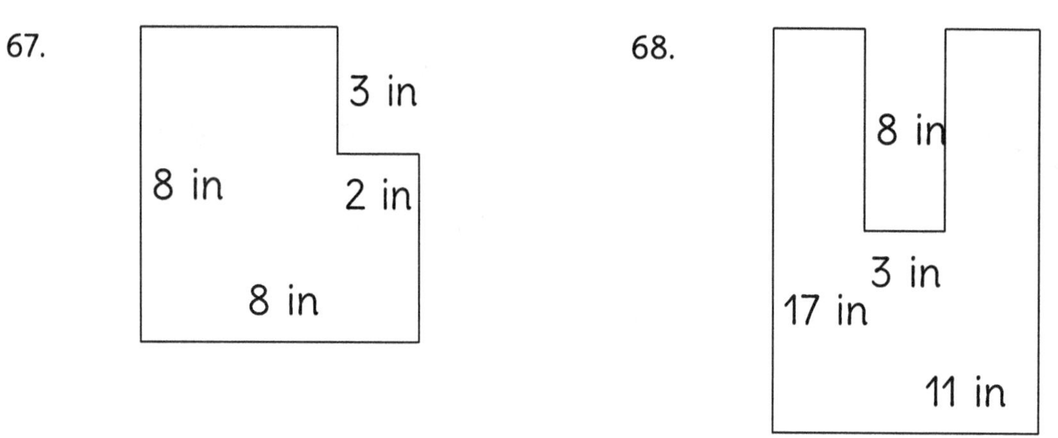

68.

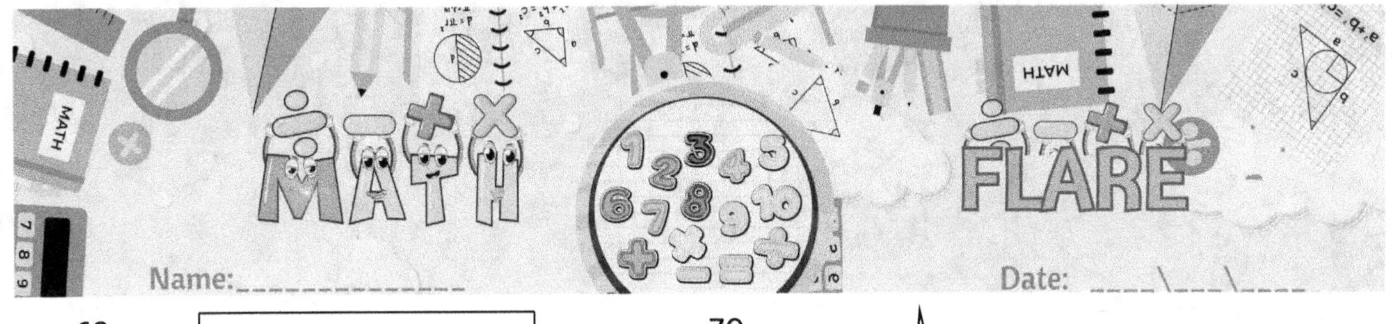

69.

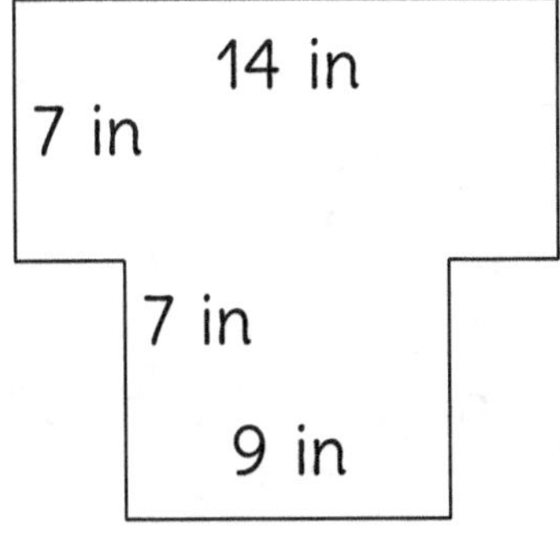

70.

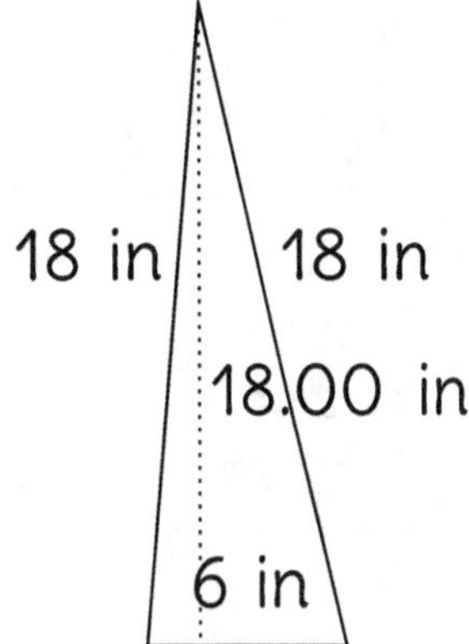

71.

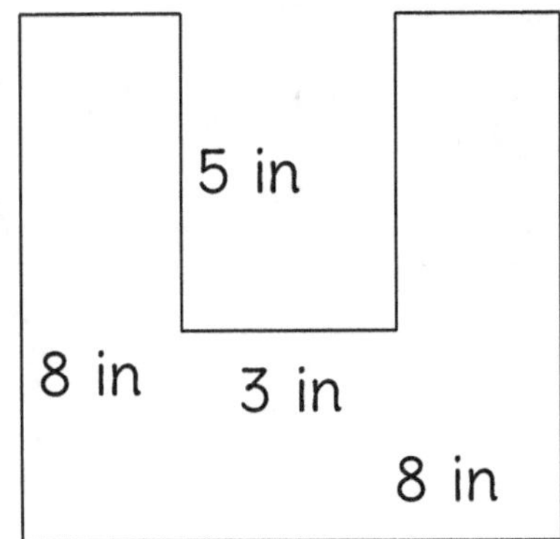

72.

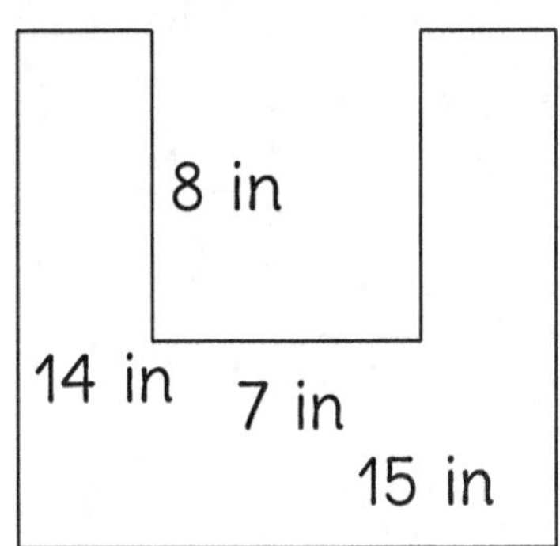

MATH
FLARE
Name:
Date:

73.

5 in
7 in
7 in 3 in

74.

9 in
10 in
9 in

75.

9 in
13 in
16 in   6 in

76.

5 in
4 in
13 in
14 in

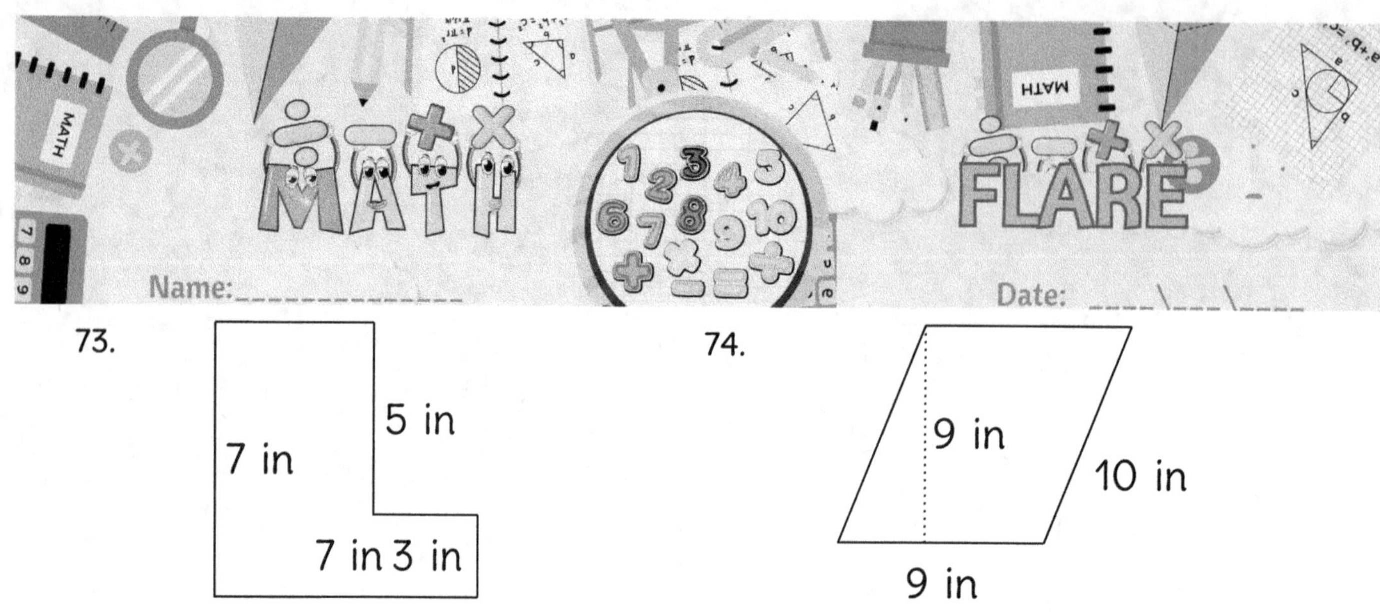

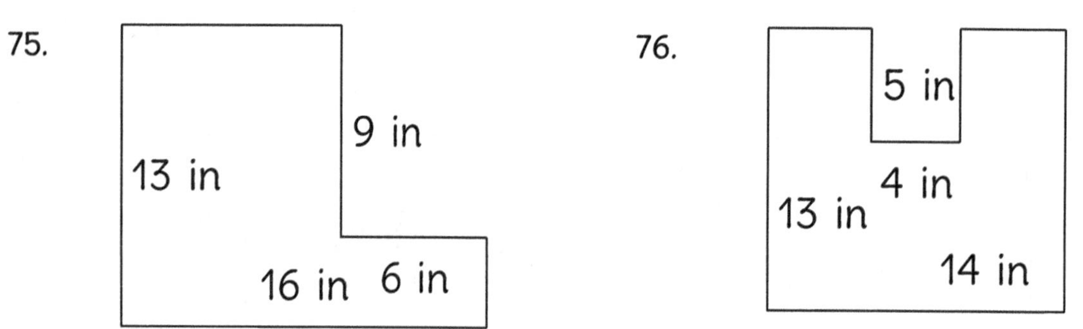

MATH
FLARE
Name:
Date:

77.

13 in
8 in
5 in
5 in

78.

12 in
6 in
7 in
7 in
7 in

79.

7 in
7 in
6 in
6 in
4 in

80.

5 in
8 in
5 in
8 in

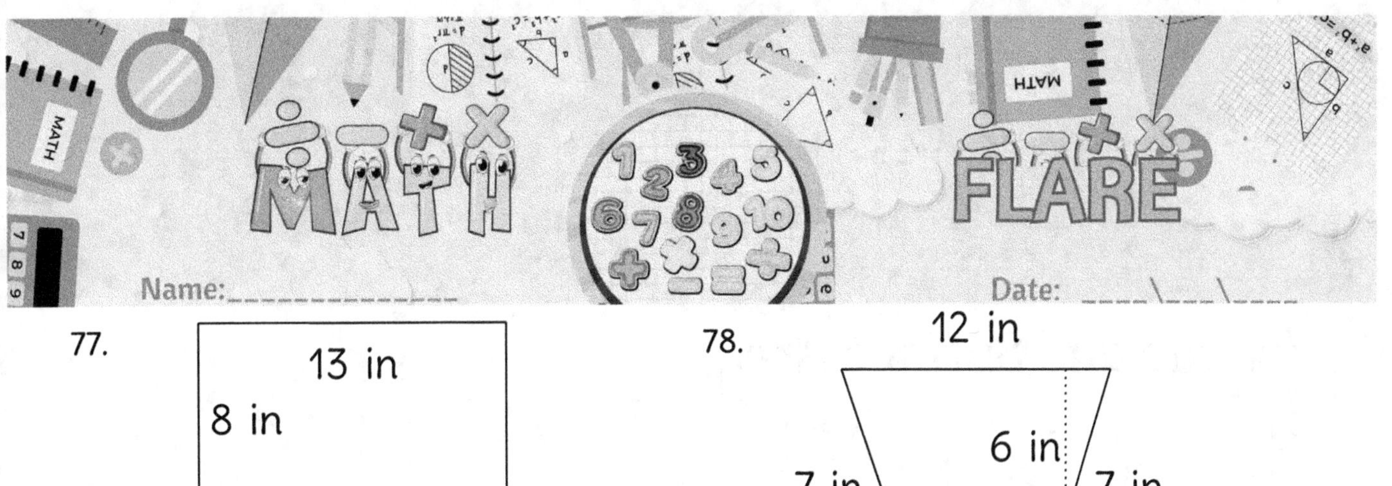

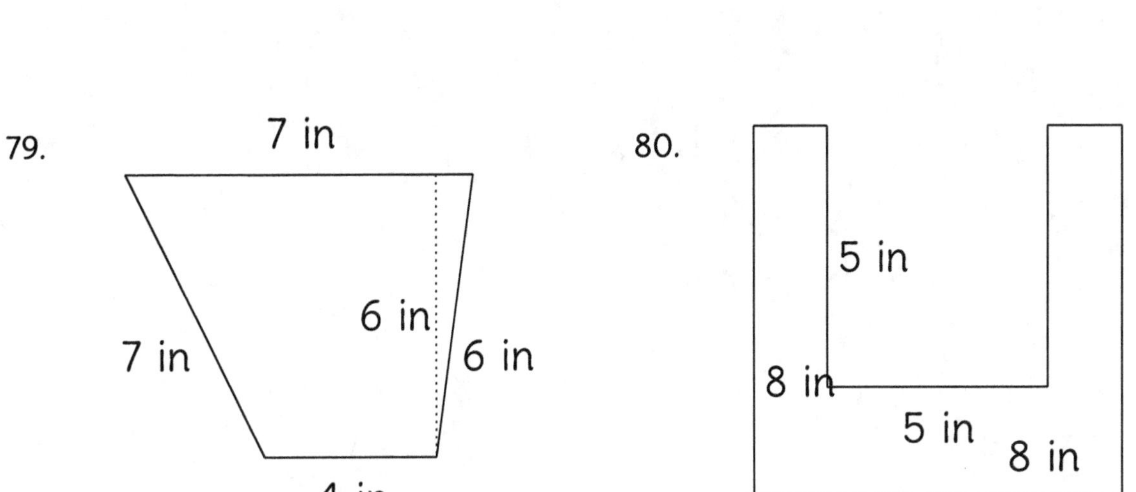

Volume and Surface Area

1.

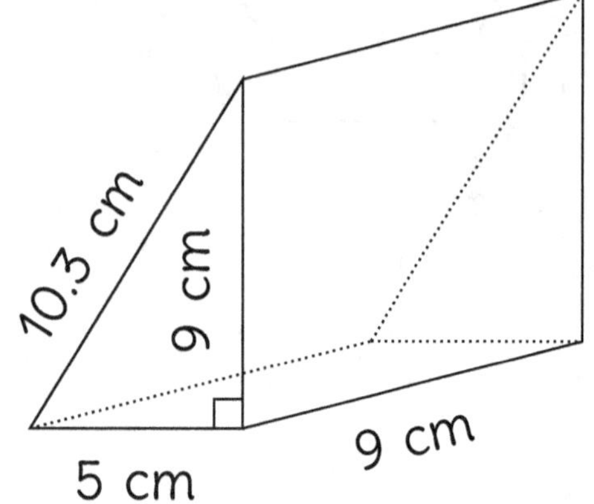

2.

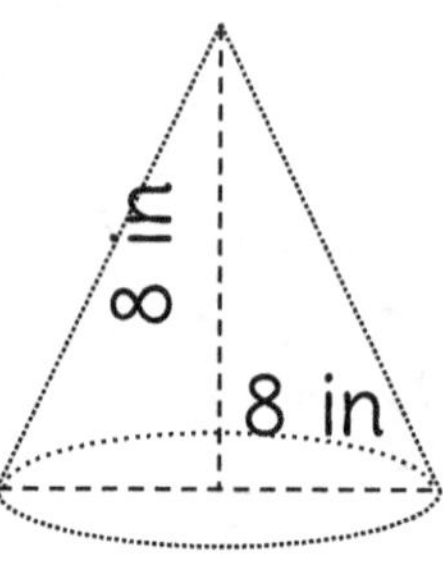

3.

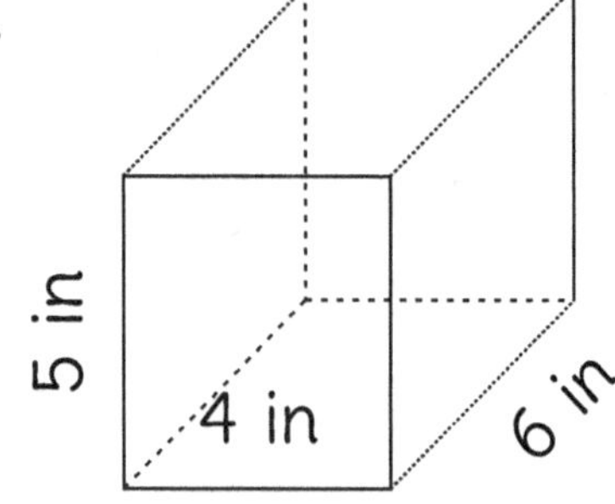

4.

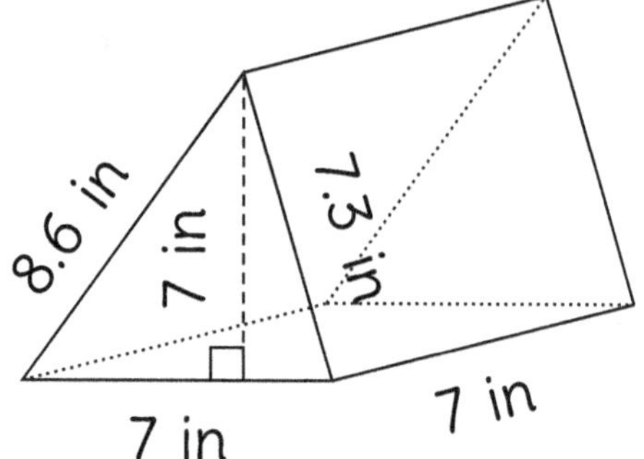

5.

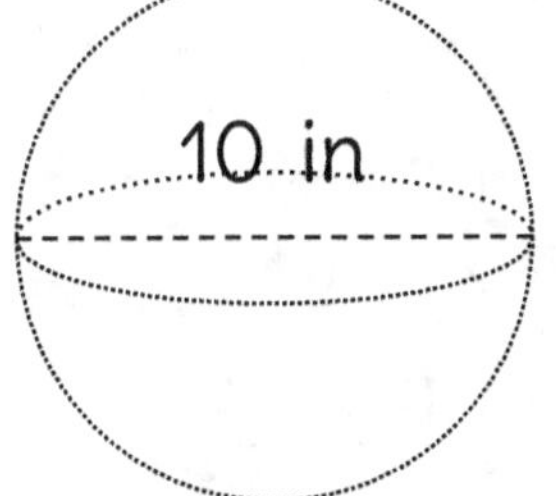

6.

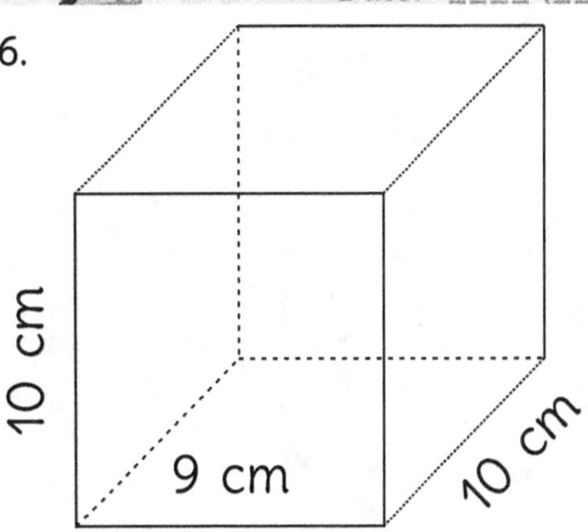

7.

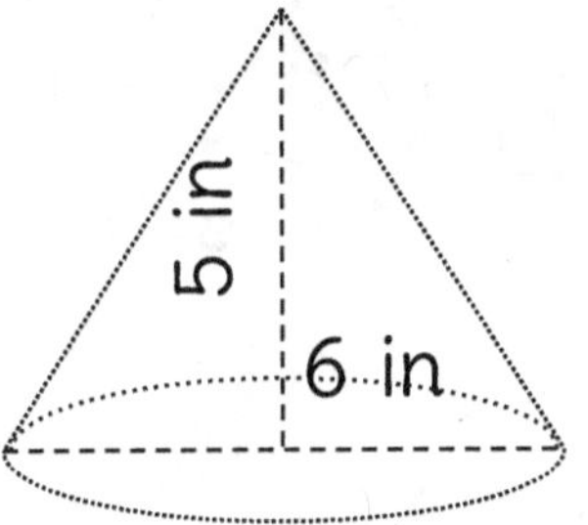

8.

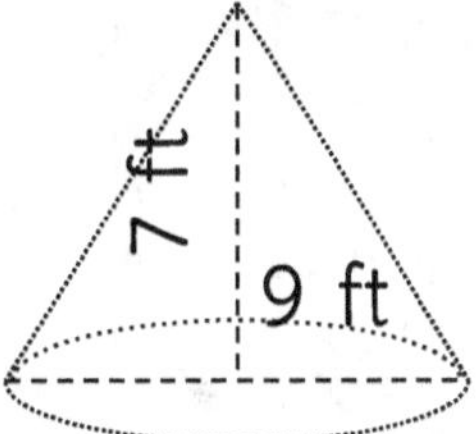

9.

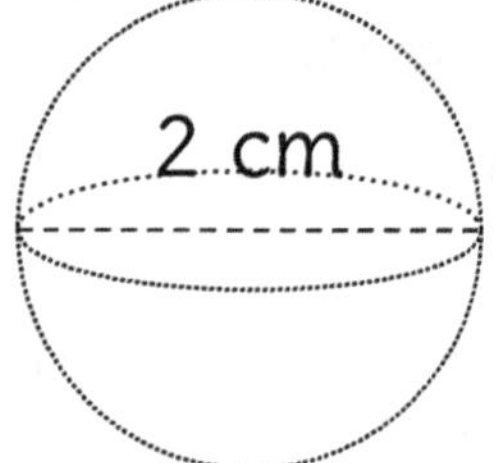

10.

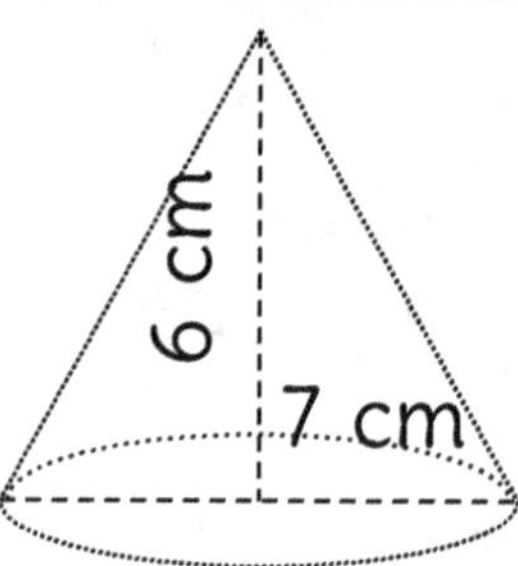

11.

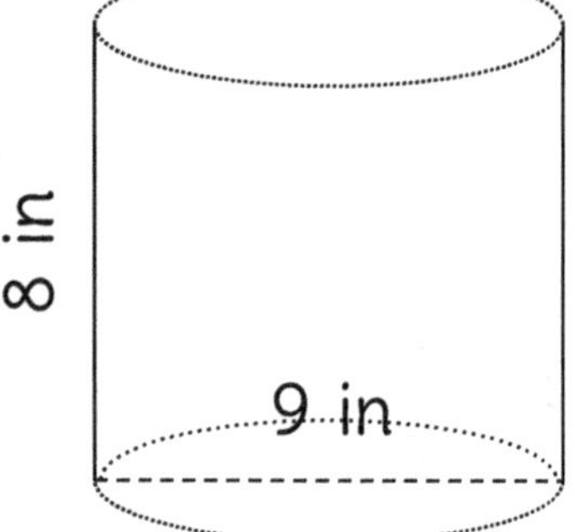

12.

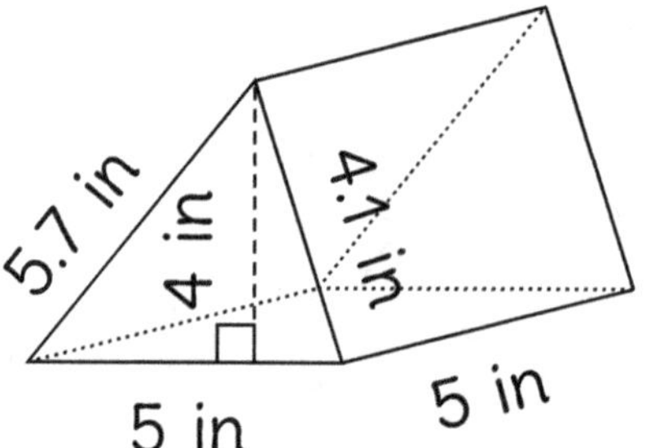

MATH
FLARE
Name: _______________
Date: _______________

13.

3 ft
4 ft

14.

11.2 ft
10 ft
10.2 ft
7 ft
11 ft

15.

9 ft
6 ft

16.

6 ft
7 ft
5 ft

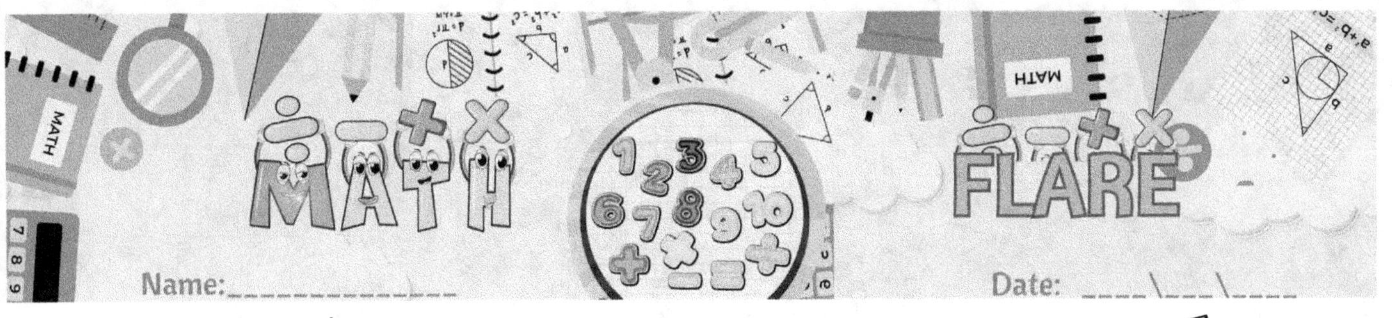

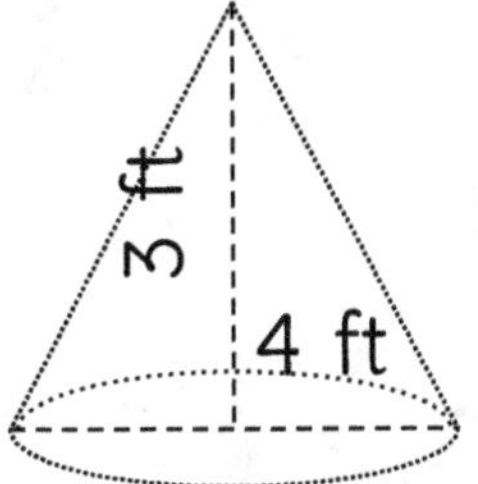

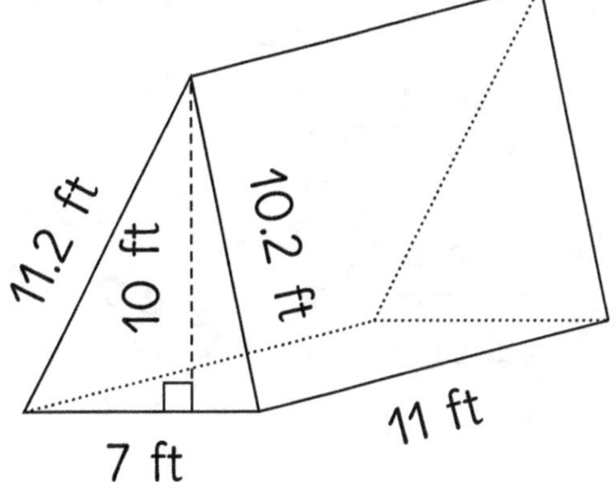

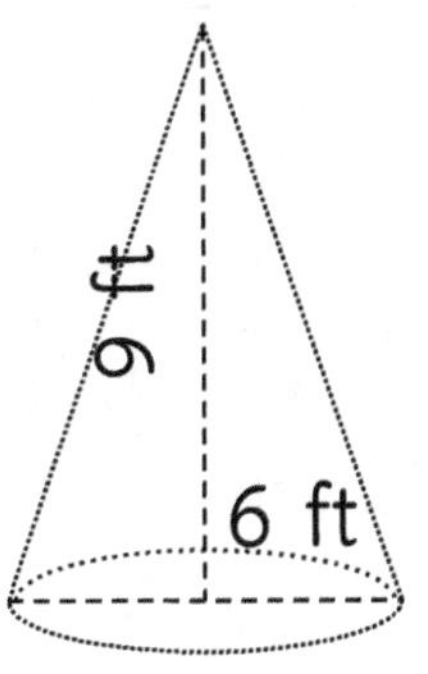

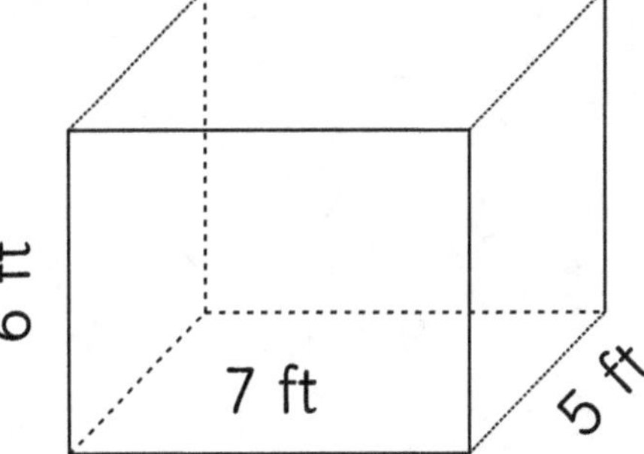

MATH
FLARE
Name:
Date:

17.

2.8 cm
2 cm
2 cm
2 cm
3 cm

18.

8.1 ft
8 ft
8.9 ft
5 ft
10 ft

19.

9 cm
9 cm

20.

2 ft
3 ft
2 ft

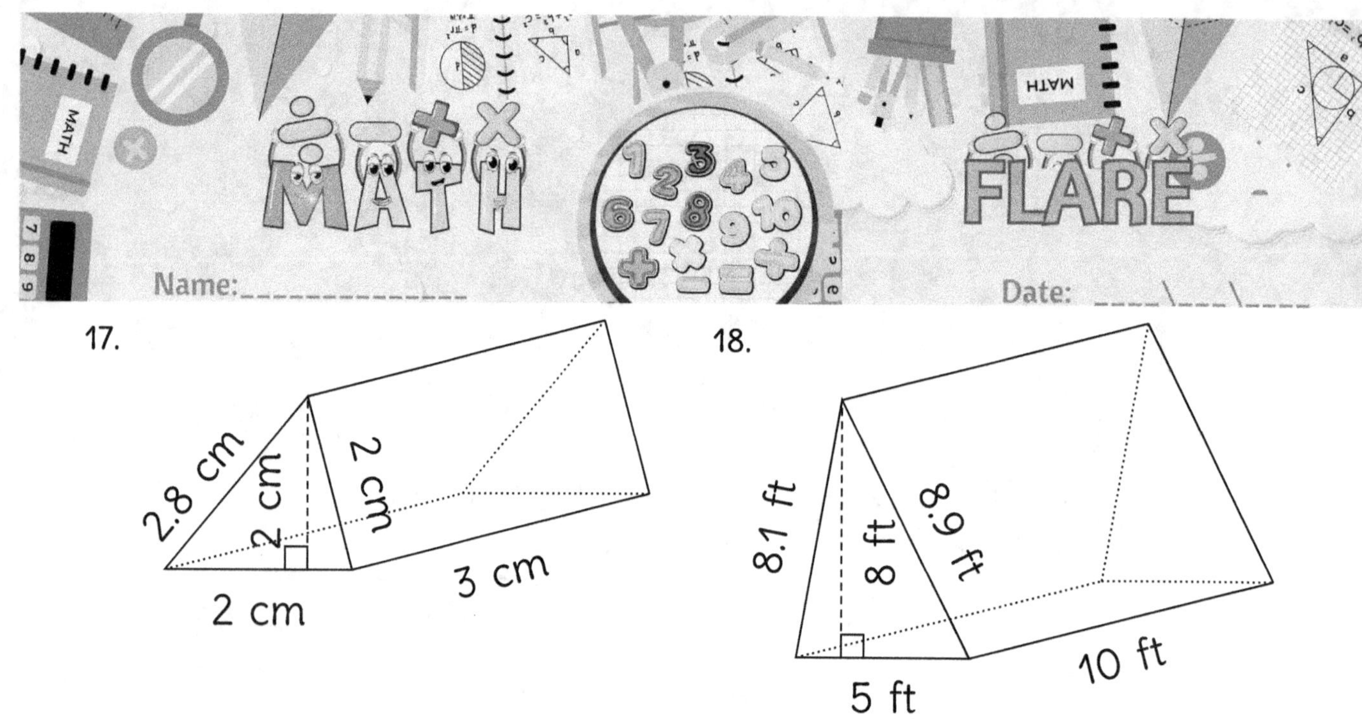

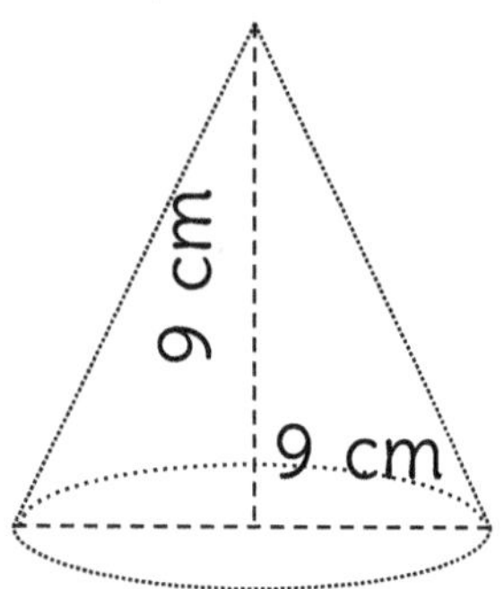

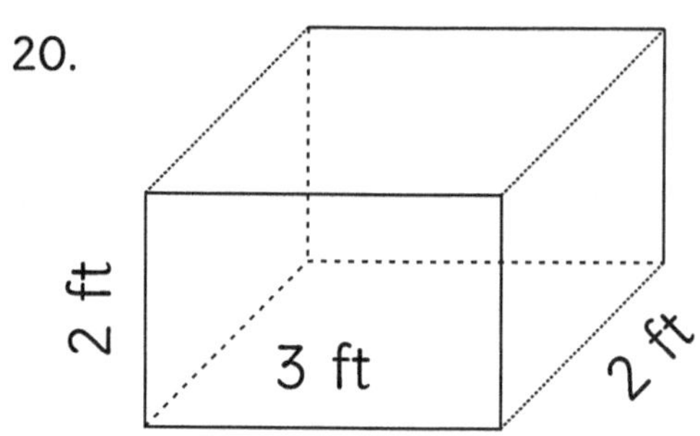

21.

10.0 ft
10 ft
11.2 ft
6 ft
11 ft
3 cm
3 cm
3 cm

22.

23.

5 in
4 in
4.1 in
4 in
4 in
7 cm
5 cm
6 cm

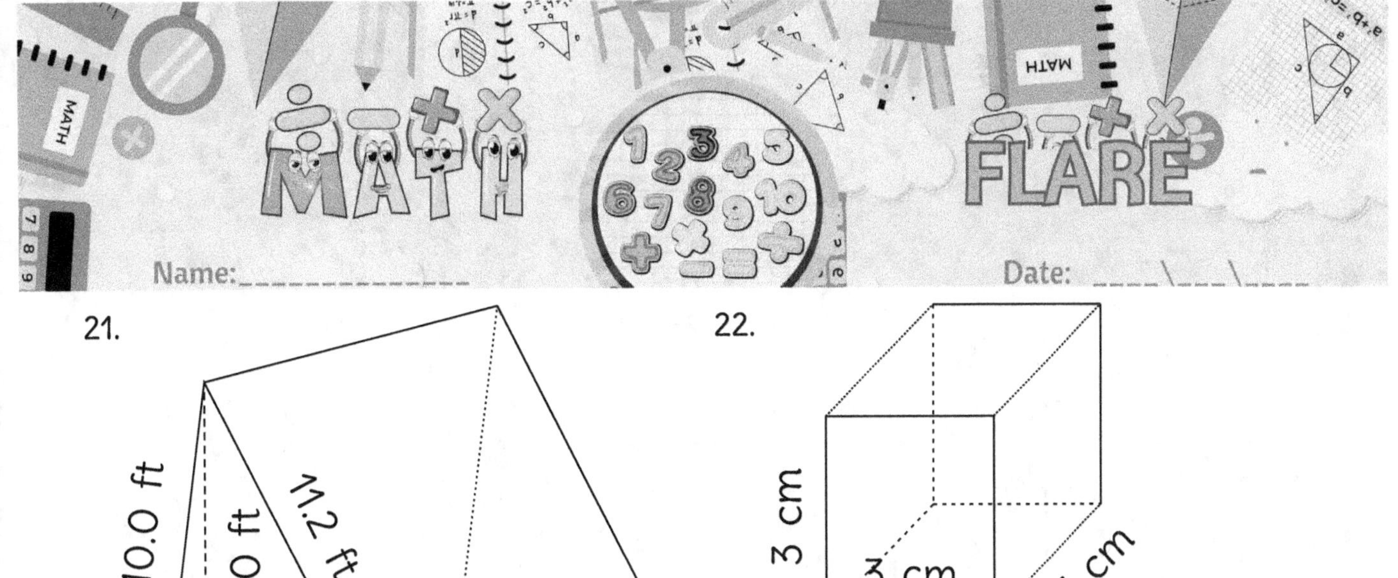

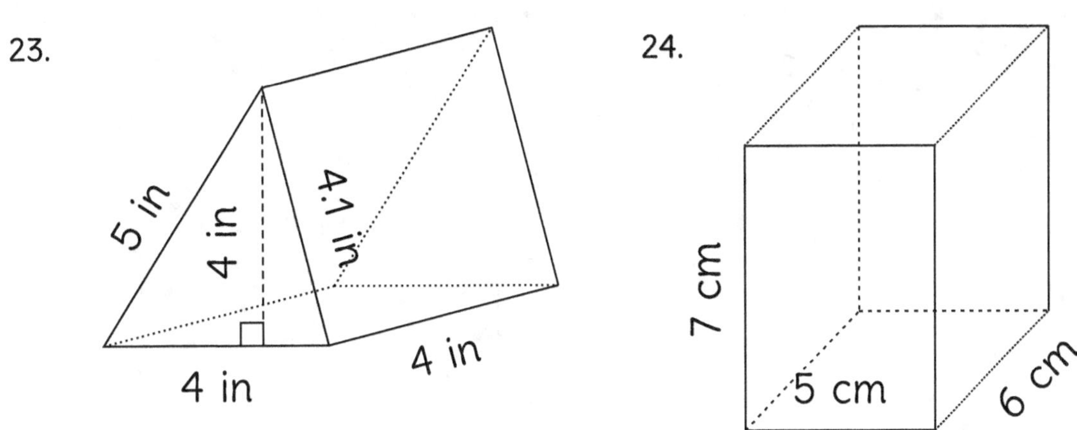

24.

MATH
FLARE
Name:
Date:

25.

6 ft
5 ft
6 ft

26.

4 in
3 in

27.

9.2 cm
6 cm
7 cm
8 cm

28.

4 ft
6 ft

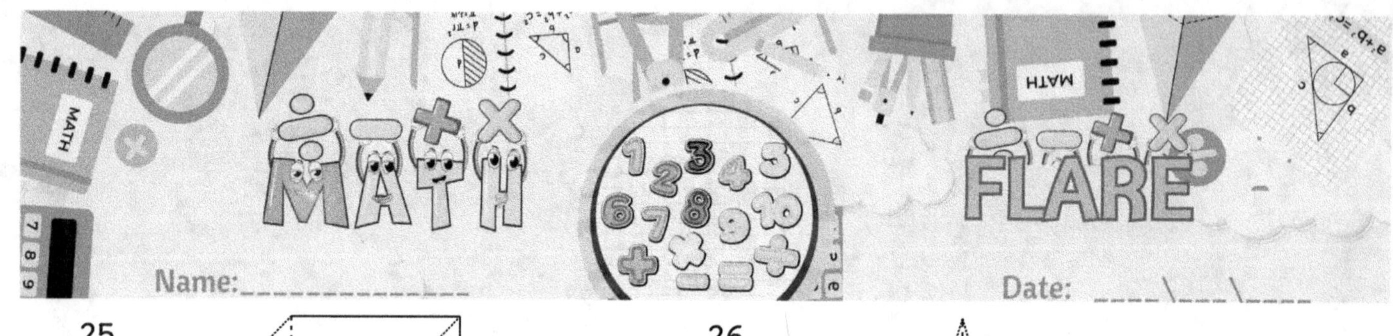

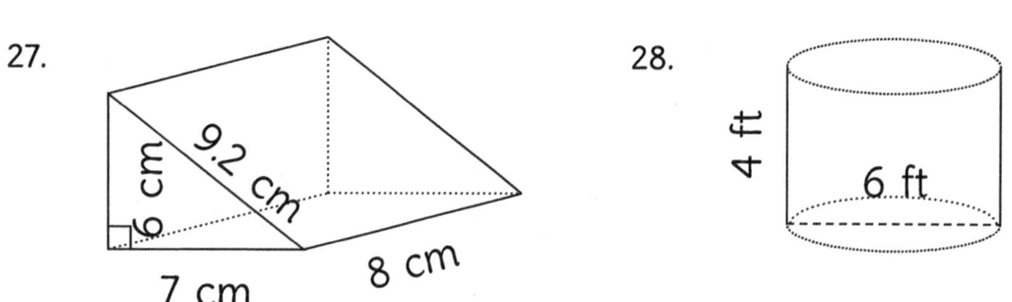

Name:
Date:

29.

4.1 ft
4 ft
4.5 ft
3 ft
4 ft

30.

7.8 in
5 in
6 in
5 in

31.

6 cm
7.8 cm
5 cm
4 cm

32.

4.1 in
4 in
5 in
4 in
4 in

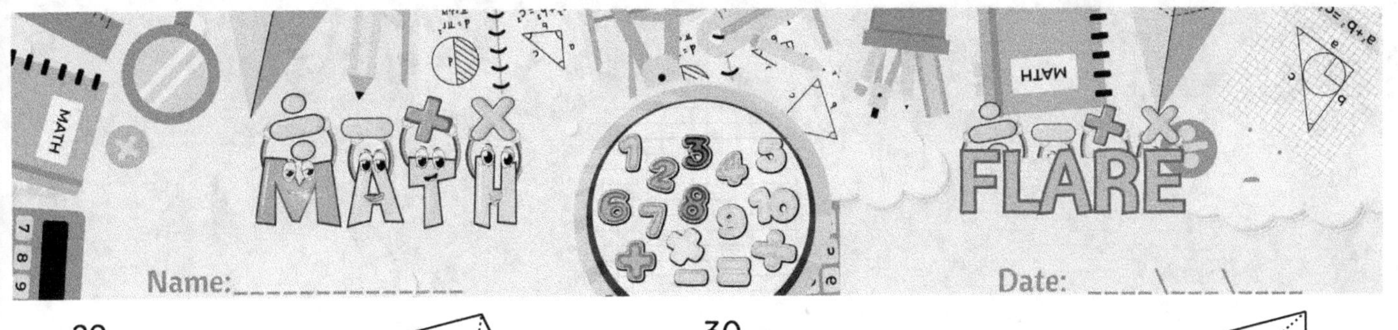

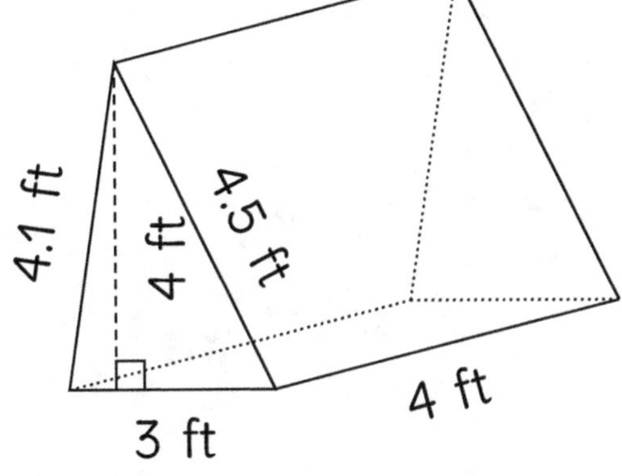

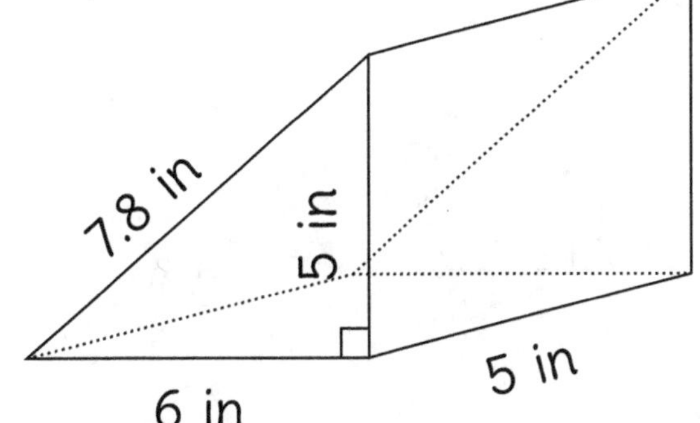

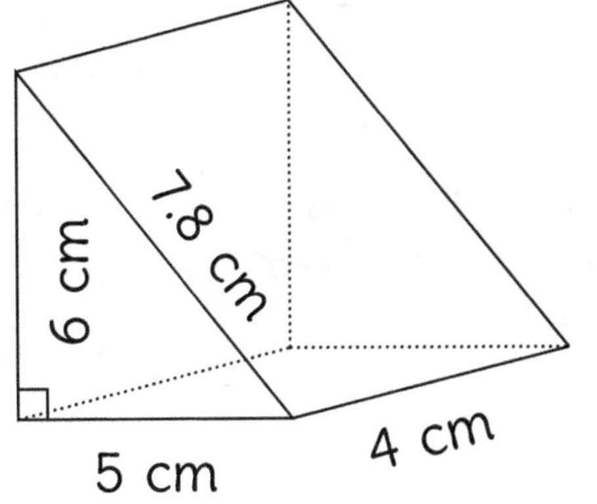

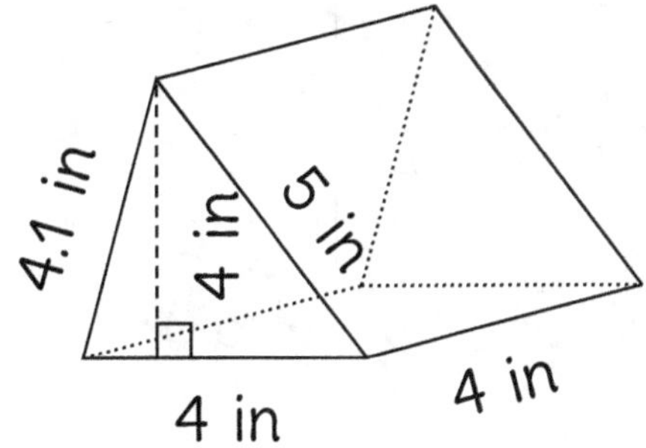

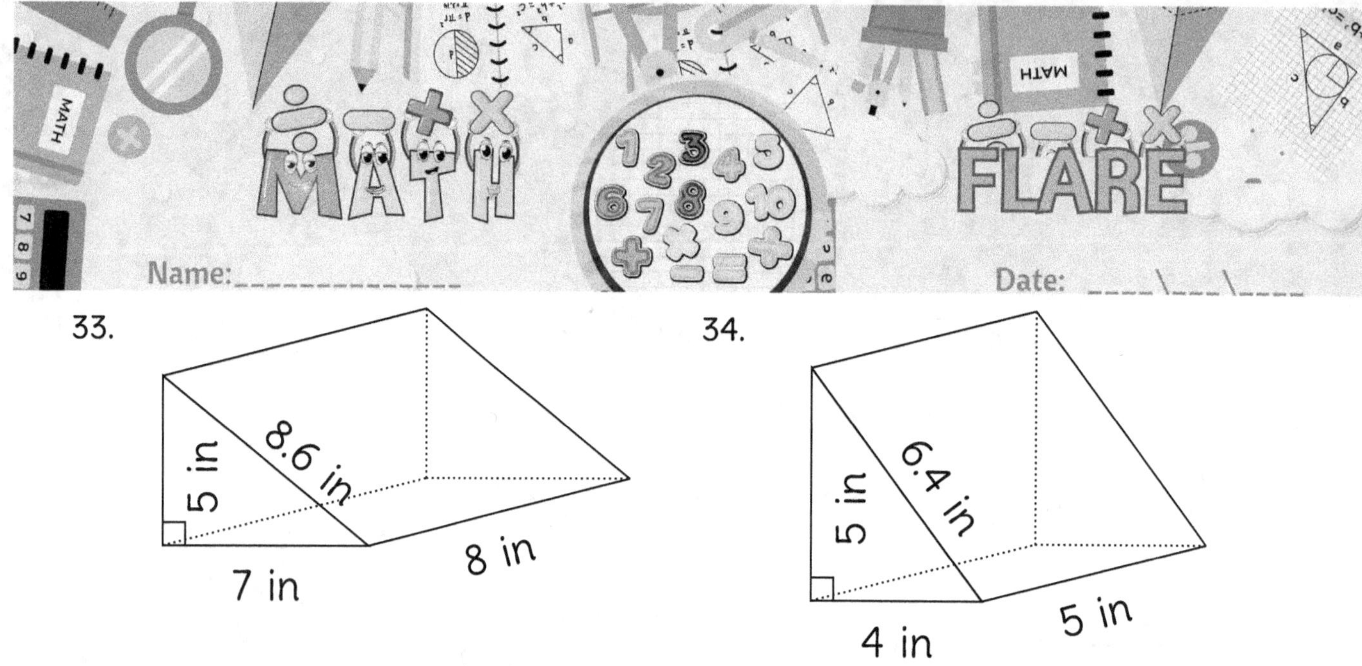

Name:
Date:
33.
5 in
8.6 in
7 in
8 in
34.
5 in
6.4 in
4 in
5 in

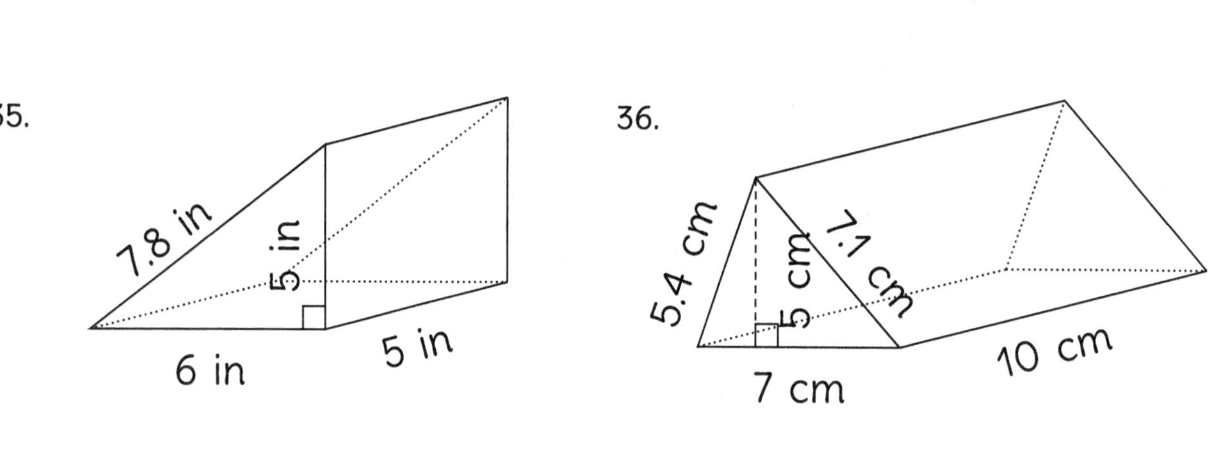

35.
7.8 in
5 in
6 in
5 in
36.
5.4 cm
7.1 cm
5 cm
7 cm
10 cm

MATH FLARE
Name:
Date:

37.

6 ft
6 ft
9 ft

38.

10 ft
10 ft

39.

10.6 cm
7 cm
8 cm
10 cm

40.

3.2 in
3 in
3.2 in
2 in
3 in

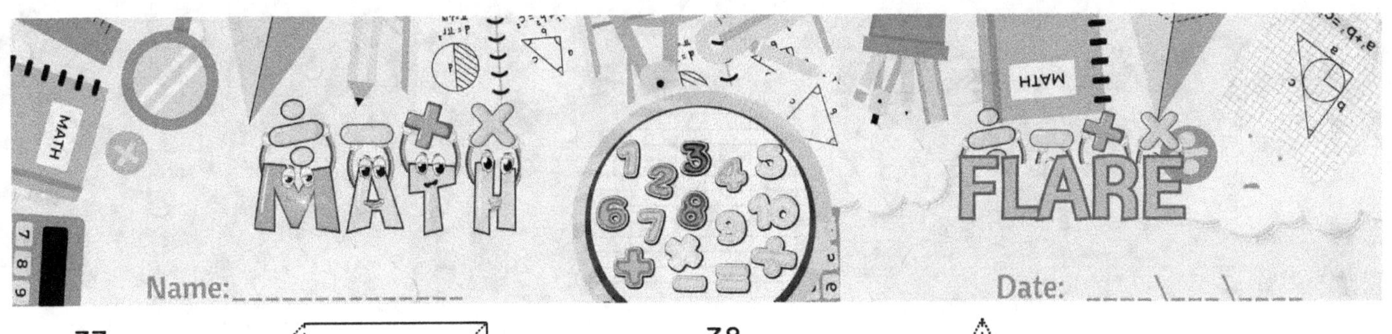

MATH
FLARE
Name:
Date:
MATH

41.

6 in
4 in

42.

3 in
4 in
5 in

43.

3 in
4 in
5 in

44.

5.8 cm
5 cm
5.8 cm
6 cm
4 cm

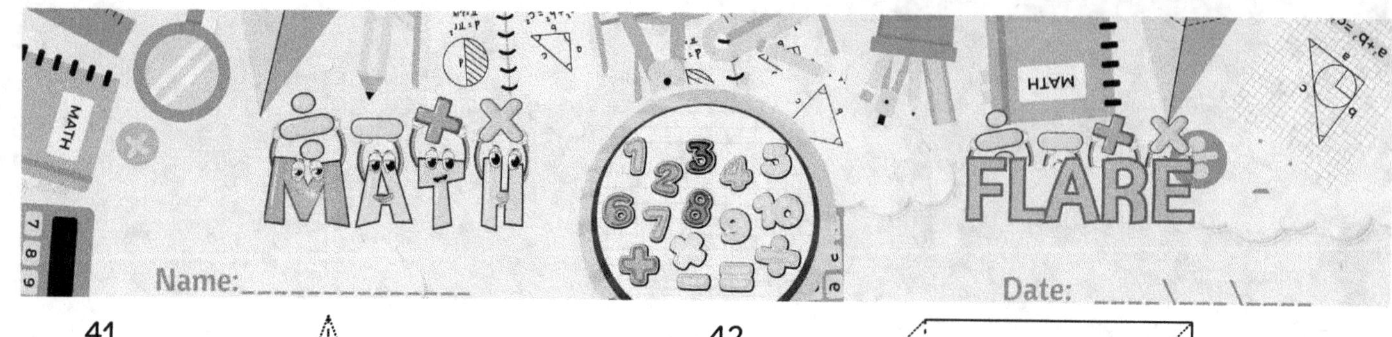

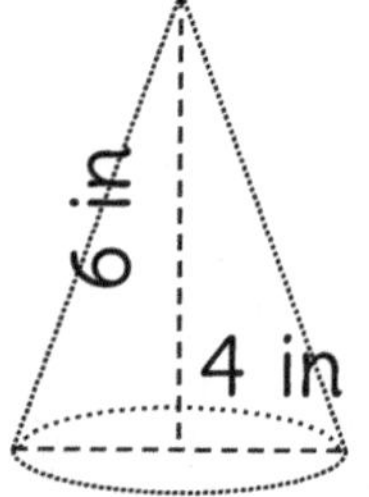

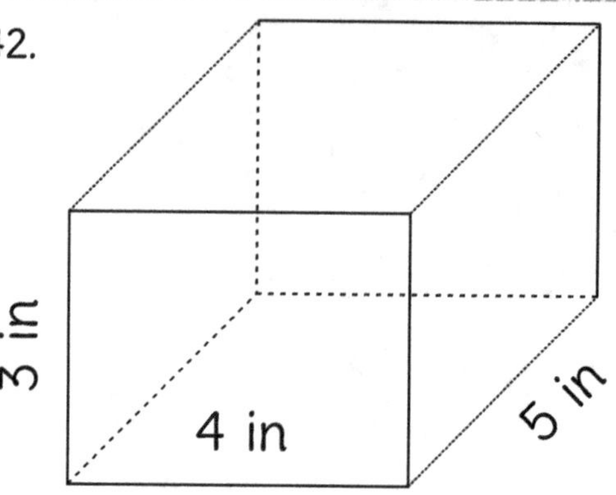

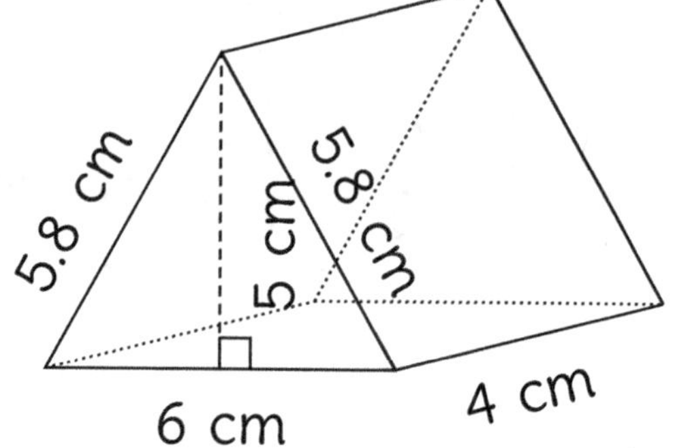

MATH
FLARE
Name:
Date:

45.

3 cm
2 cm
2 cm

46.

4 in
4 in
5 in

47.

3 in
4.2 in
3 in
4 in

48.

5 ft
5 ft
6 ft

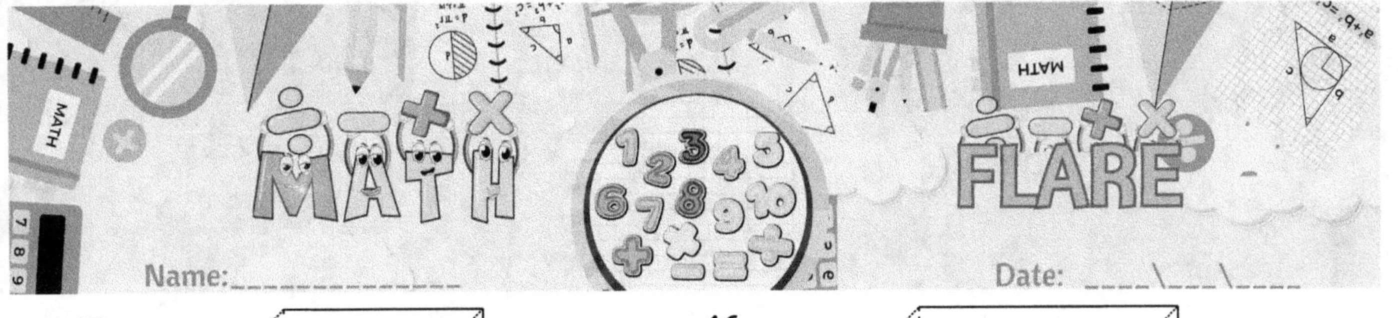

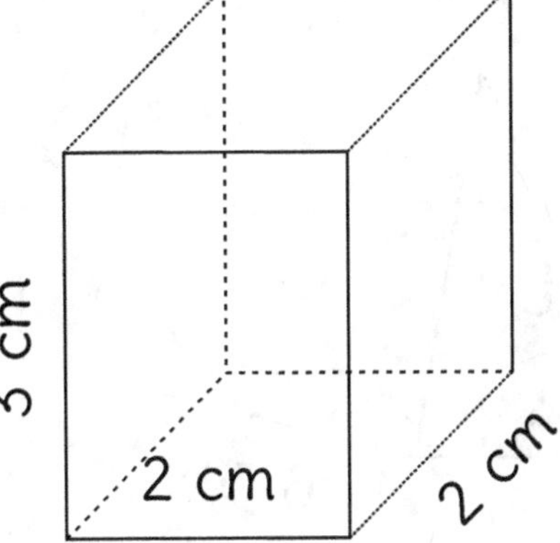

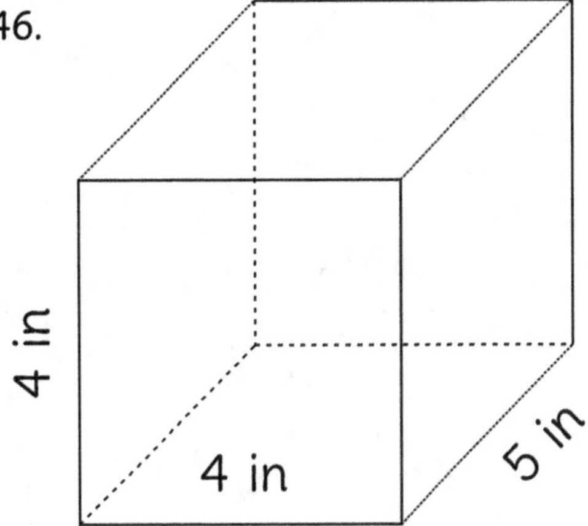

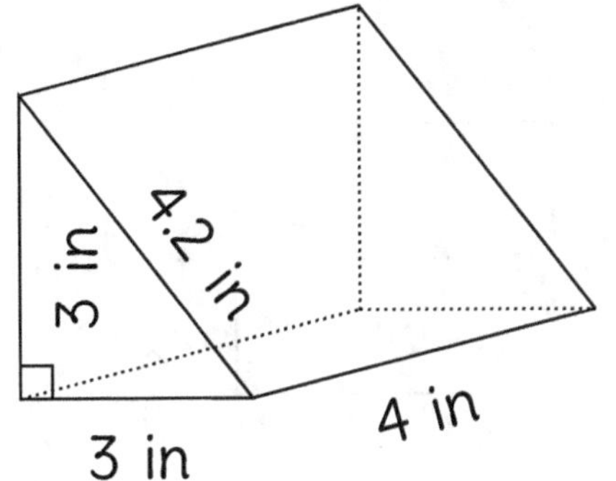

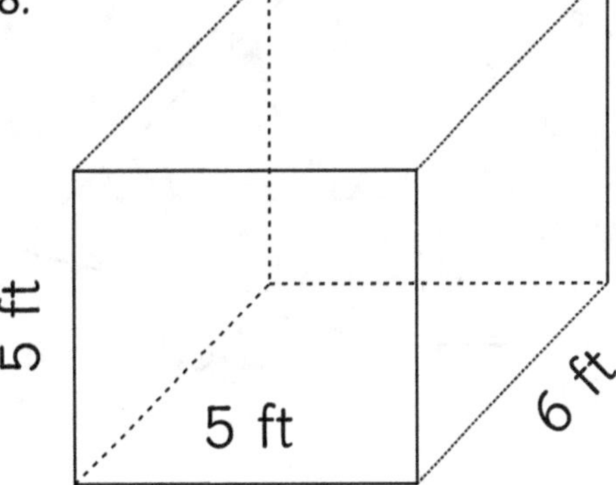

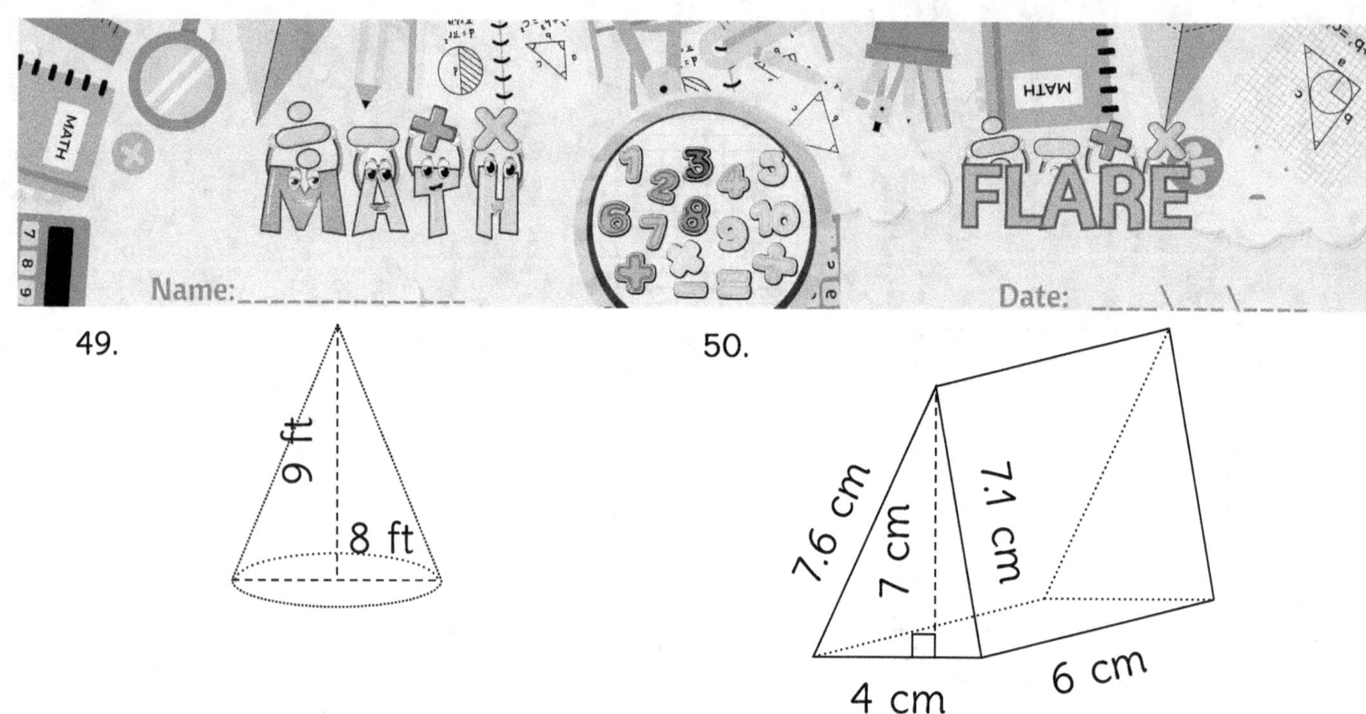
Name:
Date:
MATH
FLARE
49.
9 ft
8 ft
50.
7.6 cm
7 cm
7.1 cm
4 cm
6 cm

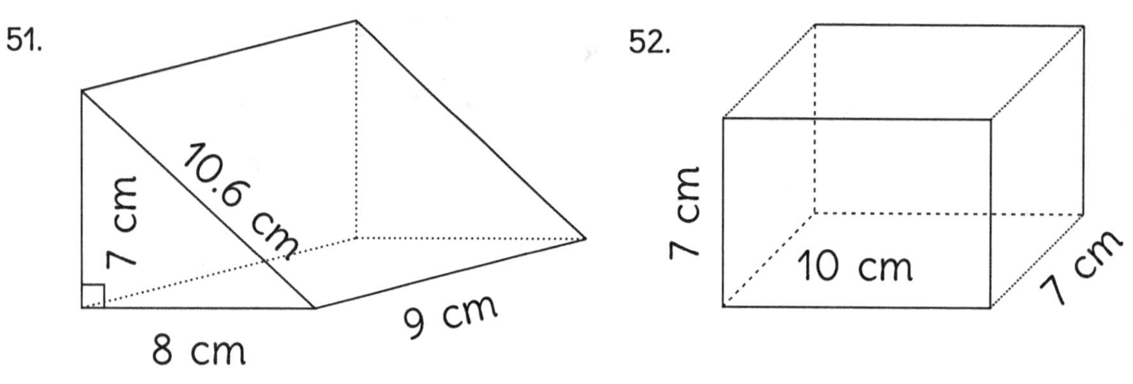
51.
7 cm
10.6 cm
8 cm
9 cm
52.
7 cm
10 cm
7 cm

Name:
Date:

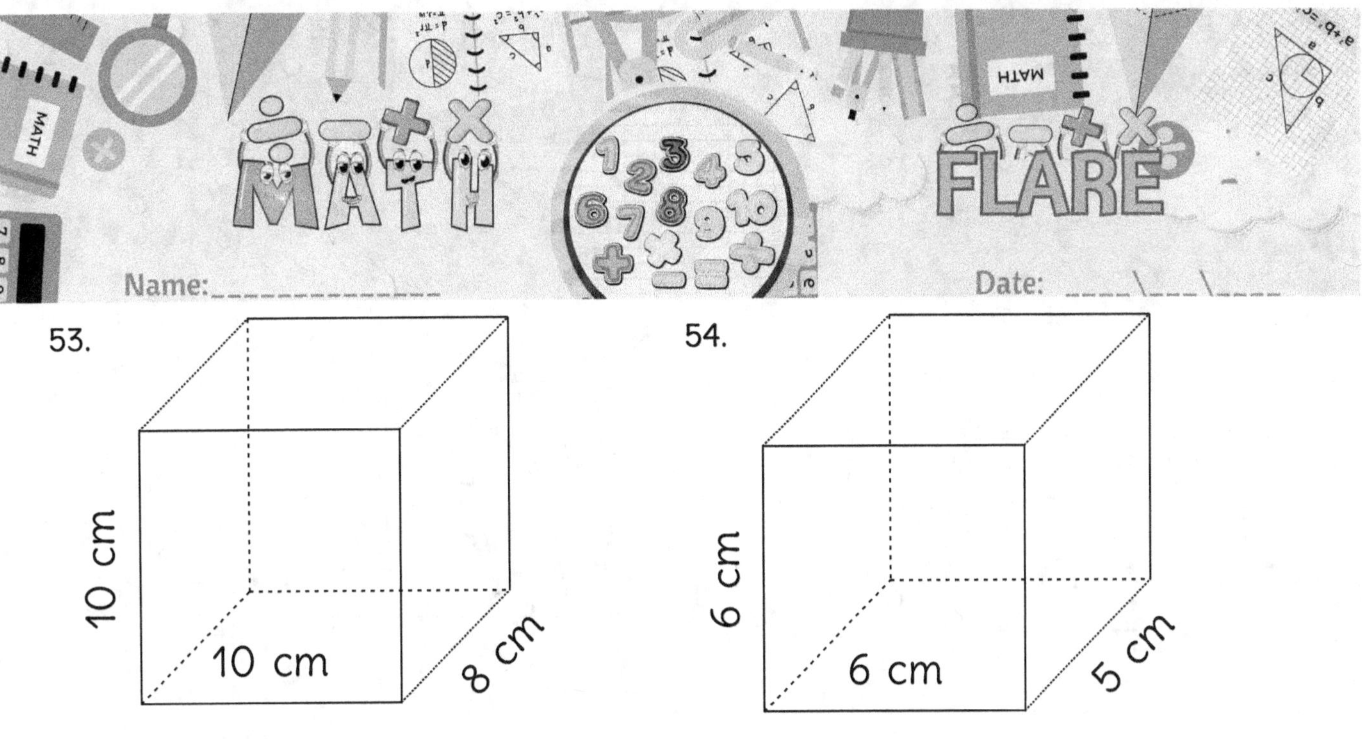

53.
10 cm
10 cm
8 cm
54.
6 cm
6 cm
5 cm

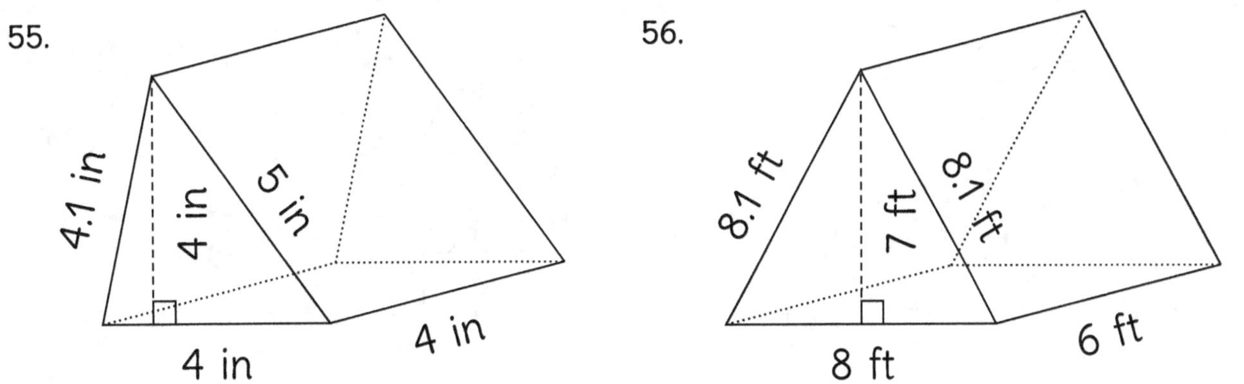

55.
4.1 in
4 in
5 in
4 in
4 in
56.
8.1 ft
7 ft
8.1 ft
8 ft
6 ft

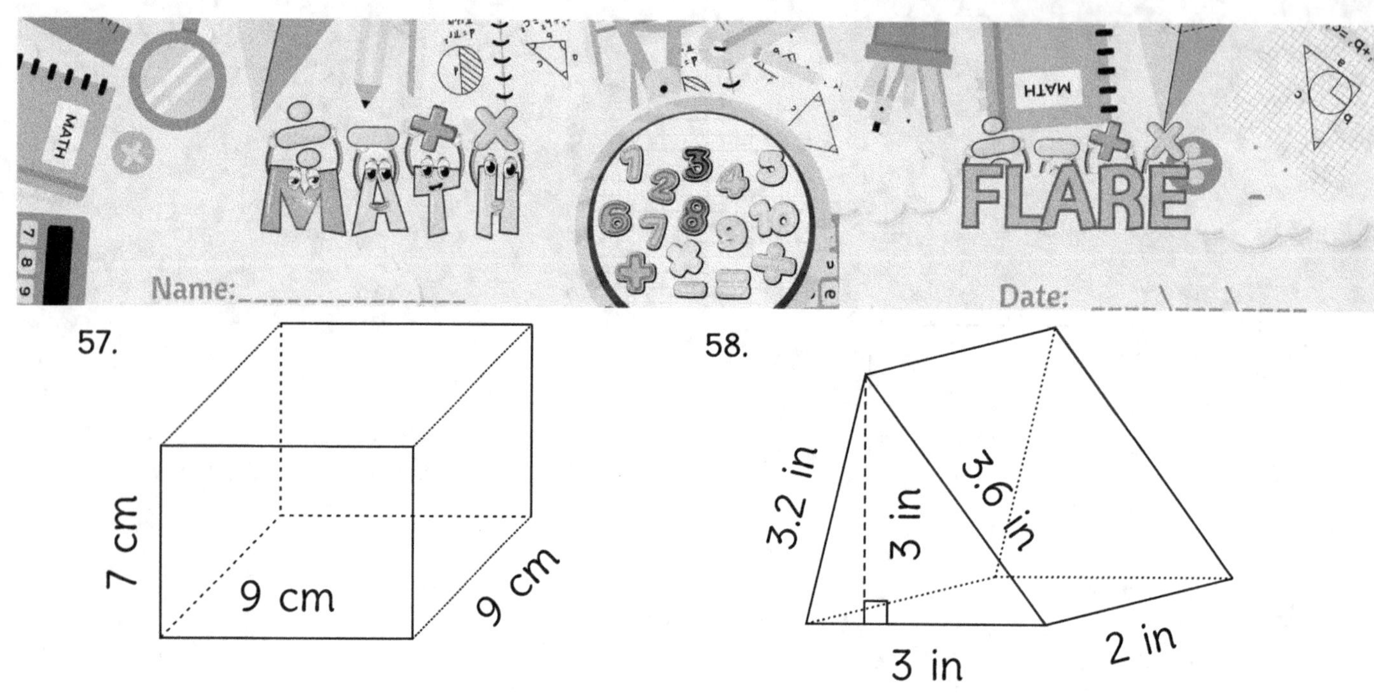
Name:
Date:
57.
7 cm
9 cm
9 cm
58.
3.2 in
3 in
3.6 in
3 in
2 in

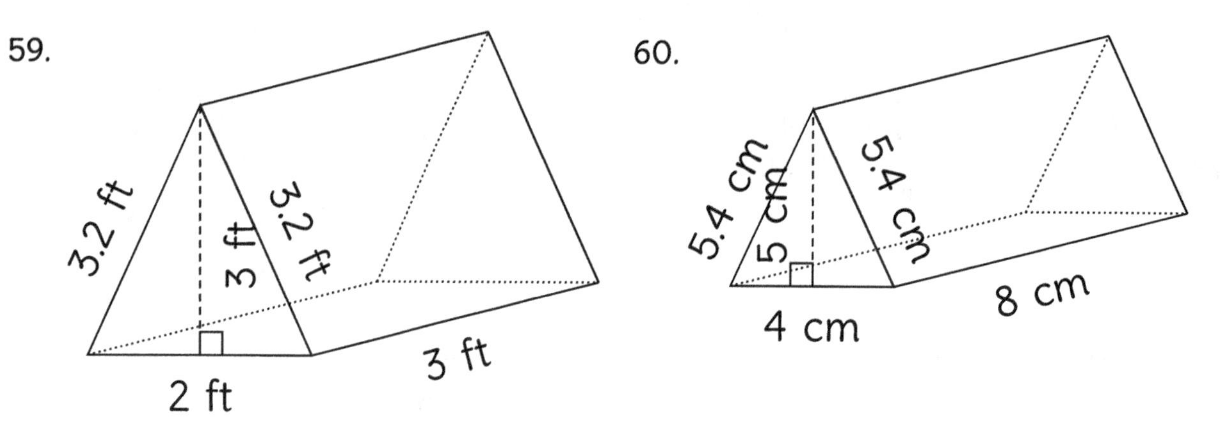
59.
3.2 ft
3 ft
3.2 ft
2 ft
3 ft
60.
5.4 cm
5 cm
5.4 cm
4 cm
8 cm

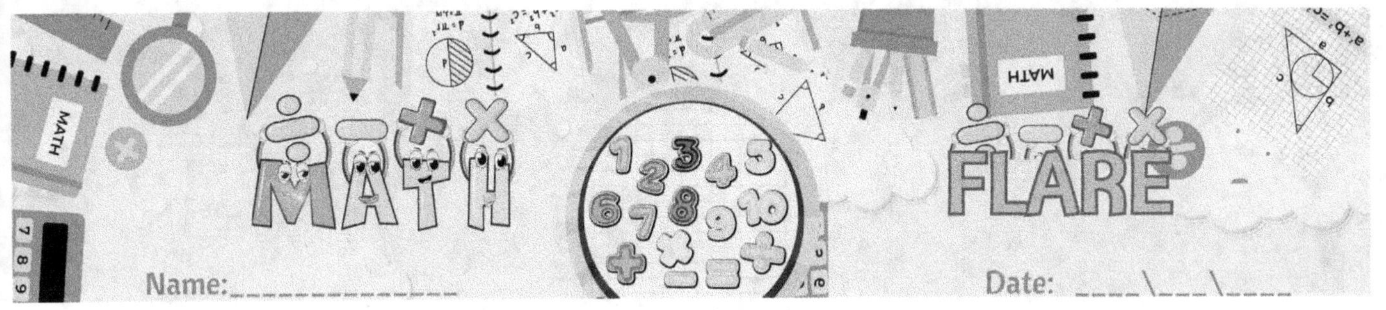

Pythagorean Theorem

1.
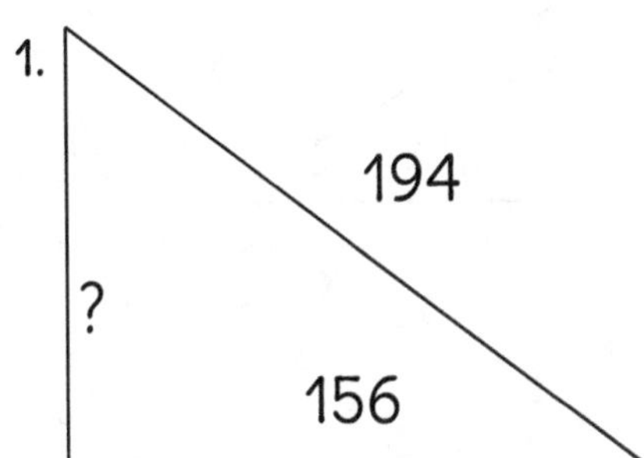

2.
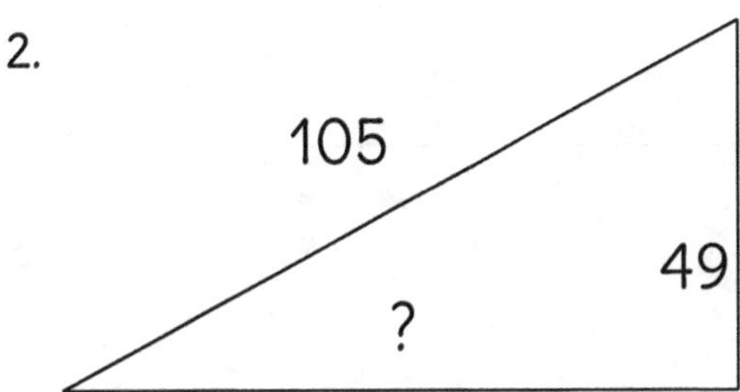

3.
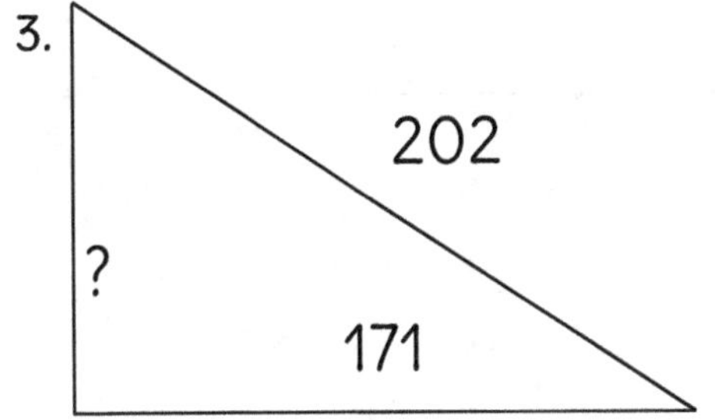

4.
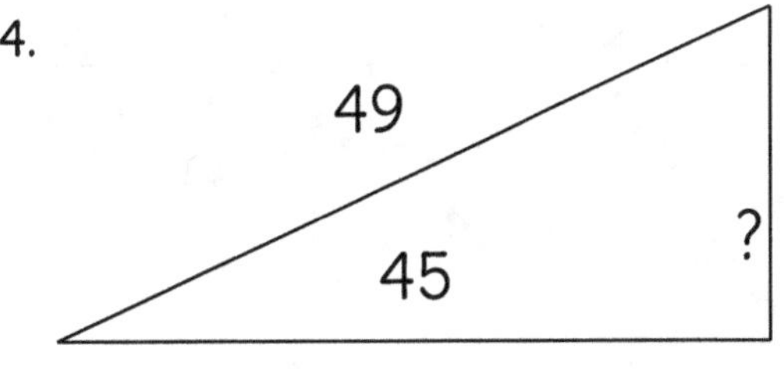

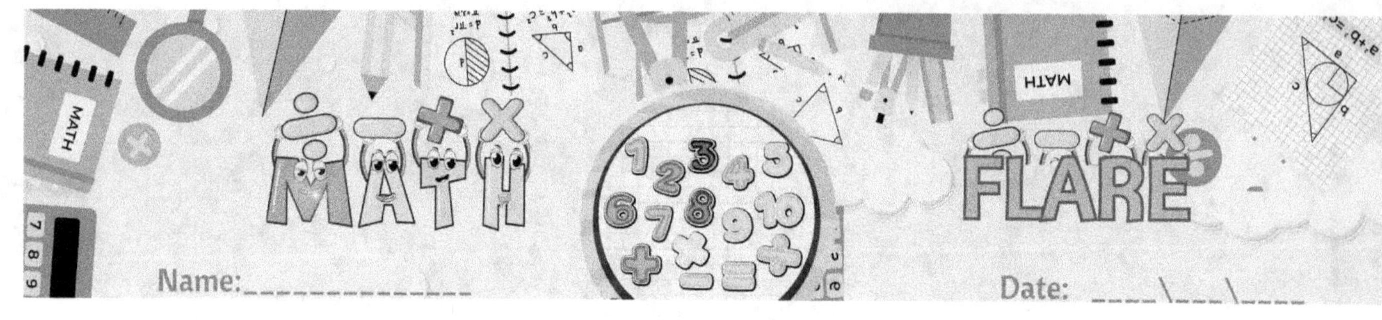

5. 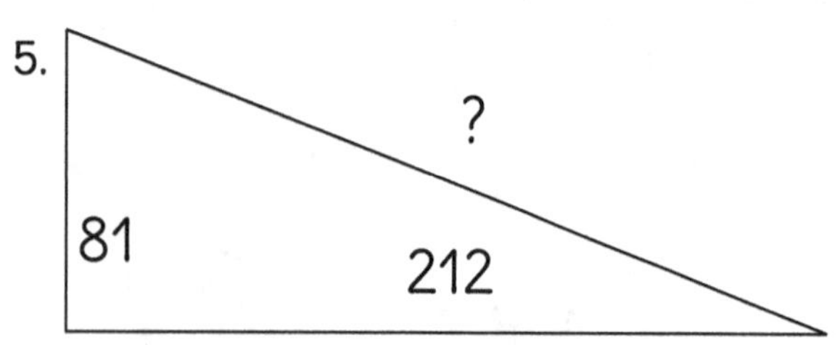

6. 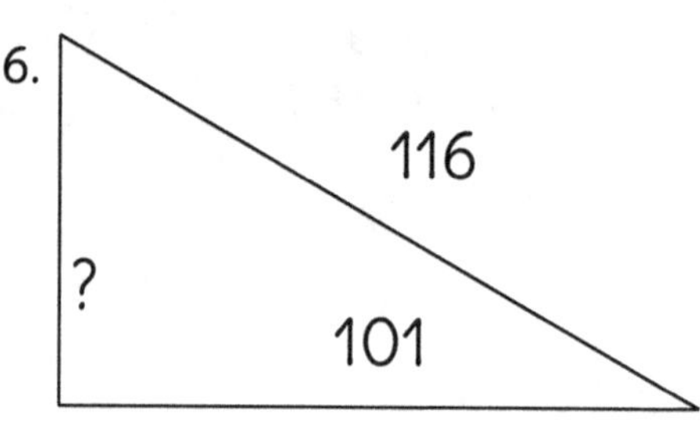

7. 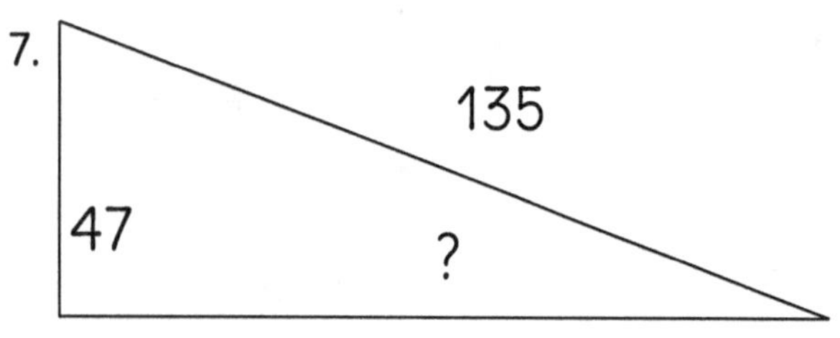

8. 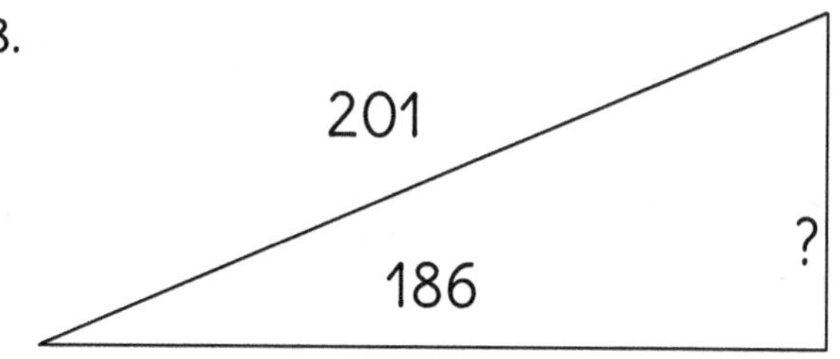

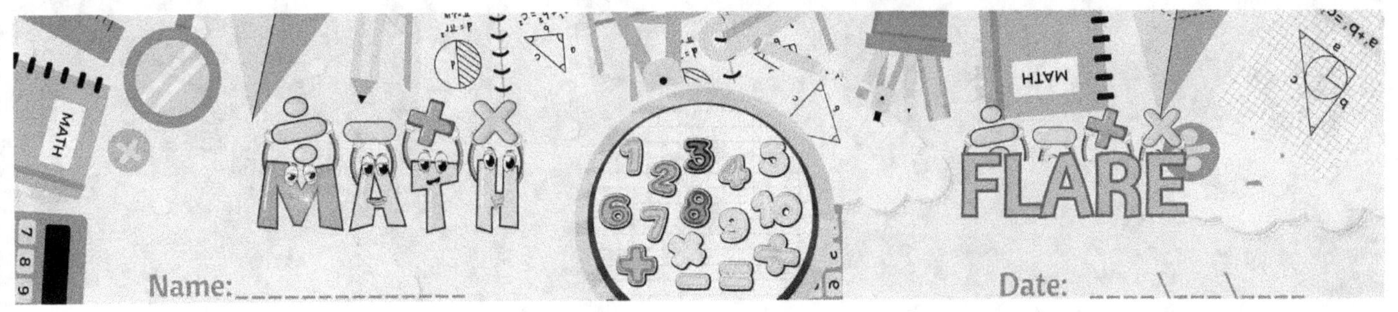

9.

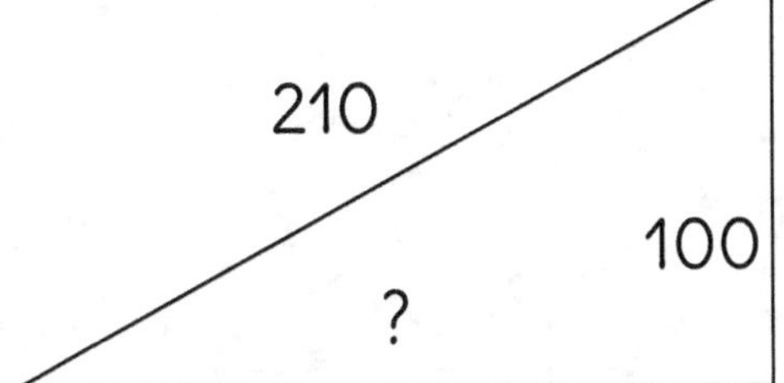

10.

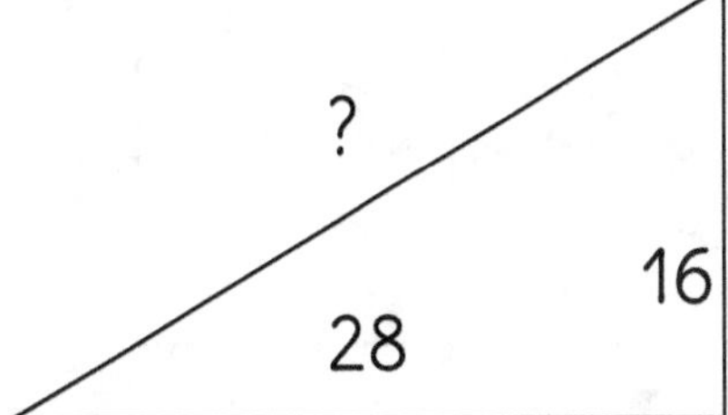

11.

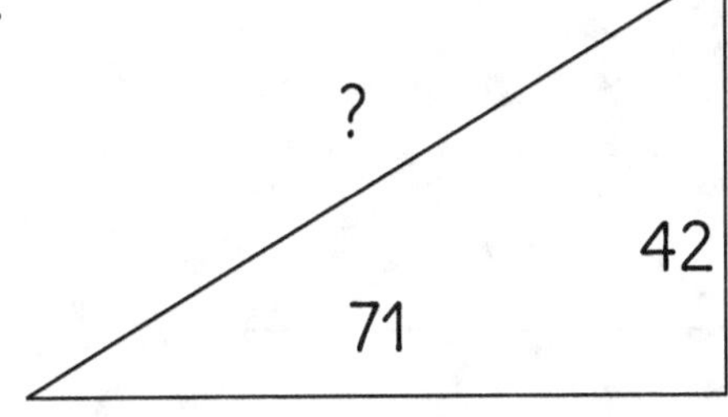

12.

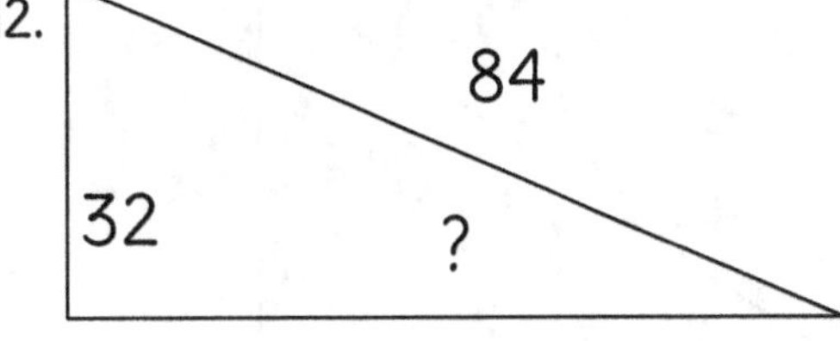

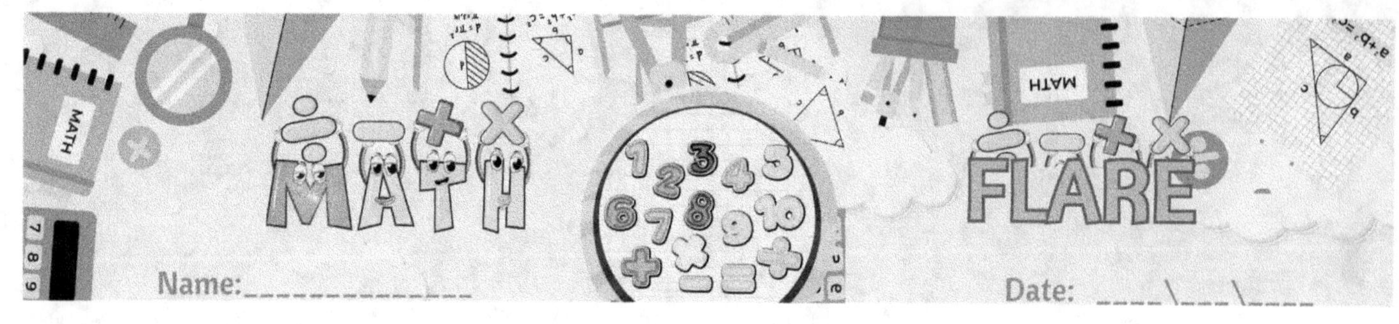

13.

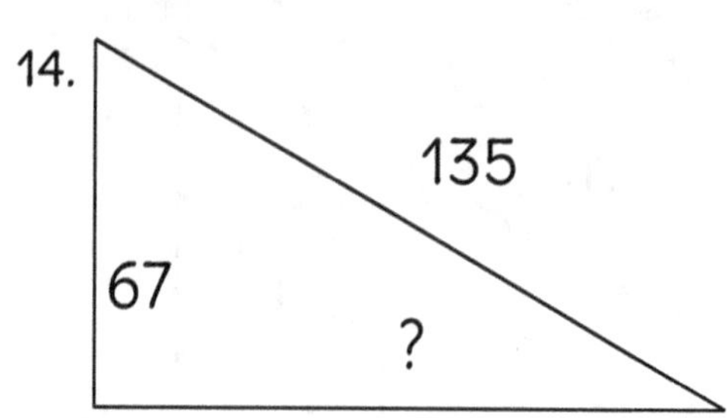

14.

15.

16.

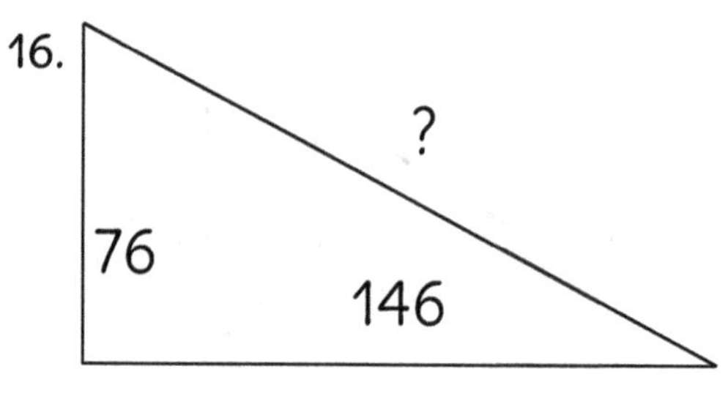

17.

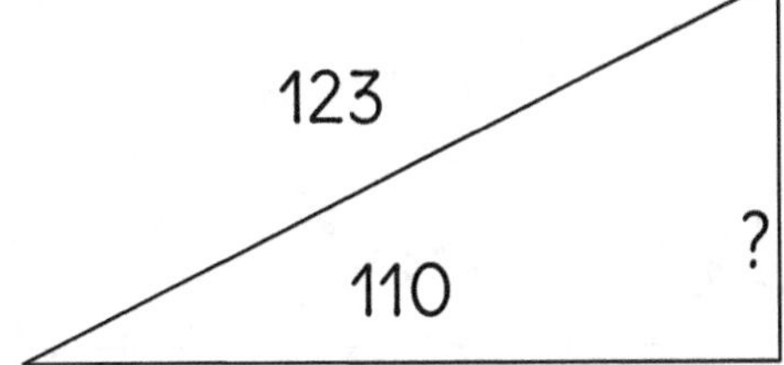

18.

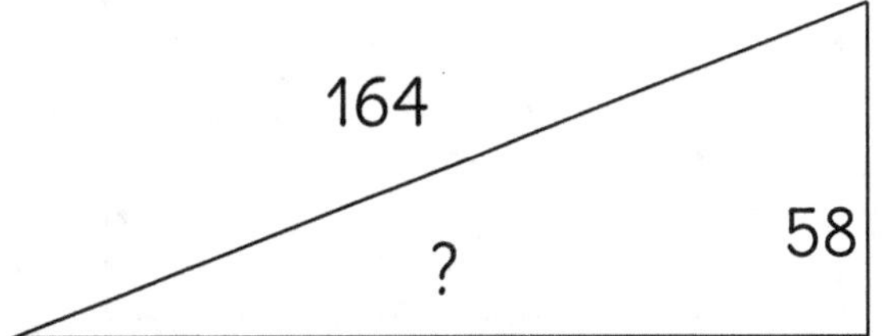

19.

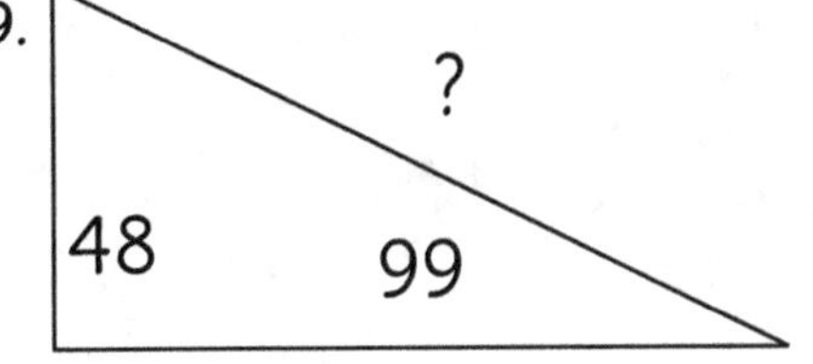

20.

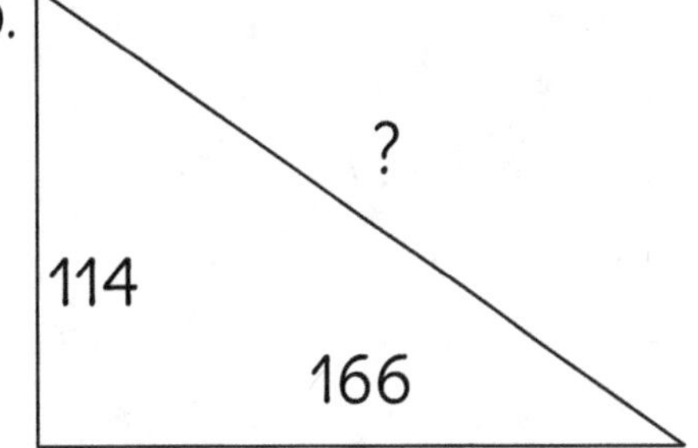

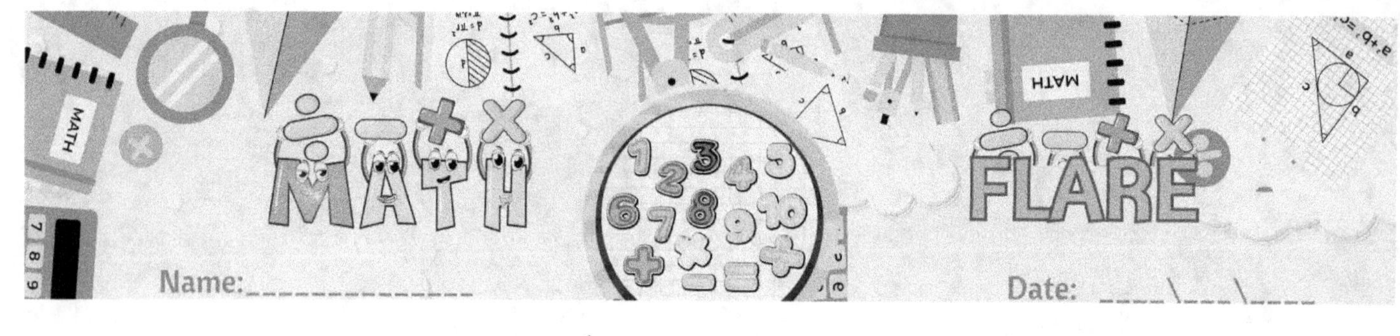

21.

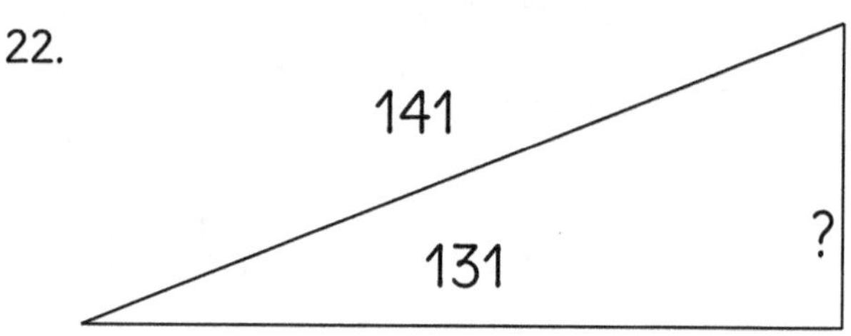

22.

23.

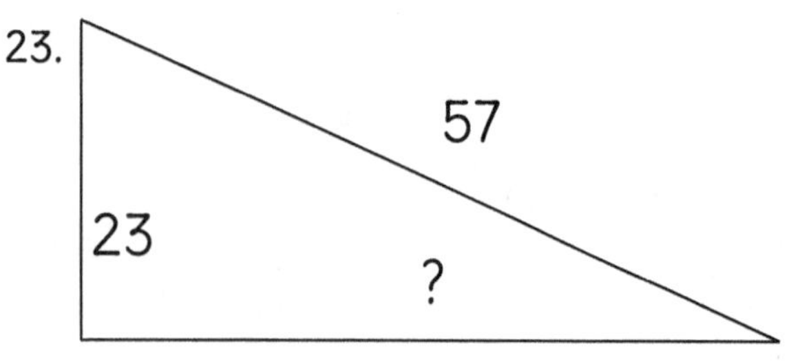

24.

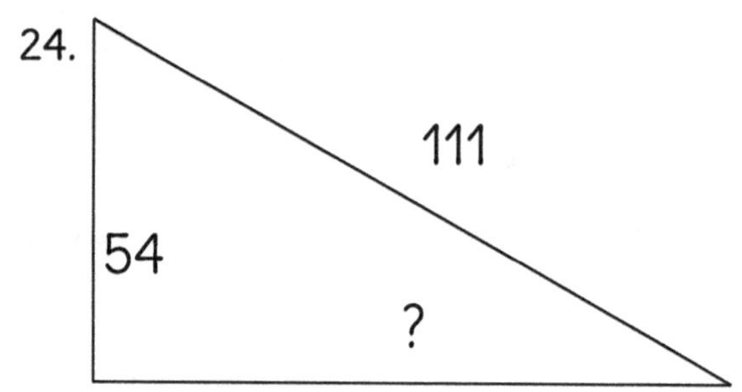

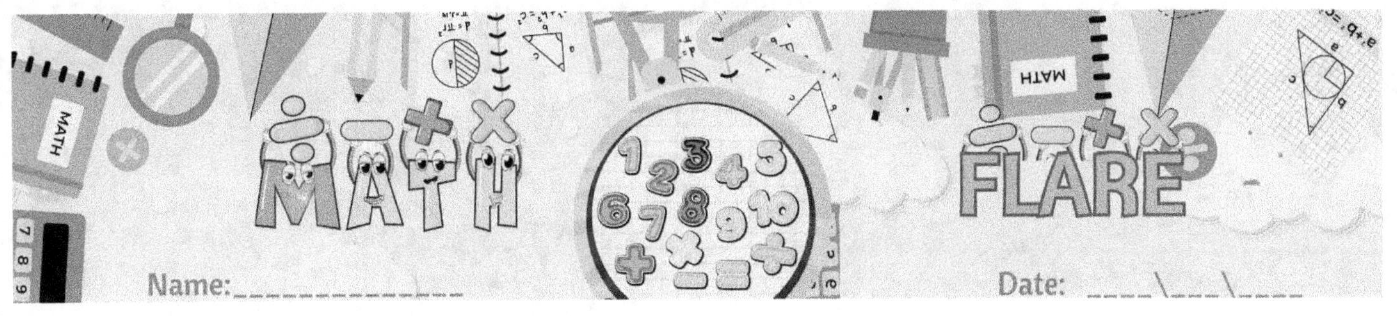

25.

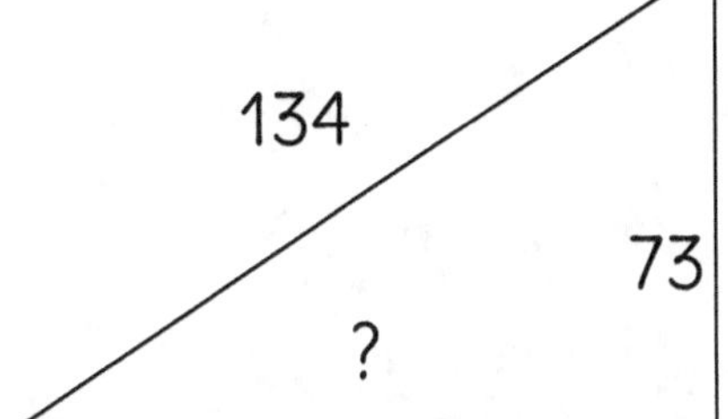

26.

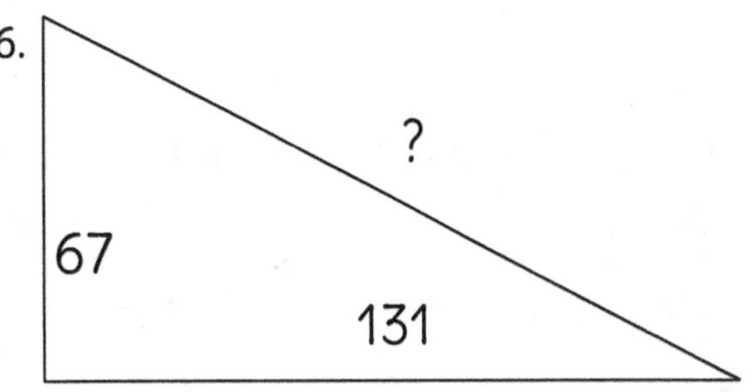

27.

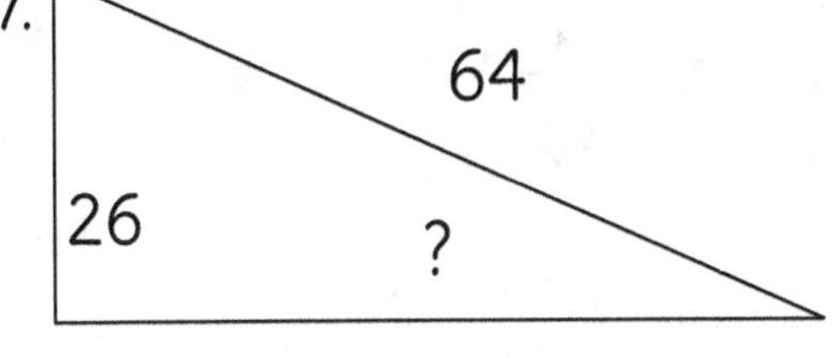

28.

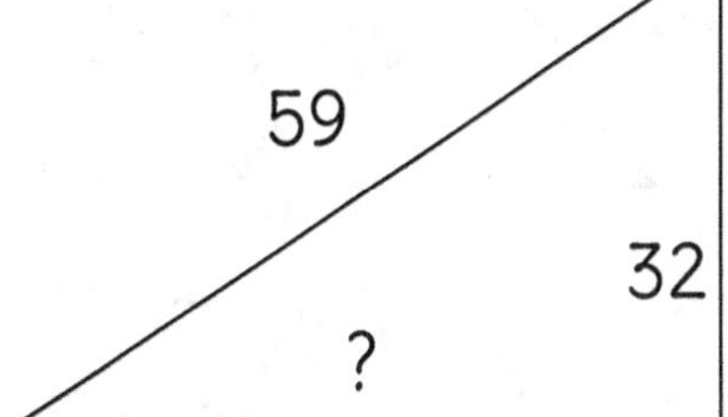

ANSWERS

Page 1: Simplify Expressions

1. -9z + 2	2. 25k - 13	3. -28m + 4
4. -14m + 30	5. 13z + 28	6. 10x + 18
7. -22x - 36	8. -9y + 14	9. -7y + 22
10. 7k + 15	11. 16k + 10	12. 9z + 18
13. -y - 6	14. -2z - 1	15. -18y
16. 13z + 11	17. 10x	18. 22m + 12
19. 0	20. 12m + 20	21. 14y + 13
22. 10x + 4	23. -8z	24. 14k + 3
25. 25z - 13	26. 12k - 15	27. 16m - 23
28. -22k - 24	29. 9z + 5	30. 16y + 1
31. 31k + 28	32. 13z + 3	33. 5y + 20
34. 7z + 22	35. -3k	36. 5x + 4
37. 16z + 7	38. -8y	39. -17k + 20
40. 19x + 11	41. -12x	42. 3y + 17
43. -39m + 22	44. 2x + 9	45. 24z + 17
46. -6k - 18	47. -26y + 30	48. -22y - 3
49. 11z + 2	50. 6y	51. 20k
52. 15z - 35	53. 14m + 6	54. -28m + 204
55. 38m + 9	56. -18m - 7	57. 9m + 11

58. –38m + 13   59. –7m   60. –340z + 230

61. 2k – 37   62. 20m + 25   63. 6y + 24

64. –4k – 15   65. –11z + 5   66. –17m – 6

67. –k – 4   68. –27y   69. 18y + 28

70. 35k – 8   71. 2k   72. 18y

73. 10m + 17   74. –136m + 341   75. 12

76. 21k + 2   77. 3k + 4   78. –m + 27

79. –133k + 75   80. –13z   81. 30m – 161

82. –24x + 3   83. 15m + 21   84. –14m

85. 15x   86. –6k   87. 37x + 24

88. –28x + 3   89. 12y + 10   90. –17y – 16

91. 7m + 10   92. 11y + 3   93. –6x

94. –204m + 259   95. 4m + 8   96. –14k + 15

97. 0   98. –24m + 20   99. 11y

100. 12y – 12

Page 21: Solving Equations

1. 1   2. 2   3. 2   4. 12   5. 1   6. 7   7. 2   8. 3   9. –6   10. 8

Page 22: Solving Equations

1. 2   2. –2   3. 14   4. 13   5. 170   6. 7   7. 6   8. –1   9. 28

10. 1

Page 23: Solving Equations
1. 1   2. 0   3. 26   4. 11   5. 4   6. 12   7. 4   8. 8   9. 1   10. -1

Page 24: Solving Equations
1. 8   2. 43   3. 41   4. 2   5. 1   6. 15   7. 83   8. 19
9. 27   10. 0.1

Page 25: Solving Equations
1. 8   2. 216   3. -28   4. 339   5. -4.2   6. 320   7. 5
8. 140   9. 26   10. -6.6

Page 26: Solving Equations
1. 18   2. 1   3. 1   4. 2   5. 5   6. 21   7. 10   8. 23   9. 8   10. 1

Page 27: Solving Equations
1. 0.2   2. 46   3. 2   4. 34   5. 108   6. 35   7. 68   8. 1   9. 23
10. 91

Page 28: Solving Equations
1. 70   2. 3   3. 1   4. 8   5. 1   6. 42   7. 84   8. -16   9. 9
10. 0

Page 29: Solving Equations
1. 18   2. 5   3. -6   4. 7   5. 16   6. 3   7. 18   8. 90   9. -3   10. 9

Page 30: Solving Equations
1. 56   2. 10   3. 1   4. 92   5. 12   6. 12   7. -13   8. -13   9. 56
10. -3

Page 31: Solving Equations
1. 14   2. -3   3. 6   4. 20   5. 40   6. 80   7. 13   8. 80   9. -18

10. 45

Page 32:   Solving Equations

1. 28   2. 7   3. 108   4. 288   5. 14   6. 13   7. 5   8. 20

9. 24   10. 1

Page 33:   Solving Equations

1. 0   2. 2   3. 4   4. 4   5. 29   6. 15   7. 8   8. 12   9. 3

10. 21

Page 34:   Equations (One Side)

1. 15

2. 18 or -18

3. 14

4. 20

5. 19

6. 7

7. 15

8. 10

9. 9

10. 8

11. 18

12. 7

13. 18

14. 11

15. 19 or -33

16. 16

17. 14

18. 15

19. 18

20. 2

21. 1

22. 5

23. 5

24. 11

25. 17

26. 4

27. 7

28. 9 or -10

29. 16

30. 2

31. 16

32. 1

33. 14

34. 5

35. 10

36. 6

37. 17

38. 19 or -19

39. 4

40. 15

41. 3

42. 7

43. 20

44. 4

45. 6 or -6

46. 3

47. 11 or -12

48. 10

49. 1

50. 3

51. 8

52. 3 or -3

53. 3

54. 5

55. 9

56. 6

57. 3

58. 2

59. 4

60. 9

61. 1

62. 2

63. 6

64. 4

65. 9

66. 2 or -3

67. 14 or -14

68. 19

69. 3

71. 8

73. 5

75. 7

77. 9

79. 16 or -16

81. 12

83. 16

85. 7

87. 13

89. 12

91. 18 or -18

93. 6

95. 19

97. 19 or -20

99. 13

101. 5

103. 12

70. 18

72. 7

74. 4

76. 9

78. 7 or -8

80. 1

82. 16

84. 16

86. 20

88. 18

90. 16

92. 9

94. 3

96. 6

98. 18

100. 6

102. 9

Page 60: Equations (Two Sides)

1. $y = 5$
2. $y = 8$
3. $x = 4$
4. $x = 1$
5. $m = 5$
6. $m = 6$
7. $z = 5$
8. $m = 1$
9. $z = 5$
10. $k = 6$
11. $y = 7$
12. $x = 6$
13. $m = 1$
14. $k = 3$
15. $x = 8$
16. $k = 2$
17. $y = 3$
18. $x = 9$
19. $z = 7$
20. $m = 7$
21. $m = 6$
22. $z = 4$
23. $y = 8$
24. $k = 9$
25. $m = 4$
26. $m = 7$
27. $k = 6$
28. $m = 9$
29. $x = 4$
30. $k = 2$
31. $x = 1$
32. $x = 5$
33. $x = 1$
34. $x = 7$
35. $z = 5$
36. $k = 8$
37. $z = 3$
38. $y = 2$
39. $k = 2$
40. $y = 4$
41. $m = 3$
42. $k = 9$
43. $k = 9$
44. $k = 7$
45. $x = 4$
46. $y = 9$
47. $k = 8$
48. $m = 3$
49. $m = 2$
50. $k = 3$
51. $z = 8$
52. $z = 1$
53. $m = 2$
54. $z = 9$
55. $y = 6$
56. $y = 5$
57. $z = 2$
58. $m = 1$
59. $m = 5$
60. $z = 7$
61. $m = 3$
62. $x = 5$
63. $z = 4$
64. $y = 7$
65. $x = 1$
66. $m = 6$
67. $z = 4$
68. $z = 8$
69. $k = 9$
70. $x = 6$
71. $k = 2$
72. $z = 6$
73. $m = 9$
74. $k = 8$
75. $z = 3$
76. $m = 4$
77. $y = 7$
78. $y = 2$
79. $y = 3$
80. $y = 1$
81. $k = 8$
82. $z = 2$
83. $k = 5$
84. $x = 8$
85. $m = 3$
86. $y = 7$
87. $k = 7$
88. $y = 3$
89. $y = 8$
90. $k = 9$
91. $k = 9$
92. $x = 2$
93. $x = 2$
94. $k = 1$
95. $x = 8$
96. $y = 9$
97. $k = 8$
98. $x = 3$

Page 70: Understanding Linear Functions

1. 0	11. -18	21. 11	31. -22	41. 30
2. 33	12. -8	22. -2	32. -2	42. 14
3. -3	13. -2	23. -9	33. -2	43. 1
4. -15	14. 2	24. 8	34. -2	44. 1
5. -17	15. -7	25. 6	35. -19	45. 15
6. 4	16. 13	26. 19	36. 3	46. -4
7. 14	17. 32	27. 15	37. -18	47. -12
8. 28	18. -2	28. -23	38. 9	48. 31
9. 24	19. 2	29. -11	39. -19	49. -9
10. 6	20. 17	30. -5	40. 7	50. 8

Page 75: Solving Linear Functions

1. 7	21. 5	41. -10	61. 5	81. 2
2. -2	22. -8	42. -2	62. -9	82. -5
3. -2	23. -8	43. 8	63. 7	83. -7
4. 2	24. -8	44. -8	64. 3	84. 8
5. 2	25. -8	45. -1	65. 5	85. -4
6. 3	26. -10	46. -8	66. 4	86. 0
7. -7	27. 9	47. 3	67. -10	87. -8
8. -3	28. 6	48. 7	68. -7	88. 7
9. 9	29. 8	49. 5	69. 3	89. 6
10. -4	30. -6	50. 2	70. 5	90. -2
11. 6	31. 2	51. -1	71. -3	91. 9
12. 9	32. -1	52. 0	72. -5	92. -1
13. -3	33. 5	53. -8	73. 7	93. -1

14. 9	34. -4	54. 4	74. -9	94. 2
15. -10	35. -5	55. 7	75. 7	95. 2
16. 6	36. -10	56. -6	76. -5	96. 3
17. -6	37. -5	57. -10	77. 6	97. -6
18. -7	38. 9	58. -8	78. 8	98. 8
19. 1	39. 3	59. -9	79. 2	99. -10
20. 5	40. 4	60. -1	80. -9	100. 2

Page 85: Find Slope from Two Points

1. -7	21. -7	41. 4	61. 0	81. 4
2. 10	22. -7	42. 5	62. -3	82. -6
3. -10	23. -4	43. -1	63. -3	83. 9
4. -7	24. 3	44. 2	64. 9	84. 2
5. -5	25. 0	45. 3	65. -3	85. 3
6. 7	26. -8	46. -8	66. 7	86. 0
7. -4	27. 0	47. 1	67. -2	87. -4
8. 9	28. -4	48. 6	68. 10	88. 2
9. -1	29. 3	49. 4	69. 5	89. 1
10. -2	30. -10	50. -1	70. 2	90. 0
11. -5	31. -9	51. -5	71. -9	91. 10
12. 9	32. 7	52. 9	72. -7	92. 5
13. 5	33. -6	53. 8	73. 7	93. -5
14. -5	34. 3	54. 6	74. 2	94. 3
15. 6	35. 7	55. 9	75. 0	95. 9
16. 0	36. 5	56. 8	76. 6	96. 2
17. -7	37. -1	57. 2	77. -2	97. -6
18. -3	38. -7	58. -1	78. -9	98. 0
19. -3	39. 2	59. -1	79. 7	99. 8
20. 3	40. -1	60. -8	80. 2	100. -7

Page 95: Plotting Lines

1.

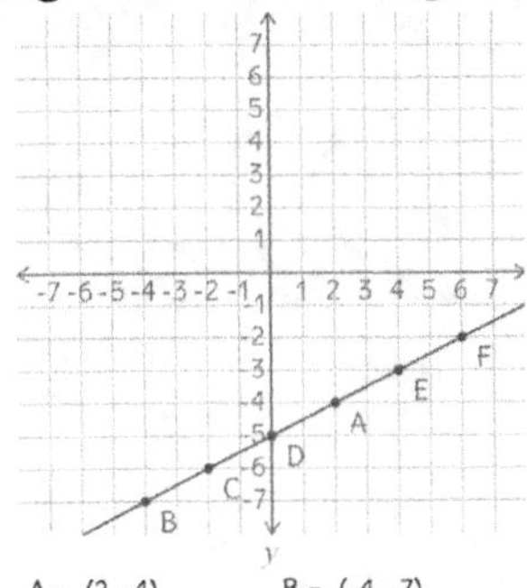

A = (2, -4)   B = (-4, -7)

C = (-2, -6)   D = (0, -5)

E = (4, -3)   F = (6, -2)

2.

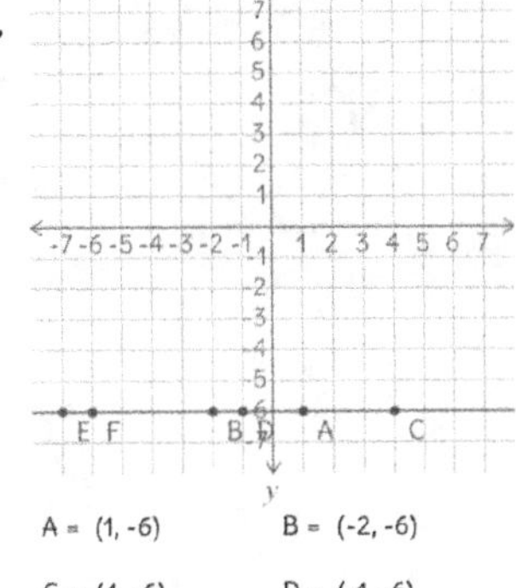

A = (1, -6)   B = (-2, -6)

C = (4, -6)   D = (-1, -6)

E = (-7, -6)   F = (-6, -6)

3.

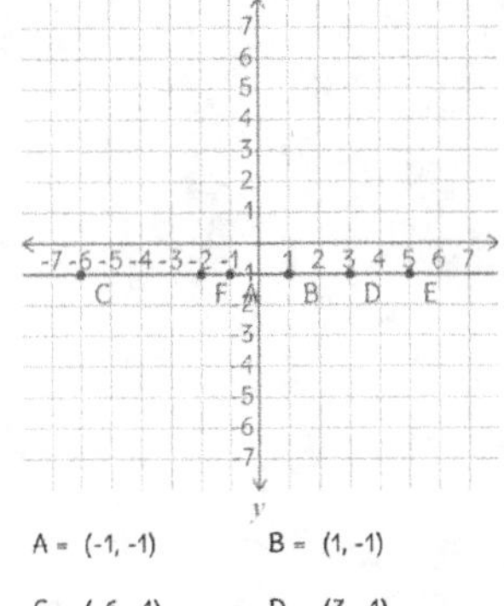

A = (-1, -1)   B = (1, -1)

C = (-6, -1)   D = (3, -1)

E = (5, -1)   F = (-2, -1)

4.

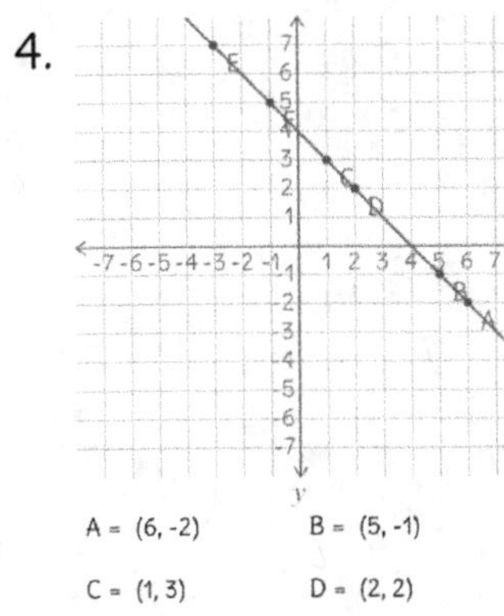

A = (6, -2)   B = (5, -1)

C = (1, 3)   D = (2, 2)

E = (-3, 7)   F = (-1, 5)

5.

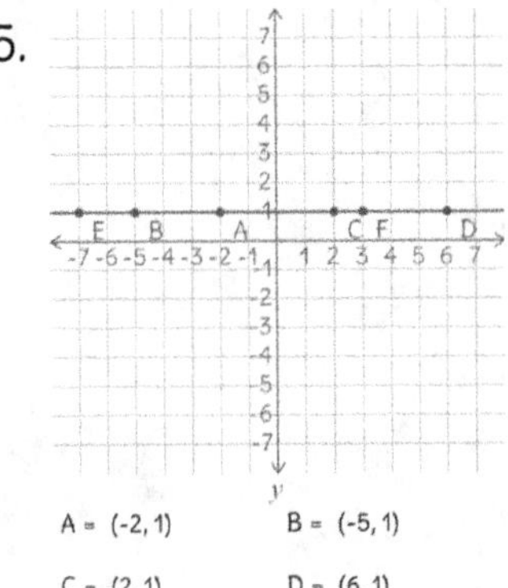

A = (-2, 1)   B = (-5, 1)

C = (2, 1)   D = (6, 1)

E = (-7, 1)   F = (3, 1)

6.

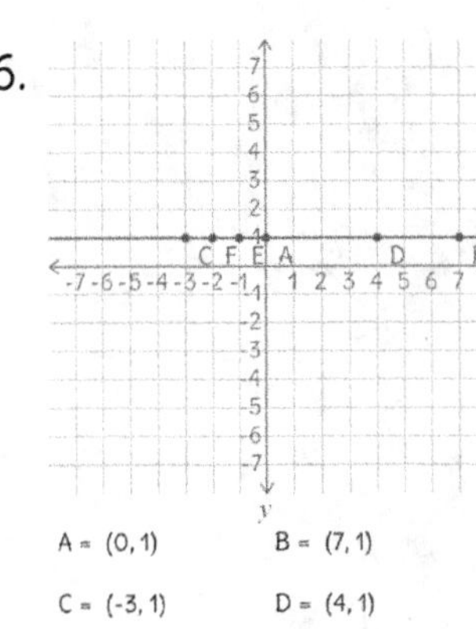

A = (0, 1)   B = (7, 1)

C = (-3, 1)   D = (4, 1)

E = (-1, 1)   F = (-2, 1)

7.

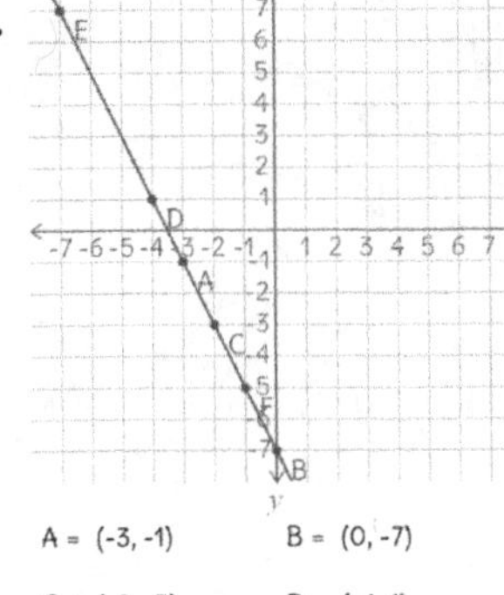

A = (-3, -1)   B = (0, -7)

C = (-2, -3)   D = (-4, 1)

E = (-7, 7)   F = (-1, -5)

8.

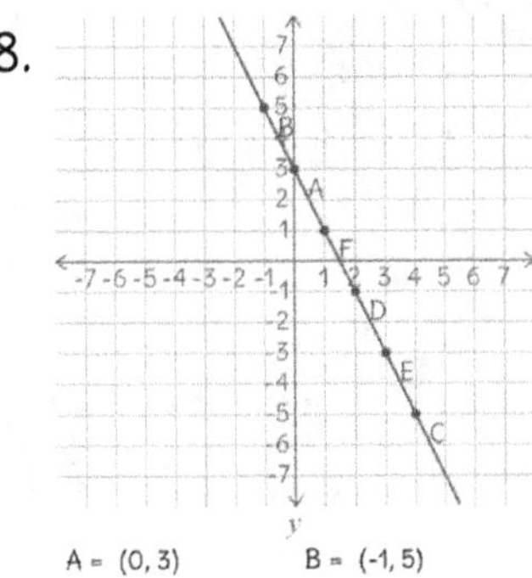

A = (0, 3)   B = (-1, 5)

C = (4, -5)   D = (2, -1)

E = (3, -3)   F = (1, 1)

9.

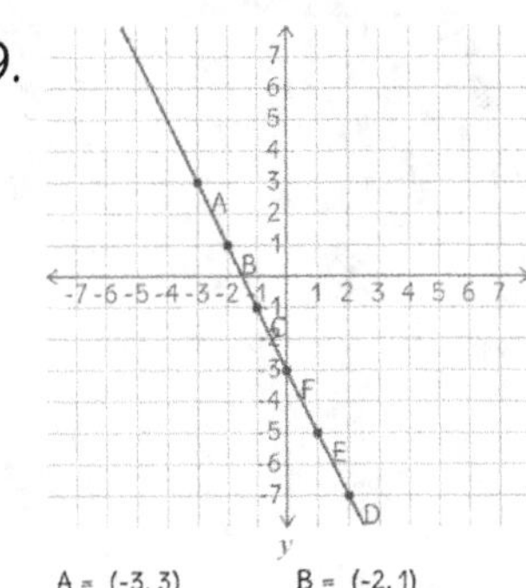

A = (-3, 3)   B = (-2, 1)

C = (-1, -1)   D = (2, -7)

E = (1, -5)   F = (0, -3)

10.

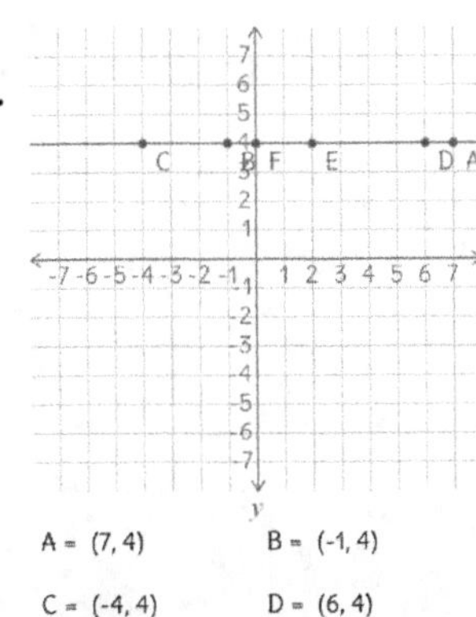

A = (7, 4)   B = (-1, 4)

C = (-4, 4)   D = (6, 4)

E = (2, 4)   F = (0, 4)

Page 105: Graphing Linear Equations

1. $y = \frac{-3}{4}x + 4$

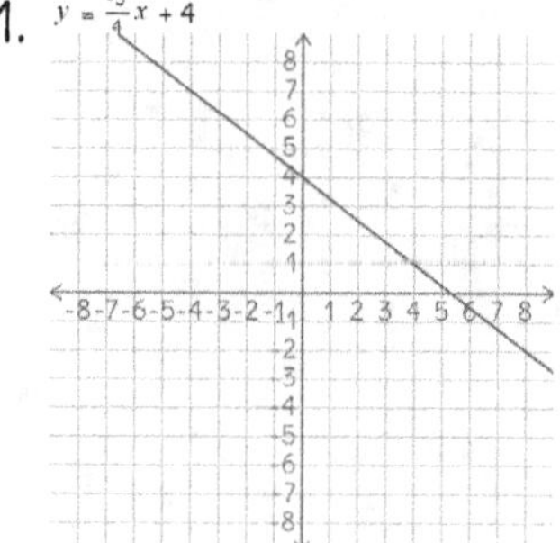

2. $y = \frac{-5}{4}x - 5$

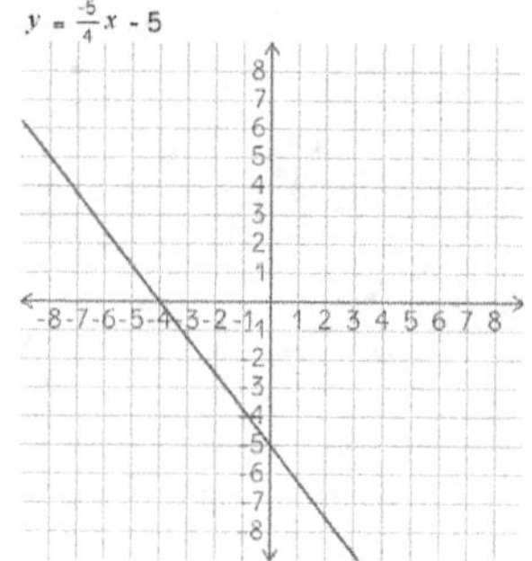

3. $y = 2x + 7$

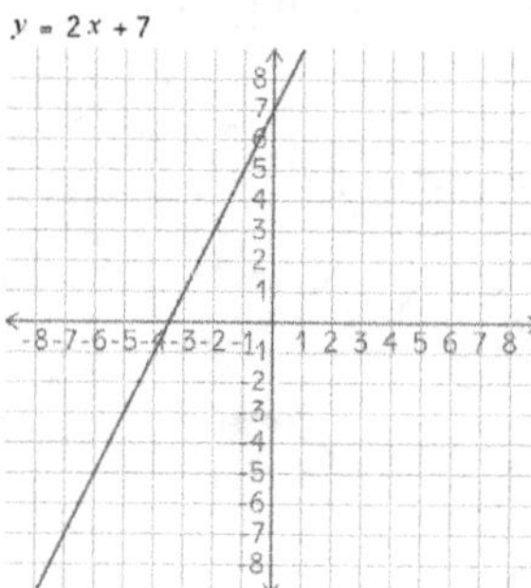

4. $y = x - 7$

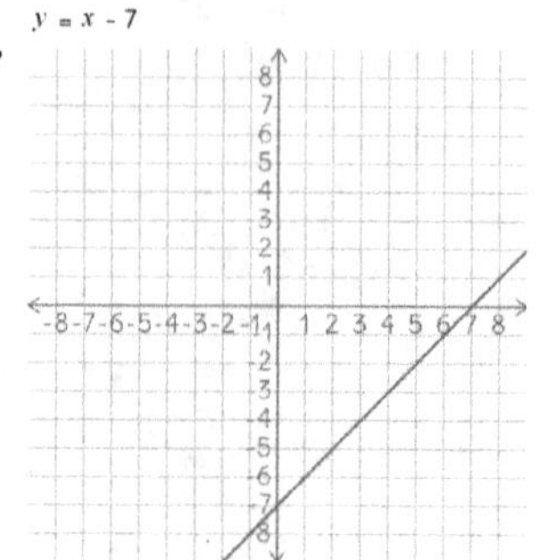

5. $y = \frac{11}{4}x + 4$

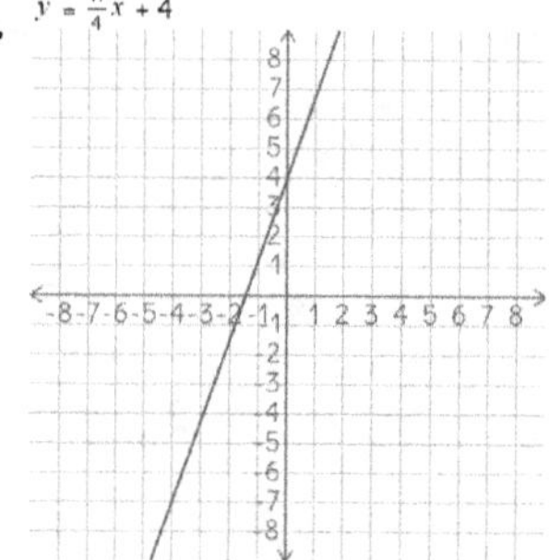

6. $y = \frac{1}{2}x - 6$

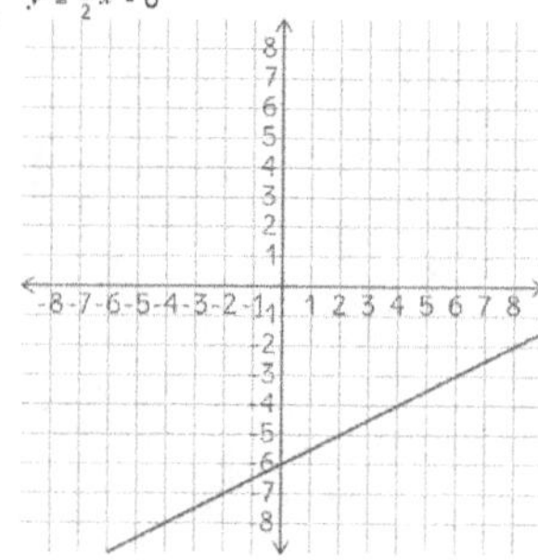

7. $y = -x + 5$

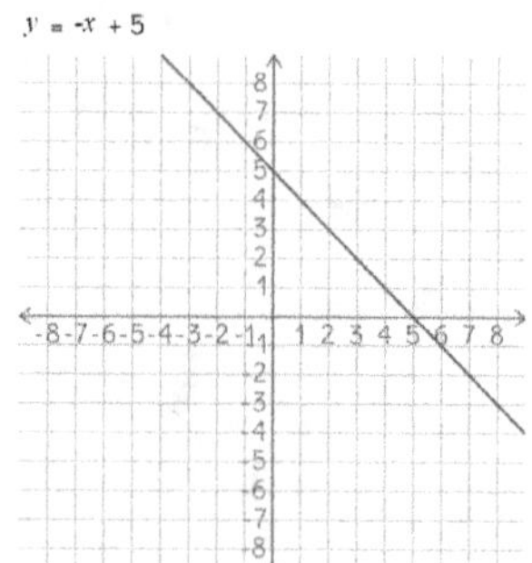

8. $y = \frac{9}{4}x + 6$

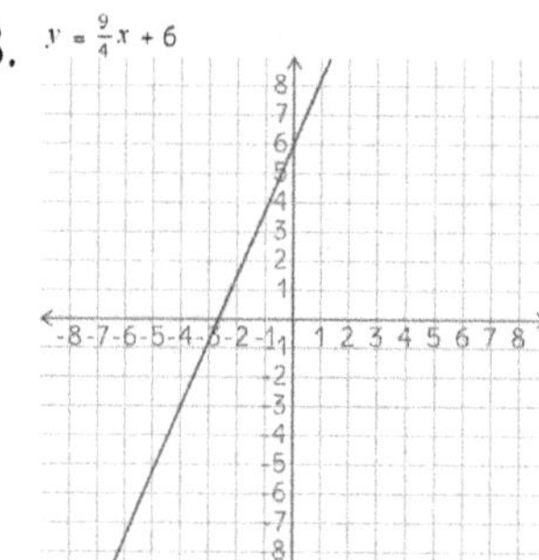

9. $y = 2x + 4$

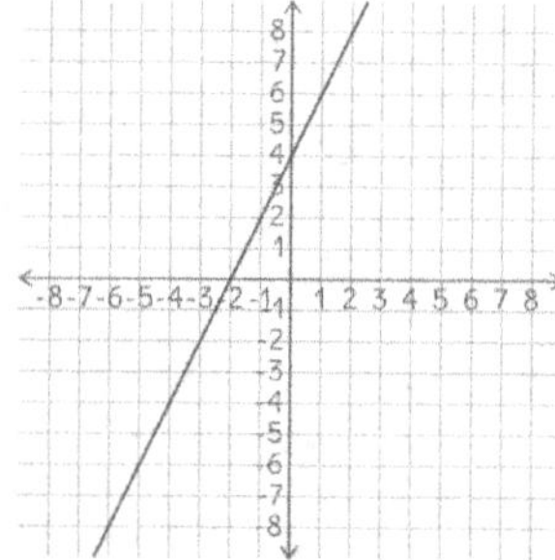

10. $y = \frac{5}{2}x - 1$

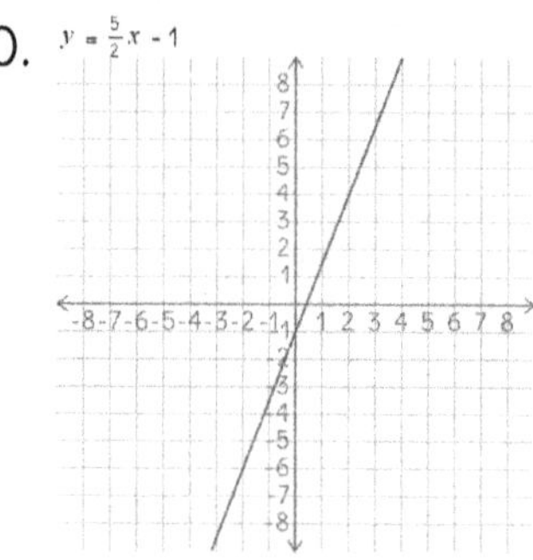

1. x = -0.87, y = 1.93

2. x = -0.25, y = 0.55

3. x = -0.71, y = 2.86

4. x = 0.64, y = -0.1

5. x = 1.13, y = -1.03

6. x = 2.0, y = -0.5

7. x = -3.0, y = 2.33

8. x = -0.0, y = 0.38

9. x = -1.57, y = 1.14

10. x = 0.82, y = 0.14

11. x = -0.5, y = 1.0

12. x = 11.67, y = -14.33

13. x = 8.5, y = -1.75

14. x = 6.0, y = -1.75

15. x = 0.85, y = 0.52

16. x = -1.67, y = 3.67

17. x = 1.37, y = 0.17

18. x = -0.8, y = 2.8

19. x = 1.0, y = -0.0

20. x = -1.94, y = 2.77

21. x = 0.55, y = -0.18

22. x = 0.74, y = 0.34

23. x = 0.42, y = 0.42

24. x = 0.09, y = 0.64

25. x = -0.08, y = 0.92

26. x = 0.52, y = -0.07

27. x = 7.33, y = -1.67

28. x = -4.29, y = 4.76

29. x = 0.36, y = 0.55

30. x = 8.67, y = -5.0

31. x = 1.02, y = 0.29

32. x = -1.08, y = 4.92

33. x = 0.38, y = 0.88

34. x = 1.21, y = 0.87

35. x = -3.0, y = 5.17

36. x = 0.1, y = 1.01

37. x = 5.25, y = -2.58

38. x = 0.44, y = 0.06

39. x = 1.68, y = -0.53

40. x = 4.19, y = -4.06

41. x = 1.0, y = 1.0

42. x = -0.0, y = 0.62

43. x = 1.71, y = -0.56

44. x = 1.04, y = -0.14

45. x = 1.11, y = 1.44

46. x = 7.0, y = -6.0

47. x = 2.67, y = -2.0

48. x = -0.03, y = 1.18

49. x = 3.25, y = -2.42

50. x = 4.2, y = -4.4

Page 132: Quadratic Equations

1. (0.302, -0.302)
2. No real solution.
3. (0.229, -0.729)
4. (3.5, -3.5)
5. (-2.449, 2.449)
6. (-1.595, 1.881)
7. (3.333, -3)
8. (4.5, -4.5)
9. (-3, 2.2)
10. (-1.584, 1.473)
11. No real solution.
12. (0.136, 0.614)
13. (-4, 13)
14. (-1, 1)
15. (-4.236, 0.236)
16. (-11, 6)
17. (1.354, -1.354)
18. No real solution.
19. (-3.833, 4)
20. (3.2, -2)
21. (3, -12)
22. (-1, -2)
23. (3, -7)
24. (2.283, -1.533)
25. No real solution.
26. (-1.58, 0.58)
27. (3, -2.333)
28. (-1.228, -9.772)
29. (-1, -1.25)
30. (5, -5.6)
31. (5.422, -0.922)
32. No real solution.
33. (3.8, -2)
34. (1, -0.5)
35. (-2.393, 1.393)
36. (-1.907, 2.307)
37. (0.743, -0.943)
38. (3.333, -4.5)
39. (0.836, -3.586)
40. (3.351, 0.149)
41. (3.317, -3.317)
42. No real solution.
43. (0.735, -1.36)
44. (-1.671, 0.762)
45. (0.91, -1.465)
46. (10, -10)
47. (1.483, -1.483)
48. No real solution.
49. (0.577, -0.577)
50. No real solution.
51. (1.298, -3.698)
52. No real solution.
53. No real solution.
54. (-1, 1)
55. (2, -0.333)
56. (-1.362, 2.112)
57. (-1.743, 1.885)
58. No real solution.
59. (-0.225, 2.225)
60. (-1.634, 1.759)

Page 140: Area and Perimeter

1. P=36 A=68
2. P=80 A=246
3. P=44 A=78
4. P=24 A=19.56
5. P=34 A=50
6. P=34 A=37
7. P=44 A=108
8. P=24 A=23.5
9. P=33 A=66
10. P=70 A=150
11. P=40 A=70.7
12. P=40 A=65
13. P=24 A=27.71
14. P=68 A=248
15. P=28 A=28
16. P=58 A=78
17. P=30 A=44
18. P=30 A=43.3
19. P=24 A=27.71
20. P=34 A=54
21. P=18 A=15.59
22. P=27 A=35.07
23. P=38 A=60
24. P=64 A=206
25. P=52 A=148
26. P=46 A=84
27. P=37 A=64.79
28. P=30 A=43.3
29. P=19 A=20
30. P=44 A=92
31. P=56 A=162
32. P=23 A=22.2
33. P=36 A=62.35
34. P=62 A=186
35. P=26 A=33
36. P=40 A=75.9
37. P=30 A=43.3
38. P=46 A=120
39. P=26 A=30
40. P=38 A=66.15
41. P=45 A=95.03
42. P=46 A=107
43. P=66 A=200
44. P=52 A=137
45. P=58 A=108
46. P=31 A=45.18
47. P=34 A=48
48. P=70 A=166
49. P=39 A=94
50. P=42 A=110
51. P=42 A=108
52. P=34 A=20
53. P=34 A=72
54. P=38 A=78
55. P=30 A=40
56. P=19 A=12
57. P=19 A=20
58. P=25 A=29.02
59. P=38 A=70
60. P=32 A=49
61. P=54 A=110
62. P=54 A=126
63. P=26 A=23.43
64. P=50 A=128
65. P=28 A=49
66. P=22 A=30
67. P=32 A=58
68. P=72 A=163
69. P=56 A=161
70. P=42 A=54
71. P=42 A=49
72. P=74 A=154

73. P=28 A=34   74. P=38 A=81   75. P=58 A=154
76. P=64 A=162   77. P=52 A=129   78. P=33 A=57
79. P=24 A=33   80. P=42 A=39

Page 160: Volume and Surface Area

1. V=202 cm³ cm³ SA=263.7 cm² cm²

2. V=134 in³ in³ SA=163 in² in²

3. V=120 in³ in³ SA=148 in² in²
V=172 in³ in³ SA=209.3 in² in²4.

V=524 in³ in³ SA=314 in² in²5.

V=900 cm³ cm³ SA=560 cm² cm²6.

V=47 in³ in³ SA=83 in² in²7.

V=148 ft³ ft³ SA=181 ft² ft²8.

V=4 cm³ cm³ SA=13 cm² cm²9.

V=77 cm³ cm³ SA=115 cm² cm²10.

V=508.94 in³ in³ SA=353 in² in²11.

V=50 in³ in³ SA=94.0 in² in²12.

V=13 ft³ ft³ SA=35 ft² ft²13.

V=385 ft³ ft³ SA=382.4 ft² ft²14.

V=85 ft³ ft³ SA=118 ft² ft²15.

V=210 ft³ ft³ SA=214 ft² ft²16.

V=6 cm³ cm³ SA=24.4 cm² cm²17.

V=200 ft³ ft³ SA=260.0 ft² ft²18.

V=191 cm³ cm³ SA=206 cm² cm²19.

20. V=12 ft³ ft³ SA=32 ft² ft²

21. V=330 ft³ ft³ SA=359.2 ft² ft²

22. V=27 cm³ cm³ SA=54 cm² cm²

23. V=32 in³ in³ SA=68.4 in² in²

24. V=210 cm³ cm³ SA=214 cm² cm²

25. V=180 ft³ ft³ SA=192 ft² ft²

26. V=9 in³ in³ SA=27 in² in²

27. V=168 cm³ cm³ SA=219.6 cm² cm²

28. V=113.10 ft³ ft³ SA=132 ft² ft²

29. V=24 ft³ ft³ SA=58.4 ft² ft²

30. V=75 in³ in³ SA=124.0 in² in²

31. V=60 cm³ cm³ SA=105.2 cm² cm²

32. V=32 in³ in³ SA=68.4 in² in²

33. V=140 in³ in³ SA=199.8 in² in²

34. V=50 in³ in³ SA=97.0 in² in²

35. V=75 in³ in³ SA=124.0 in² in²

36. V=175 cm³ cm³ SA=230.0 cm² cm²

37. V=324 ft³ ft³ SA=288 ft² ft²

38. V=262 ft³ ft³ SA=254 ft² ft²

39. V=280 cm³ cm³ SA=312.0 cm² cm²

40. V=9 in³ in³ SA=31.2 in² in²

41. V=25 in³ in³ SA=52 in² in²

42. V=60 in³ in³ SA=94 in² in²

43. V=60 in³ in³ SA=94 in² in²

44. V=60 cm³ cm³ SA=100.4 cm² cm²

45. V=12 cm³ cm³ SA=32 cm² cm²

46. V=80 in³ in³ SA=112 in² in²

47. V=18 in³ in³ SA=49.8 in² in²

48. V=150 ft³ ft³ SA=170 ft² ft²

49. V=151 ft³ ft³ SA=174 ft² ft²

50. V=84 cm³ cm³ SA=140.2 cm² cm²

51. V=252 cm³ cm³ SA=286.4 cm² cm²

52. V=490 cm³ cm³ SA=378 cm² cm²

53. V=800 cm³ cm³ SA=520 cm² cm²

54. V=180 cm³ cm³ SA=192 cm² cm²

55. V=32 in³ in³ SA=68.4 in² in²

56. V=168 ft³ ft³ SA=201.2 ft² ft²

57. V=567 cm³ cm³ SA=414 cm² cm²

58. V=9 in³ in³ SA=28.6 in² in²

59. V=9 ft³ ft³ SA=31.2 ft² ft²

60. V=80 cm³ cm³ SA=138.4 cm² cm²

Page 175: Pythagorean Theorem

1. S=115.326
2. S=92.865
3. S=107.531
4. S=19.391
5. S=226.947
6. S=57.053
7. S=126.554
8. S=76.191
9. S=184.662
10. S=32.249
11. S=82.492
12. S=77.666
13. S=37.736
14. S=117.201
15. S=40.398
16. S=164.596
17. S=55.036
18. S=153.401
19. S=110.023
20. S=201.375

21. S=29.597   22. S=52.154   23. S=52.154   24. S=96.979

25. S=112.370   26. S=147.139   27. S=58.481   28. S=49.568